ublished by Mills & Sanderson, Publishers
Box U, Bedford, MA 01730
Copyright © 1987 Christine A. Adamec

ry of Congress Cataloging in Publication Data

Adamec, Christine A., 1949–
There are babies to adopt.

Bibliography: p.
ption—United States—Handbooks, manuals, etc.
I. Title.
.55.A3   1987   362.7'34'0973   87-14012
ISBN 0-938179-08-X
ISBN 0-938179-04-7 (pbk.)

ed and Bound in the United States of America

t

for P

Christine A.

Lib

1. A

HV

P

Dedication and Acknowledgements

This book is dedicated to my husband, John Adamec Jr. His constant cheerleading, moral support, and willingness to watch our children so I could work on many evenings and weekends, along with his utter conviction of the importance of this task, made the book possible. It helps a lot when your husband is also your best friend. Thank you, John.

Over one hundred people were interviewed for this book and space will not allow thanking each one singly. But I would especially like to thank my support group, Lifeline for Children in Plantation, Florida, for their generous assistance. I particularly thank Juanita McKenna of Lifeline for Children for her unbounded enthusiasm and tremendous knowledge of adoption and adoption contacts. You said a book should be written for people who want to adopt babies, Juanita: here it is.

I would like to thank Jeffrey Rosenberg, Director of Public Policy for the National Committee For Adoption in Washington, D.C. for the valuable research tools he provided as well as critical information shared in several interviews.

I would also like to thank the state social services departments who so rapidly and completely replied to my questionnaire. Many states sent me copies of their state laws, annual reports, and other types of adoption information.

Two states provided the greatest amount of information: California and Connecticut. My thanks to Gordon Scott, Chief of Adoptions Field Support Bureau for the California Department of Social Services, Russell Mercer, Social Worker with the Connecticut Department of Children and Youth Services, and Joyce Clark, also a Social Worker with Connecticut's Department of Children and Youth Services. These busy people were exceptionally comprehensive in the amount of data they generously provided.

I collectively thank the many experienced social workers and agency directors, prominent attorneys, busy government officials, compassionate birthmothers, and other interviewees who so candidly shared their extensive knowledge and experiences with me and who put themselves in the shoes of prospective parents to advise my readers how they can adopt.

I would like to thank Jesse Baker, pastor of the Palm Bay United Methodist Church. His inspirational discussion of the importance of taking on the really hard jobs that you think should be done, but too often feel like someone else should do because you don't have time, made a strong impact on me. His words helped convince me I should learn as much as possible about adopting infants so I could write a book and convey what I learned to prospective parents.

The support group leaders who assisted me were extremely generous in terms of supplying both valuable information and the names of key people to interview. Especially helpful were Families Adopting Children Everywhere (F.A.C.E.) in Baltimore, Maryland, the Open Door Society of Massachusetts in Boston, Massachusetts and the Open Door Society of New Hampshire in Kingston, New Hampshire. There are too many names and organizations to list them all here, but group leaders throughout the nation were very supportive of this project.

Finally, and most importantly, I thank the adoptive parents I interviewed. They openly described the process by which they succeeded in adopting, including the mistakes they made along the way, how they felt about the process, and what advice and information they thought prospective parents needed to know. I was and still am awed by these adoptive parents' willingness to share personal stories of the triumph of adoption and why and how they succeeded. My readers and I owe you a great debt.

CONTENTS

Introduction

You want to adopt a baby, and maybe you can already imagine how excited and thrilled you'll be when you hold that child in your arms for the first time. Or perhaps you envision yourself proudly pushing a carriage or stroller containing your baby. The first smile, the first word, so many firsts!

You're emotionally prepared for this big step and you have enough time and money to support a new family member. In fact, you're ready NOW, and if the baby comes next month or tomorrow, maybe that won't be too soon!

But when you tell your friends and relatives about your big decision, they'll caution you not to get *too* excited. Because, they'll say, "Don't you know there *aren't* any babies available for adoption anymore? There's a big baby shortage, everyone knows that. You'll have to go on a waiting list for about five years or maybe even longer." They know, because they read it in the newspaper, heard it on TV, and "everyone" says so.

So, if patience is a virtue, you'll have a great opportunity to develop this trait as you wait to adopt!

These views are particularly frustrating if you're in your mid-thirties or older, because you realize you'll probably be considered too old to adopt five or seven years from now. Maybe you should consider adopting an older child?

My answer is a resounding "no!" Not if what you really crave is to adopt an infant and you're willing to devote the time and energy needed to succeed with this task. Consider it a project, and it's your job to start this project by locating a source, whether it's an adoption agency, an attorney, or even a birthmother herself!

If you resign yourself to passivity, then you *will* wait five to seven years—or forever. But if you'll educate yourself about adoption—and this book is a launching point—and if you'll act positively and assertively, your chances for success are good. Not 100%—I can't promise you success in every case—but the "odds" are far better than you've been lead to believe by *them*.

Who am I? I'm a professional writer with hundreds of interviews under my belt, including several years working for a state welfare office. I'm also an adoptive parent writing the book that I wish had been available when my husband and I wanted to adopt a baby. (We succeeded anyway, but this book certainly would have helped!) Sure, there were other books on adoption, and they were good. But they weren't solely dedicated to our goal: adopting an infant.

We knew there were plenty of older or handicapped children available to adopt, but we wanted to adopt a healthy baby. And we did.

So I decided to write this book and share what I know combined with the intensive and extensive research I've done. I interviewed social workers, lawyers, and adoption agency executive directors, nationwide.

I've talked with scores of adoptive parents throughout the country to find out what they did and how they succeeded—what were the common denominators? Are there things that you could also try in your efforts to adopt a baby? I think so, and they're here, between these pages.

Not wanting to rely on interviews alone, (and being an avid researcher), I used a search service available on CompuServe, (the largest computerized information service in the country) to run detailed and comprehensive computer searches on adoption.

Searching major newspapers in the United States, doctoral dissertation databases, the American Psychological Association database, and many other compendiums of computerized information, I located recent valuable research on adoption which you can use to a practical end.

This book provides how-to information you can use. For example, what signposts should you, your social worker, or your attorney look for in a birthmother who is making an adoption plan? What is the average birthmother like? (A birthmother is a woman who bears a baby. Adoptive parents detest the term "real mother".)

Deciding I didn't want to rely solely on the social workers' summation of birthmothers, I interviewed over 20 birthmothers to find out why they placed their children for adoption and how they felt about it now. Their responses are described in the chapter on motivation. I know you'll find their very candid responses intriguing.

CHAPTER 1
The Path Ahead

My goal is to provide you the information you need to prepare your own gameplan for achieving your dream of adopting an infant. Because I believe you *can* adopt the child you seek, whether it's a healthy White infant, Black infant, biracial child, or foreign-born baby. You set the parameters for what you want and this book will provide you with guidelines and sources so you can forge ahead.

(Note: This book concentrates on the adoption of infants ages newborn to two years. Many readers may hope to adopt newborns, while others may seek slightly older infants or toddlers. In addition, most international adoptions are of infants at least three or four months old.)

It'll take flexibility to succeed—as you begin to contact people, they'll give you the names of other people, and you may have to pursue many seemingly blind alleys before you find the agency or attorney who is right for you.

Your search will also require perseverance and you can't be a shrinking violet. You'll need a strong will and the ability to deal with some setbacks and discouragements—and people telling you "no." But others have succeeded and you can too. They're high school graduates and Ph.D.s, middle class and affluent, religious and indifferent to religion.

They all shared a single-minded determination to adopt their baby. Because, if you thought the "hard" decision was resolving to adopt, you haven't begun yet! You have so many choices ahead of you, and I'll do my best to give you hand-holding advice along the way as you make critical decisions.

You'll have unglamorous aspects to consider, such as how much you can afford for this adoption. The reactions of your family and friends must be considered—if you decide to adopt a biracial baby, will they shun you? Sometimes even when a White family intends to adopt a White baby, aunts and uncles worry about "bad genes" and advise you against the whole thing. Can you emotionally afford to alienate them? The chapter on motivation discusses these issues.

If you're single, you'll have to cope with the reactions of couples who are jealous of your adopting the baby *they* believe should have been theirs.

In fact, the amount of soul-searching you'll undergo during the adoption process may be equalled only by the amount of thought which you hopefully gave to deciding for or against marriage! Even if you refuse to confront these issues, the social worker for your home study investigation will want you to probe and analyze your values, hopes and goals, and much more. I don't want to scare you, I want to motivate and prepare you!

Before I move into definitions of some major terms and a description of what is covered in this book, let's clear the air about the "baby shortage."

A Baby Shortage?

Is there one? Experts are cautiously telling us that the precipitous drop in adoptions we saw in the 1970s is probably over. One reason for a likely increase in adoptions is that the number of births to unmarried White women has increased dramatically. (I am using figures for unmarried White women because this group is more likely to place their infants for adoption than other races, according to a Working Paper published by the National Center for Health Statistics.)

In 1970, there were 183,600 births to unmarried White women. By 1982, that figure nearly doubled to 355,180 births. In 1984, the most recent data available as of this writing, the number of births to unmarried White women was 391,929 and statisticians at the National Center for Health Statistics say the figure has been increasing every year and will very likely be higher for 1986 and 1987. Unmarried White women bear about 13% of all White children.

Of course, every unmarried woman who has an infant doesn't place the child for adoption, but the experts say the percentage of placements is probably constant. So, the increased number of births means more adoptions.

Says Jeffrey Rosenberg, Director of Public Policy for the National Committee for Adoption, a Washington, D.C.-based organization of about 135 adoption agencies, "I think the decline of infant adoptions we saw in the 1970s has at least stabilized and may even be going up a bit."

Dr. Christine Bachrach, a statistician/demographer for the National Center for Health Statistics agrees and says all the figures seem to point to an increase. Says Bachrach, "Even though teenagers don't seem to be rushing into adoption as an alternative, the increase in the total number of births has to have an effect on the number of adoptions, and we can conclude more children are being adopted."

Another interesting aspect is that the average woman who places her child for adoption is 18 years old or older. (See the chapter on motivation for more information and a profile of a typical birthmother.)

It's also fascinating that an estimated 5-6% of all adoptions are of babies born to MARRIED people! So the numbers of unmarried women don't represent the total pool of women who place their infants for adoption.

Well, How Many Babies Are Being Adopted?

This is one question I've spent many hours agonizing over. Because no one really *knows* how many infant adoptions occur in the United States today, nor have they known since 1975 when the federal government, in its great wisdom, decided we no longer needed this information. Consequently, most states do not tabulate adoption data. Individual states license adoption agencies, but they don't track the number of adoptions which agencies actually perform.

A survey of a myriad of higher and local courts nationwide might uncover that data—and that would cost Big Bucks to accomplish. (Uncle Sam can afford it better than I can!)

Not that obtaining data hasn't been tried: in 1984, The National Committee for Adoption undertook a comprehensive survey to determine the number and type of adoptions occurring in 1982, among other data.

Their outstanding efforts uncovered much valuable information. But even they were stymied on the subject of infant adoption because of underreporting by states.

According to an appendix note in the *Adoption Factbook*, published by The National Committee for Adoption, "incomplete reporting in many States may have yielded a very conservative estimate of healthy infant adoptions."

As a result, the National Committee considered their figure of 17,600 infants low, and they estimated the actual number could have been closer to 24,600 for 1982.

I'm making an educated guess that the number of infants adopted today is a considerably higher count, based on results obtained from questionnaires on adoption which I sent to all 50 states.

For example, back in 1982, Kansas reported only 264 private placements to the National Committee for Adoption. Yet in 1986, the state of Kansas estimates about 1500 independent adoptions occurred in their state. (Independent means non-agency, a form of adoption lawful in most states.) This is very high, considering the state of California has about 2200 independent adoptions— and California is a much bigger state in land and population than Kansas.

Virtually all of the Kansas independent adoptions are non-relative infant adoptions, according to Adoption Supervisor Barbara Stodgell of the Kansas Department of Social and Rehabilitative Services.

"We don't have what's commonly referred to as a 'venue' law, so anybody who wants to come to Kansas can petition to adopt if the baby is born here—they don't have to be a legal resident," explains Stodgell.

She continues, "We do require that a home study be completed and the Interstate Compact must be adhered to in those situations, so there are checks on such adoptions." (The Interstate Compact on the Placement of Children is an agreement between virtually all the states on how interstate adoptions will be accomplished legally and procedurally. The Compact offices must review the adoption before it can be approved and finalized.)

Nevada reported 79 independent adoptions in 1986 and 118 state placements of infants and toddlers, up from the 81 total adoptions of healthy infants reported in 1982 to the National Committee. (And that didn't include a statistic for agency adoptions, which would increase the number even more).

Most of the heavily populated states don't maintain data on adoptions, although the state of California generously provided extensive statistics which reveal an upswing in the number of adoptions of infants and small children.

For example, in Fiscal Year 1983/1984, about 1800 children of all ages were adopted through agencies. Since about half of the adoptions in California were for children under age three, this means about 900 children ages three and under were adopted through agencies.

During that same year, about 1800 independent adoptions occurred. Since virtually all independent adoptions are of infants or toddlers, this means about 2700 children under age three were adopted.

Two years later, in fiscal year 1985/86, independent adoptions increased to over 2200, and agency adoptions for children of all ages were nearly 2300. According to Dan Cudworth, Adoptions Consultant for the State of California's Department of Social Services, about half of all adoptions are still of children under age three; thus, we can assume about 1150 agency adoptions were in this age category. So, in 1986, California had about 3150 adoptions of children age three and under, compared to 2700 in 1984.

In the state of South Carolina, the Department of Health and Environmental Control, Vital Records Division, reports there were 312 infant adoptions of children under age one in 1986. Yet only 104 infant adoptions were reported by the National Committee for Adoption in 1982. So we're looking at a 300% increase.

I could go on and on, and I do have more statistics for other states, which are provided in the appendix. But the bottom line is I can't statistically prove to you that x number of infants were adopted in 1986, or will be adopted in 1987 or 1988, based on the sketchy information available today. And no one else can either— any numbers you hear will be guesstimates only. The information I *have* been able to amass leads me to believe that infant adoptions *are* on the rise.

One more statistic, and I'll release you from my fascination with numbers: in addition to the babies adopted in the United States, many Americans are turning to international adoption, and the majority of the more than 9,000 international children adopted by Americans in 1986 were *infants* from Korea, India, South America, and other countries.

However many adoptions *have* occurred, it is not necessarily an upper limit on how many *could* occur. As new agencies form, they need parents. Yes, believe it or not, some agencies actually *need* parents to apply. (Although they would not admit this publicly under torture!)

In addition, adoption agencies which deal with foreign countries also need parents; at this writing, there are many male toddlers available from Thailand and waiting for adoptive parents. The international adoption scene changes daily, so next month it could be another country. The point is, there are babies out there.

Also, if more birthmothers were aware there were people like you looking for a child to adopt, more of them might opt for adoption. Another related factor in adoption today is the increasing amount of information and control many agencies and attorneys are offering parents who place their babies for adoption. In increasing numbers of adoptions, social workers are allowing birthparents to choose the adoptive parents, from non-identifying resumes, face-to-face meetings, or other means. (See the chapter "A New Openness in Adoptions" for more information.)

Some adoption professionals speculate that with increasing numbers of birthparents being allowed to choose adoptive parents, will come a greater number of birthparents deciding to place a child for adoption rather than keeping or aborting it.

Demand for Infants

Let's stop here and dispel one significant myth. Once you accept the idea that there are more babies available for adoption than the general public realizes, what about the demand: Isn't that sky high?

Well, one way to look at the demand for infants is to look at the number of infertile couples in the United States. After all, isn't it logical to assume that it is infertile childless couples who represent the primary "demand" for healthy infants.

Dr. William Mosher, Statistician and Demographer for the National Center for Health Statistics in Baltimore, Maryland, has studied and reported on this problem for the United States government.

Based on this data, there are one million married couples in America with wives ages fifteen to forty-four who have tried to conceive a child for one year or more and have not succeeded. Contrary to popular belief, this number of infertile couples was the same in 1976, and Mosher says we can assume the infertility rate has remained about the same.

These infertile couples may eventually have a child *after* one or two years, or at some point in the future. But for whatever reason, they haven't achieved a pregnancy after at least a year of trying.

This one year time frame is the criteria used by physicians to define infertility. Nature often works slower.

The American Fertility Society says up to 75% of the couples who have *not* undergone sterilization will ultimately bear a child. Which leaves about 250,000 in this group of childless couples who remain infertile.

Let's make a broad assumption, and assume as many as 100,000 of them hope to adopt. Even if only 20,000 babies were placed for adoption every year, that would mean a ratio of 5 to 1! Of course the ratio may *not* be this low, and one reason is that there are couples who already have one or more children and can't have more. Maybe they want a sister or brother for little Susie or Jimmy.

As a result, some number of them also want to adopt and consequently they must be added to the "competition" for adoptable infants. I'll address that issue more later.

Perhaps 100,000 childless couples are pursuing adoption. But the probability is zero that 100% of all infertile couples have applied to adopt a child. Instead, some are opting for advanced surgical techniques to correct blocked fallopian tubes or other problems. Still others decide to go for artificial insemination, in vitro fertilization, or one of the many biological options described in chapter eleven. And some number will elect to remain childless rather than adopting, because they feel a strong need for a genetic link.

In addition, some of these couples will apply to one agency, get on their waiting list, and do nothing else. But remember, it is the people who are persistent in their efforts to adopt who reach their goal.

There are also about 300,000 married women, ages 15 to 44, who are childless and have had a hysterectomy, according to Mosher. Some of these families may seek to adopt as well. Let's assume a greater proportion of these will opt for adoption, since they *know* it's extremely unlikely they'll ever have biological children. If 25% of these families seek to adopt, that means 75,000 couples should be added to the 100,000 infertile couples who did not undergo hysterectomies, for a grand total of 175,000. Now the ratio is 8.5 to 1. Conservatively assuming a very low number of infants are available for adoption—an assumption that I challenge elsewhere in this chapter, we still wind up with much better odds than the general public realizes.

Of the people who do apply to adopt a child, some will be immediately rejected because they're over forty, not in good health, cannot afford a child, etc.

It should also be noted that according to Mosher there are another 1.4 million American couples who have what is called "secondary infertility."

These couples already have one or more biological children and they haven't succeeded in having additional children, even though they would like more. They are not infertile because of hysterectomy or sterilization: these people have some other problem.

Perhaps some of them will seek to adopt. Some will ultimately succeed in bearing more children, while others will give up.

If we assume their fertility "success" rate is about the same as childless couples, about 75%, then about 350,000 will be infertile, and some number will seek to adopt. Let's assume on the high side: let's say half of them decide to adopt, or 175,000.

Now we have 100,000 childless but healthy couples, 75,000 couples in which the women had hysterectomies, and 175,000 couples already with children but now infertile, all eager to adopt a child. With a total of 350,000, our ratio is now more like 17.5 to 1.

You can play around with statistics for hours, or weeks, or months; for example, adding in the numbers of women who already have children and had hysterectomies and may want to adopt, etc. Or the women who've had tubal ligations or their husbands who've had vasectomies and want them reversed.

The basic point is that not all infertile couples will want to adopt. And that the number of *childless* couples, your primary competition, is much smaller than most people realize—when you hear that two to three million people are infertile, don't you automatically assume they are all childless? Well, they're not.

It's also important to know that childless couples are generally given a higher "priority" by many adoption agencies and even attorneys handling independent adoptions will turn down people with one or more children; consequently, families with children should not be perceived as primary "competition" by childless couples.

So the bottom line is that although there are many infertile couples who are probably pursuing adoption, these numbers should not discourage couples who hope to adopt.

Don't worry if an agency tells you they get 5,000 calls a year! Not every casual caller puts in an application. And if one agency has a waiting list of seven years, then find another agency with a shorter waiting list, in or out of your state. Or adopt independently or adopt internationally. But don't say it's impossible to adopt because there aren't enough babies and too many people want them. It may take one year or it may take three or four years. But don't give up because of numbers the media—or I—throw at you.

A Few Terms

Most people probably have an idea what a "social worker" is. As far as an adoptive parent is concerned, your social worker will determine if your family would make suitable parents for the type of child you want, and she or he also follows up after placement of your child to see if there are any problems.

The social worker does a "home study," which is not just an evaluation of whether your home is nice and clean, but is really primarily an analysis of you and your family. (More information on home studies is included in a later chapter.)

A birthmother is the person who, with the birthfather, conceived the child. She bears the child, sometimes placing it immediately for adoption, other times waiting a period of weeks or even months.

A birthmother is *not* referred to as the "real" mother, because this would imply the adoptive parents are unreal. Many social workers still use the word "natural" mother instead of birthmother, but if the birthmother is "natural," then the adoptive parent is "un-natural," an idea which has negative connotations.

Birthmothers don't "give up" their babies, they "place" or "release" them for adoption. Or they "make an adoption plan." It's not just quibbling over semantics: there's a genuine sense of difference if you use one word over another. (Think about it— "place" sounds like the person has control over her actions.)

Sometimes adoptive parents already have children. They are not referred to as "children of their own", but as "biological" children. Personally, I don't particularly like this word, because all children are biological, but, for want of a better word, I will use it.

An Overview of The Book

Before plunging into the nitty-gritty of it all, I want to strongly recommend that you read the entire book. Okay, if you MUST, skim through and read the sections that interest you the most, but then, go back and read everything. Although you may think a topic is not relevant to your needs, that section may contain valuable advice that could bring you nearer to your baby.

For example, if you're one of the many people who think *all* "special needs" children are severely disabled, mentally or physically, read the special needs chapter. A Florida family adopted two perfectly healthy boys, ages two and four, who were defined as special needs children simply because they were brothers and could not be separated.

Another example: I cover the question, "Should I apply to more than one agency?" in the chapter on agency adoption. But this question is also relevant to someone interested in international adoption.

Moving along, let's begin an overview of the material covered.

I've devoted an entire chapter to adoptive parents' groups because I'm convinced they're a key to success in so many adoptions, not only in helping you find your child, but also in assisting you with retaining your sanity during the home study. (No, it's not normally that horrendous, but most people have an inordinate dread of the home study. A support group can help!)

Also, no matter how kind and friendly your social worker is, many adoptive parents feel inhibited about asking questions or expressing concerns. Your adoptive parent peers will tell you the way it really is, with no qualms. In addition, many adoptive parents have told me very bluntly that they wouldn't have their child today without the support group's referral and help.

If there's a brand-new agency opening up, an adoptive parents' group knows. If an attorney is successful in placing infants—or if he's been very UNsuccessful and is a problem—the group will know. Without the knowledge and moral support of a parents' group, you're flying blind.

The next chapter discusses motivations of both birthmothers and adoptive parents and also reactions of the adoptive parents' family. Why would anyone place their child for adoption? And what is the average birthmother like: age, socioeconomic status and other ways. How does she feel about her decision?

I'm convinced that it's important for adoptive parents to try their best to understand their child's birthmother. You don't have to meet her and have an ongoing relationship with her—although some families do—but you should strive for an understanding. Your child's birthmother may have different reasons for making an adoption plan than did the women I interviewed, but you'll get a good "feel" for some basic motivations from this section.

The motivations of adoptive parents are also covered. Beyond the obvious reason that they *want* to adopt a child, *why* do they want to? And what thought process do they go through before, during and after the adoption?

This chapter is also important because it's an area virtually all social workers will cover. Have you really worked through any infertility problems you may have? Or are you trying to replace the phantom child you should have had with an adopted child—rather than seeing the child as a separate person? These and many other questions related to motivation are covered.

The reactions of family members to an impending adoption are also very important. What do you do if your parents or an in-law is very negative about the adoption you're planning? And do they usually "come around" if they are opposed to the idea?

What about questions that people in general ask you? What do you say when you're asked to speak for all adoptive parents in America, merely because you've adopted one child? And how do you handle negative reactions of strangers—whether you've adopted a child who resembles you or a child who looks very different from your family? These are all important issues discussed in the motivation chapter because they can affect your motivation to adopt. For some of you, making you more resolute than ever!

Of course, no book on adoption would be complete without a discussion of adoption agencies, and a chapter on this subject is provided. However, there are literally hundreds of adoption agencies in the United States, and I can't list them all because that would require a directory rather than a few pages. I'll list at least a few for each state, but expect your research to go beyond that.

Some agencies are publicly supported through United Way donations or church contributions, while others are private self-supporting non-profit corporations. Some specialize in placing biracial babies and others turn their attention to foreign infants, although I have separated the international adoptions into another chapter. And yes, there are agencies who place White infants, too.

I'll discuss how to find the agency which suits your needs, how to deal with the agency, and general agency philosophies; for example, what kinds of parents are they looking for?

Agencies have their own personalities and vary radically in their services and their costs to applicants. Some have many rules and regulations, while others are more flexible. The more flexible agencies are the ones that offer the greatest input to the birthparents; who often have very different ideas of what a "good" family for the child is.

I'll also cover a new entry into the adoption arena: identified adoption. This is an option offered in such states as Connecticut and Massachusetts, where non-agency adoption is banned. This option enables a couple to identify a birthmother and with her permission adopt her child under an agency's supervision. I'll discuss the pros and cons of this option.

The home study investigation of prospective adoptive parents is a source of considerable fear and gnashing of teeth and consequently worthy of an entire chapter. What do they want to know about you? Must you bare your deepest darkest secrets? And must you really steam-clean the carpets before the social worker comes to your home?

Another chapter will concentrate on international adoption. Although this is a continually changing scene, with countries dropping in or out on an almost daily basis, there is still some basic information every prospective parent needs, and I'll do my best to cover that information.

How hard is it to adopt internationally? How old are the kids? And what kinds of diseases, if any, might you expect them to have? Will society accept your Asian-born or Hispanic infant? These and many other questions are answered.

Independent non-agency adoption is lawful in most states, yet it has often received extremely "bad press." Although it's difficult to impossible to know how many independent adoptions occur each year, experts estimate that at least half of all infant adoptions are private placements.

It's a controversial topic and the chapter on independent adoption is a comprehensive overview of the pros and cons, based on in-depth nationwide interviews with adoptive parents, attorneys, support group leaders, and adoption experts.

I'll also discuss methods used to find a birthmother, ranging from sending out resumes and networking with friends and associates, to actually advertising your desire to adopt in a newspaper. For those who decide to advertise, I'll discuss what to say, where to advertise, how to respond to a birthmother, etc.

I'll also explain the difference between lawful independent adoption and baby buying, which still goes on. You certainly don't want to get caught up in an immoral or illegal scam.

The special needs chapter will include a broad spectrum of categories of infants considered hard to place, as well as a discussion of foster children who are adoptable.

Not all special needs kids are profoundly retarded or severely disabled: many have correctable problems and some, for example, sibling groups or biracial children, are perfectly healthy. And some problems are outgrown as the child matures. (I don't want to be overly-optimistic, but feel the average person is overly-pessimistic.)

Transracial adoptions are covered in the special needs chapter. Should a White family be allowed to adopt a biracial Black/White child? This is a "hot" issue today.

Most state agencies will not place a biracial child in a White home, but many private agencies insist a good permanent home in a White family is preferable to long-term foster care, which is often in a White home!

This book covers other heatedly discussed issues in adoption today. For example, increasing numbers of singles are adopting infants, some from abroad and some from the good old USA. What kind of problems do singles face in adopting? How long did it take for them to succeed? And why did they opt to take on single parenthood voluntarily, rather than have it thrust on them through divorce, widowhood, or an unplanned pregnancy?

"Open adoption" is another very important and hotly disputed topic in adoption and of increasing interest to social workers, birthparents, and adoptive parents. What are the risks and the benefits of actual contact with a birthmother? And how "open" is open? Adoptive parents, birthparents, and adoption professionals answer these questions.

I'll also discuss other options to obtain an infant, including surrogate motherhood, artificial insemination, and in vitro fertilization.

These are all biological options in which you or your spouse contribute to the genetic makeup of the child. Now that the Pope has condemned these options, it will be interesting to see if the demand for them will decrease. Apparently he is encouraging couples to pursue adoption.

In addition, in the celebrated Baby M case, a New Jersey surrogate mother went to court to regain the child she no longer wished to relinquish. The child's father and his wife were equally adamant that they would keep the child. The surrogate mother lost the first round when the judge awarded the child to her father, but, as of this writing, she has appealed the ruling and the case may drag on for years. And as a result of this case, many states are considering passing legislation restricting surrogate mothers.

The concluding chapter sums up everything and briefly discusses future issues of interest to adoptive parents; for example, adoptive parents must realize that adoption isn't over after finalization. In the future, children may wish to "search" for birthparents, or vice versa.

An appendix in the back of the book includes important resources: state adoption agencies, private and publicly-funded agencies, adoptive parents' groups, and a summary of current laws on adoption. (Remember, laws *do* change, so these are not cast in granite for all time.)

I wish I could promise you that everyone who reads this book will adopt an infant, I can't. My goal is to make you so aware of the whole process, from finding a baby to finalizing an adoption, that your chances of success will be greatly increased. Ignorance is *not* bliss! Instead, knowledge is power, and I want you to avoid the trial and error mistakes so many of us have made, and get a good headstart.

As you begin your quest to adopt an infant, I want you to know how exciting this is! It'll be an adventure you'll never forget, and worth all the hard work and introspection you must endure. Because at the end of the line is YOUR baby!

CHAPTER 2
Adoptive Parent Support Groups

"I wouldn't have my baby today if I hadn't joined my parents' group!" emphatically stated an adoptive mother in the South. "They referred me to an attorney who handled adoptions and he knew of a birthmother seeking a good family."

A northern mother describes her extreme frustration with solo attempts to understand how and where to apply for an infant. She read about the support group in the newspaper and says, "I picked up the phone and called the parents group and they told me about a new agency which just opened up. And that's where our daughter came from!"

And from a Connecticut father, "We adopted a biracial child and were concerned the state might disapprove of the adoption, since they had a policy against transracial adoption. I think maybe meeting social workers at support meetings helped a lot—they knew us and we didn't have any trouble with the adoption."

A Florida father was not so sure he wanted to adopt internationally—until he went to his first support group meeting. There were children there from Columbia, Korea, and many other countries. A little Korean girl charmed him and he told his wife, "I want one just like her!" The family later adopted twin Korean girls!

Another adoptive parent said her support group was a great morale booster. She recalls, "It really helped to see other people in the group *were* getting their babies—I knew it WAS going to happen for us too, and it would be our turn soon!" Soon after joining the group, they *did* succeed.

Similar words were chorused by one parent after another interviewed. They told me they didn't know how they'd have succeeded in adopting without the very real help their support group provided.

"The members have been there before!" said another parent. "They know what kind of emotions you're facing: your fears, your anticipation, the whole gamut."

"It's a great way to network and help get the word out that you want to adopt!" said an adoptive mom.

As an adoptive parent myself and a member of several support groups, (The Lifeline for Children in Plantation, Florida and OURS, based in Minneapolis, Minnesota), I'm 100% convinced that a support group is a necessity for a prospective adoptive parent as well as for a parent who has already successfully adopted.

In addition to the two groups I've joined, I've also sat in as an observer at other parent group meetings—and have been consistently impressed by the sincere desire members have to help each other. In fact, I've often thought that people who *haven't* adopted their children are really deprived of a great benefit!

Why Your Search Should Start Here

If you're a childless person seeking to adopt a baby, do NOT be embarrassed to walk into a parent group filled with adoptive parents who've already succeeded. Instead, think of the wealth of free advice available in that room! And stride in purposefully and eager to learn!

Because whether you want to adopt a domestic infant or toddler or you wish to adopt an international child, a support group can offer invaluable tips.

Let's say you want to adopt internationally—often your group can tell you which countries have children available for adoption, and which agencies members have dealt with. They can also direct you to members who've recently received their children from that country.

Did they have to travel there? Where did they stay? What did they bring, and what did they *wish* they had brought with them? You're probably beginning to see how people who've already faced the situation you're planning to face can provide you with do's and don'ts to help you avoid problems they may have experienced, as well as tell you how they successfully solved problems.

Did they adopt through an agency or did they do a parent-initiated placement—meaning they found the orphanage or foreign attorney who handles adoptions themselves? What was it like dealing with the United States Immigration and Naturalization Service? And so on. (We'll cover many more details of international adoption in the chapter devoted to that subject. But I want to encourage you early on to find a support group!)

If you want to adopt a domestic child, your support group can often tell you which agencies are accepting applications, and they know about new agencies that have just opened for business and *don't* have a waiting list, because they never existed before!

And if you're applying to an established agency which does have a waiting list, how long *is* the wait? Sometimes social workers tell callers the wait is longer than it actually may be to discourage people who aren't really committed to adoption.

Support group leaders can direct you to individual members who have adopted the way you want to adopt: Are you interested in a biracial child? They'll refer you to a member who has adopted one. Do you want to adopt a "special needs" child—a baby with physical or emotional problems? It's very likely someone in the group has succeeded in this kind of adoption and can offer you pointers. (Read the chapter on special needs adoption for some pointers from *this* writer!)

Many, and perhaps most, of you will want to adopt a perfectly healthy infant, and your group can tell you about the latest rules and regulations in your state. If you want to adopt independently, you can ask them for a listing of recommended attorneys. Some groups are heavily oriented to either international or domestic adoption, so you should ask what they lean toward before you join. If you're interested in adopting a child from South America and everyone in the group is adopting locally, they could have trouble meeting your needs.

During the adoption process, you may need some mental hand holding from a member. (I did!) Why is everything taking so long! Does this or that mean there's a problem? Why is this social worker standing between you and the thing you want the most: your child!

Fellow members can calm you down and assuage your fears.

Sure, you can talk about it with your friends or relatives—but they'll usually be as uncertain as you are and will probably end up making you feel worse! It's far better to talk with someone who's been there before and who cares passionately about adoption.

It's also true that sometimes birthmothers will contact support groups directly and ask for assistance in finding a family for their child. Some groups maintain resume files for birthmothers to review, while others will describe prospective parents, with their permission, to pregnant women.

If a birthmother walks into an attorney's office one week before her due date—or sometimes even *after* her child is born—he may need help in finding good parents for this baby. Who is the logical group to call? A parents' support group! Although this doesn't happen every day, it does happen. . .and you'll want to hear about it!

In addition, many groups have invited social workers and attorneys to join, and consequently, you'll have a chance to meet and rub elbows with these professionals and begin a friendly relationship.

Educating Yourself in a Congenial Atmosphere

Most groups meet monthly or bi-monthly and members are open to newcomers and their questions. You can ask your social worker questions too, of course, but maybe you don't *want* to ask her everything!

Some groups have elaborate programs and guest speakers, while smaller groups provide informal get-togethers centered loosely around a topic. They share a common bond. "There's a special feeling we have for each other," explained an adoptive parent. "We care, and when you're on that other side of the fence and haven't adopted yet, you can sometimes feel it's almost a hopeless situation. A support group really helps."

She's talking about one of the really big pluses of joining a support group: the strong camaraderie which can develop between people dedicated to the common goal of adopting and raising children. Members are morale boosters who will actively encourage you to pursue your goal of adoption—they won't tell you it's impossible, they'll tell you how to *make* your dream come true! You'll have to do your "homework" too—they're not going to drop a baby in your lap. But they know the ins and outs of various forms of adoption.

In these days when your extended family is probably spread all over the United States, with grandma in California, your sister in Idaho, and maybe your brother in Kansas, it's really nice to share child rearing tips with others who are as committed as you are.

These are people who truly love children and are willing and eager to share what they've learned. One adoptive father who adopted a two-year old who was emotionally disturbed said, "When my wife and I had a problem, we could call up and find out how others solved this or that problem. Or talk about it at meetings. They'd make suggestions, and they'd usually work!"

Said one adoptive mother referring to her teenage daughter, "She never told anyone she was adopted." After the family joined the group and her daughter met other adoptees, the child become more open. "She started casually mentioning in school that she was adopted and to her amazement about a half dozen other kids she'd known for years said they were adopted too!" says her mother. "Now she really sees adoption as normal."

If you decide to adopt internationally, other members will help you face the varied reactions of strangers who may comment when your children don't look like you—say you're as pale as a ghost and you've adopted a Hispanic child.

Even if you adopt a child which the general public will assume is your own, a support group is tremendously valuable. Some members want to breast-feed their adopted infants—it is possible, and help is available. When should you tell your child he is adopted? What should you do if she grows up and wants to search for her birthmother? If members don't know, they'll generally try very hard to help you find the resources you need to answer these questions.

Not everyone is a member of a support group, and that makes it harder on them. Several people I interviewed, who were not members when they adopted, described the difficult research they did and the many calls they made to learn information that would have been easily obtainable from a support group. Why duplicate all that effort—wasting your time when you could be spending time searching for your child? Some of these people later joined a support group and said how much they wished they'd known about a group when they were in the adoption process— how much it would have helped!

Many support groups offer workshops on adoption in general, parenting, or special topics of concern—such as drug abuse in birthmothers. In fact, the adoption workshop held by F.A.C.E. (Families Adopting Children Everywhere) of Baltimore, Maryland is held in such high regard that most local adoption agencies require prospective parents to take this course before they can adopt. Now that's credibility!

Newsletters and Books

Most groups also produce monthly or bi-monthly newsletters that are packed with information and sometimes photos. For example, the OURS magazine is devoured immediately by over 10,000 readers in the United States (Including me, it's fascinating!).

Why? Because this magazine of about seventy-five pages is filled with candid articles written by adoptive parents who describe the trials, tribulations, and successes of adopting. Problems they've faced, how they've coped with the reactions of strangers and family, and much more. The magazine also includes photos and descriptions of "waiting children" throughout the world, and yes, some of those kids are under two! (I fell in love with a photo of a little two year-old boy from Thailand!)

Most parent newsletters include listings of families who've recently adopted, discussions of pending legislation in the state or federal government, and serious and thoughtful debates on such issues as transracial adoption, special needs problems, foreign-based diseases, childhood adjustments, and other topics.

The latest books and newsletters are often reviewed, including an overview of the newest resources on adoption.

Some large groups produce books for members. For example, F.A.C.E. offers a bound book entitled *They Became Part Of Us,* (Mini-World Publications, 1985), which is nearly 200 pages of the experiences of adoptive parents.

The organization also produces a coursebook of helpful information which is very up-to-date. (*Family Building Through Adoption* was published in 1987.) Oriented to families in the Maryland/ Virginia/D.C. area, these books are also valuable references to adoptive families nationwide, as well as those considering adoption.

What If the Nearest Group Is Over 200 Miles Away?

Maybe you're not near a support group—I'm not. My support group is over a three hour drive for me. But they're also as close as the phone, and worth those toll calls! Why? Because when you have a question on adoption, they can advise. And if the person you call does *not* know the answer, she or he will generally find someone who does know.

I interviewed a New Hampshire woman who lived several hundred miles away from her support group; the Open Door Society of New Hampshire. She intends to stay a member, even though she rarely goes to meetings and has successfully adopted her child.

"I don't want to detach myself from them," she says. "They helped me tremendously in finding my child and I want to remain a member so that when she's a little older, we can go to meetings together and she can meet other adopted children."

Of course the social aspect of a support group is important too, and many groups offer dances, holiday parties, and special dinners to bring members together in a relaxed social environment. Often, there are Halloween or Valentine parties for the kids, too!

Support groups carry a lot of weight with state legislatures on adoption-related issues, too. After all, the logical ones for legislators to go to for help are the very people involved. One adoptive mother said a social worker asked her support group for help in banning independent adoption in the state.

"She said she couldn't get it outlawed without our help," said the mother. Since many members of the group supported independent adoption, they refused to help the social worker and her efforts failed.

Helping others is an important aspect of many support groups. Some assist the local welfare office by taking pictures of waiting children for the photo listing book. Others solicit money for children in less developed countries. Many perform drives for toys around Christmas/Hanukkah time for needy children in the area.

Speaking out loud and clear to the media on the issue of adoption is also important to parents' groups. Every so often there will be a scandal about someone selling babies from Mexico or some other country, and a reporter may make the grand leap in logic that all international adoption is tainted. If he does, he'll hear from a support group!

Of course, not all members of a group are vocal and activist— as in any group, some members opt for a lower profile. And that's okay too! There's room for everyone.

Finding a Parents' Group

I thought I'd list all the parents' groups for you in my appendix, but there are so many groups nationwide, that one state could fill up several pages! So I've tried to list at least one group per state. Contact the group which is closest to you and tell them you want to adopt a baby or toddler. (Tell them my book "sent" you!) If they're very far from you, ask them to recommend a group which is closer to your home.

If the group nearest you is primarily oriented to international adoption and you want to adopt domestically, tell them so. Ask if there are any other local groups, more oriented to your needs, which could help you.

Write to the branch of your state social services office that handles adoptions and ask them for a listing of parent support groups. (Addresses for state adoption offices are listed in the appendix.)

If you're adopting through an agency, ask them if they know of any support groups in your area—some agencies help parents form groups. And some agencies form their own groups for adoptive parents. For example, the Southwest Maternity Center of the Methodist Mission Home, in San Antonio, Texas prides itself on its groups.

"We have 25 chapters in all major cities in Texas and one chapter in Colorado, one in Louisiana and one in New Mexico," says Bryce Hatch, director of the agency.

Another source to contact is the national headquarters of OURS in Minnesota and ask them for the nearest OURS chapter. (See the appendix for their address.)

Conclusion

Whether you have no children and want to adopt, have biological children and seek to adopt, or have already adopted, I recommend you find the nearest parent support group and join up! You'll find it a positive experience and well worth the ten to twenty dollars in annual dues: especially if it leads you to your child!

"I'm an active member because we all get along really well," said an adoptive mother. "My son will grow up knowing other adopted kids and knowing adoption is okay—it's a normal way to create a family."

CHAPTER 3
Motivations and Feelings of Birthmothers and Adoptive Parents

It takes a strong commitment from a birthmother to make an adoption plan in today's social climate. Many single pregnant women consider two alternatives only: abortion or keeping the baby. The woman who opts for adoption often finds herself the subject of considerable social disapproval.

"I had three girls last month who really wanted to place their babies for adoption, but they couldn't withstand the social pressure," sighed a social worker.

"One girl's parents told her she could come home from the hospital *with* the baby—or she could stay away from home."

The girl was seventeen and no one would support her on the adoption. All her friends said things like, "How can you give up your own flesh and blood?" So she very reluctantly kept the baby, tearfully asking the social worker if she'd still be there if she needed her. Yes, of course.

Another teenager opted for abortion. If she remained pregnant, it would soon become obvious to the world. Abortion seemed an easy way out—no one would have to know about it.

"I wish society would leave these girls alone to make their own decisions," says Dorothy Barkley, Executive Director of the Texas Cradle Society in San Antonio, Texas. "Today there is extreme peer pressure to keep your baby, whether it's right for you or not."

This chapter covers the motivations of birthmothers who do and who don't decide to make an adoption plan, as well as motivations of adopting parents. A general overview profile is also included for birthmothers and adoptive parents, discussing who they are in relation to age, socioeconomic status, education, and other factors.

Knowledge is power and the more you understand *why* birthmothers place and why they don't, the better handle you'll have on the whole subject and the more confidence you'll have that you can and will succeed in adopting.

Also discussed are the feelings and reactions of the adoptive parents' extended family about an adoption—what if your Mom or Dad is strongly opposed to adoption?

Who Places Babies for Adoption

The stereotype of the average pregnant woman considering adoption is the fourteen or fifteen year old girl who is "only a baby herself." She is poverty-stricken and uneducated, and just doesn't know any better. Instead, agency directors and social workers nationwide told me that these are generally the girls who *keep* their babies and it's far more frequently the blue-collar/middle class women *over* seventeen or eighteen who place their babies for adoption.

"Most of the women we see placing their babies for adoption are over eighteen and they can see beyond what's happening to them today," says James Timmens, Director of Placements for Adoption Services Associates in San Antonio, Texas.

Some of them already have children. Says Timmens, "Many of them are nineteen, twenty, or twenty-one and have one or more children they've kept. They now know what it's like to be a single parent." And they also know they can't handle any more children. So they make an adoption plan for their child.

Jeffrey Rosenberg is Director of Public Policy for the National Committee For Adoption in Washington, D.C., and he agrees with Timmens that birthmothers who place their babies for adoption are more future-oriented than those who keep their babies.

Says Rosenberg, "One thing research has definitely shown is that birthmothers who place their children for adoption have a clear future perspective in their thinking. They can picture themselves five or ten years down the road and make a decision based on that future orientation. The teens who parent have not developed that concrete future orientation."

A recent study by Dr. Michael Resnick of the University of Minnesota also appears to support this view. His study was one of numerous adoption-related studies funded by the Adolescent Family Life Program, under the United States Department of Health and Human Services.

According to a release by the Department of Health and Human Services, Resnick interviewed and analyzed information received from 120 teen mothers, including 60 who kept their babies and 60 who placed them. One intriguing finding: the teenagers who placed their babies for adoption came from more affluent families than teen parents.

In addition, placers were more likely to continue their education, while the teenagers who kept their babies had lower educational and occupational goals.

Unfortunately, the lower socioeconomic status of the teenagers who keep their babies usually continues throughout their lifetimes. A national survey on adopted children and adoptive parents by Dr. Christine Bachrach of the National Center for Health Statistics revealed that teen parents who decide to keep their babies never catch up economically with their peers.

Often they do not finish high school and rarely do they graduate from college. Dr. Bachrach's study revealed that the average years of education among never married birthmothers was 10.7.

Their social and financial status obviously affects their children, and according to Bachrach's study, 62% of the children living with never-married birthmothers were living below the poverty level.

If the birthmothers *did* marry, their status was raised; yet 11% were still below the poverty level. (Compared to the two percent of adopted children whose parents lived below the poverty level.)

Of course, it's true money and education can't buy happiness, but living on welfare in a public housing project is no picnic either.

Other experts agree that the public perception of the woman who makes an adoption plan for her baby is in stark contrast to reality.

"The poor girl, the runaway, the delinquent, the irresponsible, downtrodden, and hopeless have always clung to their babies," says David Keene Leavitt, a Los Angeles attorney who has overseen over 7,000 adoptions.

He continues, "That's really the only treasure this girl is going to ever have in her lifetime—she's not going to give it up! In the more marginal parts of society, motherhood is still the only real destination a woman has in the world. The sooner she's a mother, the sooner she's a grownup."

Then who *are* the birthmothers who opt for adoption? Says Leavitt, "They are generally middle class girls from the silent majority to whom bringing home a baby without a husband is just plain against the rules."

Mothers Who Place for Adoption Are Not All Teens

Increasing numbers of birthmothers are in their twenties and even thirties. "Every once in awhile we have a woman in her thirties who may be divorced and have a couple of teenagers already and just can't handle a new baby," says Timmens.

An adoptive mother told me about her child's birthmother: a woman in her late thirties who was working overtime and struggling to support two teenagers.

Deciding her options were abortion, keeping the baby and leaving her in daycare all the time, going on welfare, or placing the baby for adoption, she chose adoption: it seemed the only logical answer to her.

She wrote her daughter a letter to read when she's grown, explaining to her that when she had her two other children, she was happily married. Now everything was different, and she felt she was doing the one right thing for the baby.

Adds Timmens, "I also see birthmothers who are in the middle of college—it's an unplanned pregnancy in their junior year. They'll place the baby for adoption, and I can predict their future: they'll graduate from college and do well."

Leigh Ann Johnson, Director of Adoptions for Shepherd Care Ministries in Hollywood, Florida, agrees, and says, "The girls who are most likely to relinquish for adoption have career goals and educational goals and have a better relationship with their fathers than the girls who keep their babies. They have more to lose by single parenting."

She adds, "Society views adoption as a nice way for infertile couples to get a baby, but they haven't really viewed it as a good thing for the girl. But girls who place their babies for adoption are more likely to get married later, continue their education, not go on welfare, and be involved in some kind of a church. So it can be a very good choice for the girl as well."

Leavitt agrees and says, "Society sees adoption as a one-way street, with the adoptive parents as the big winners and the birthmothers as the big losers. But the girl I see going through with an adoption is relieved and thankful she was able to find a couple who is going to love her child and keep it safe and give it everything."

Looking for Love in All the Wrong Places

In contrast to the birthmothers who make adoption plans for their infants, are the young teens who are convinced that keeping and raising the baby is the only way to go.

Says Timmens, "The fifteen and sixteen year olds who get pregnant keep the baby. They have romantic visions in their heads and imagine a Knight in Shining Armor will arrive on his horse and they'll all live happily ever after. They just can't see beyond their noses."

He adds, "The young teens have various motivations for keeping their babies: for example, they want somebody to love them."

The reality is far grimmer.

About ten years ago I worked for a state welfare department investigating whether or not welfare and food stamp recipients were truly eligible for the benefits they were receiving.

The saddest cases I saw were the teenage mothers on public assistance, such as the sixteen year old mother living alone and lonely with her baby in a tiny dark apartment. She gave me a photo of the baby's father so I would recognize him when he came out of the factory where he worked. (Part of my job was to ask the alleged birthfather if: a.) he was the father of the baby and b.) he provided any financial support to the girl.)

I tried to convince her to take some legal action against the man so she could obtain support for herself and her baby. "If he doesn't want us, then we don't want him," she said firmly.

At her request, I crossed-my-heart-and-hoped-to-die that I would return her one and only picture. Later that afternoon I talked to the young man, who denied her "lies" about his paternity. I sent back the picture to the girl the next day.

Another sad case: I went to see a thirty-five year old divorced woman on welfare. During the interview, her seventeen year old daughter announced that she was pregnant, too. "Can I get welfare and still live with Mom?" she asked anxiously.

Voluntary Adoptions of Newborns

Perhaps one reason the public thinks all pregnant single women are the same is that many people confuse women who opt for adoption with women whose children are involuntarily taken from them by the welfare system.

Attorney Leavitt feels it's important to understand that there's a distinctive difference between an older child adoption and a baby adoption.

"It's as different as pediatrics is from obstetrics!" he says. "The older child is generally seized by the welfare system from its parents, against their will, and thrust into adoption because its parents have fumbled the ball and been declared unfit."

And the baby adoption? "In this case, the newborn is placed in the adoption system because its mother makes a voluntary decision that parting with the child is indispensable both to her and her child's future happiness," says Leavitt.

Other Findings on Birthmothers

Other fascinating findings about birthmothers are available from such sources as Ph.D. disserations. Elizabeth Lindner of the University of Wisconsin did a study in 1984 on maternal-fetal attachment in the pregnant adolescent, and studied self-esteem, the birthmother's relationship with her own mother, and how it all related to the decision to keep or release her baby for adoption.

Her findings: "adolescents who planned to keep their infants obtained significantly higher maternal-fetal attachment scores than those who planned to release." Which makes sense: if a woman has a very strong emotional tie to her fetus, it seems logical that she would lean towards keeping the child.

No significant differences in self-esteem were discovered between women who kept their babies and women who placed them for adoption.

Another factor among the "keep" group was a strong ongoing relationship with the baby's father. And finally, Lindner found a strong relationship between the birthmothers' decision to keep or release and the preferences of their mothers.

Concluded Lindner, "The results support the idea that the environment in which the pregnancy is sustained and relationships with significant others are important factors in facilitating maternal-fetal attachment in pregnant adolescents."

A more recent dissertation by Kathleen Herr of Brandeis University backs up Linder's findings. According to the conclusions in Herr's 1986 social work dissertation on adolescent pregnancy, the adolescents most likely to make an adoption plan were those whose mothers favored adoption. In addition, she found the teenagers placing their infants for adoption had few peers who had chosen to parent.

The implications for adopting parents are clear: it's very important for adoptive parents to determine if the birthmother and birthfather are still "involved," because if there's any uncertainty on the birthmother's part, it will be heightened by a continuing relationship with her baby's father.

It's equally important to ask your social worker or attorney to find out how the birthmother's own mother feels about the adoption. Is she supportive, neutral, or negative?

An antagonistic attitude could lead to problems before finalization, whereas a very positive attitude means the birthmother will probably feel more confident she's doing the right thing.

I interviewed a "birthgrandmother" in her mid-forties who encouraged her eighteen year old daughter to place her baby for adoption.

"Maybe I'm selfish, but I just didn't want to raise any more babies, and I knew who would be doing most of the work—me!" she said. So she advised her daughter to find an adoptive family, and she and her daughter asked the obstetrician to help them find a family who would be interested in an open adoption with continuing contact between the birthmother and the adoptive parents.

Three days later, the doctor received a resume and photos of a couple living several thousand miles away who were eager to adopt a baby and interested in open adoption. Both women took this to be a "sign," and the child was ultimately adopted by the couple.

Some Statistics

How about a basic statistical profile of the average birthmother? According to Bachrach, in 1982, women aged fifteen to forty-four had borne almost seventy-one million babies, and had placed about 594,000 for adoption. (In an interview with Bachrach, she said this estimate is probably conservative.)

Her research revealed that 88% of the children born to those mothers who opted for adoption were unmarried, 6% were born to women who were previously married but not married at the time of the birth.

The shocker: 6% of the babies placed had married parents.

Married people are still placing infants for adoption, whether because of a bad financial situation or a rapidly dissolving marriage. They don't believe in abortion, but they can't cope with an infant, either.

Says Timmens, "I have married couples placing their babies for adoption, and they're always high school dropouts with a lack of skills. They have two or three kids already and are unemployed. They may have a fairly stable marriage, but it is so tough raising the other chidren that they decide to go for adoption, and they both sign the relinquishment paper."

He adds, "These are the people who generally answer the want ads. They want expenses taken care of, but agencies are going to negotiate that with them and half of them would not want to provide them with any support." As a result, such couples place their infants in a private adoption.

Timmens reflects, "Ironically, the kid they place for adoption has got a better destiny than the ones that they're keeping. The kid who is adopted will go to college, but the ones they keep will probably drop out of high school." (Further evidence bearing Timmens out: I attended an adoption seminar at which an adoptee who found his birthmother said she was astounded that he was a college graduate: her other children were all high school dropouts.)

Race was another factor among birthmothers in Bachrach's study. Bachrach found White mothers were more likely to place their babies for adoption than Black mothers: 12% vs. less than 1%.

It wasn't that Black single moms were so much more maternal: often they depended on their mothers, aunts, or other relatives to watch and sometimes raise their children.

Another intriguing finding of the study: White mothers were more likely to place their babies for adoption if their own fathers had some college education than if their own father had not completed high school.

Perhaps, the father's college education inspired the birthmothers to want something better for themselves and their children than single parenthood.

When we talk about birthmothers who opt for adoption, the bottom line is we're generally talking about women who are mature enough to know they can't handle a child, and mature enough to consider the child's interests above their own. At least, that's what the experts say. But what about the birthmothers themselves—how do they feel?

The Birthmothers Speak

I interviewed over twenty birthmothers. A few had placed their infants fifteen or twenty years ago in a very "closed" and traditional adoption. Others had placed within the past year or two. Yet even the mothers who had placed long ago remembered details with amazing clarity!

Here's one woman's story, and although she has unique aspects to her tale, there are many feelings she shares in common with all birthmothers. She placed her child last year, when she was twenty-three.

"I was adopted myself when I was three months old, too. I loved my parents but they passed away when I was little so I didn't have it too easy. I lived with an aunt and uncle and then moved into foster care. I ended up becoming what you'd call a troubled teenager. I'm a Christian now.

"I think there's a lot of social pressure to keep the baby, and part of that is so you won't get an abortion. Some people get pregnant and run down to the abortion center before they've thought through all the alternatives.

"I placed my baby last year, through a Christian attorney. I already had a three year old, and they have different fathers. I didn't give him up right away—I kept him for three months.

"But I wasn't really bonding to him the way we should have. I knew what bonding was like because of my first son, and I had this feeling he wasn't really supposed to be with me. So I went to a lawyer and told her I was thinking of giving the baby up for adoption.

"She pretty much picked out the family for me, and that was okay with me. I'm supposed to get pictures and a letter once a year and I can send him anything I want, gifts and cards and letters.

"But everytime I write him a letter, it says basically the same things, I love him, hope he's all right, and he's always in our thoughts and prayers.

"I think it helps me keep my sanity so long as I know he's being well taken care of. I did what was best for him, I'm sure of it.

"Some of the people around me were very rude about me giving him up for adoption. They said, 'If you're giving up this one, why don't you give up your other son?' They didn't understand.

"The hardest part was the day after he left, it was the worst. People don't understand, it's like someone died. Even though you know that baby is alive, inside you're still grieving as if that child died.

"But you don't have a funeral and you don't grieve with other people. Most people who give up their babies are in the hospital, surrounded by people having babies! I think that would be harder than the way I did it.

"I think if you're in love with who the father of the baby is, that makes a difference. I just made a mistake and I couldn't care less about him.

"I still have the pictures I took of the baby and I hope the parents send me pictures, too. I know parents have to keep their guard up, but I hope they wouldn't be so paranoid as to not allow the birthmother some kind of joy in seeing pictures. If my son and I received more pictures, it would make our day.

"If we ever ran into each other, like maybe in the supermarket or something, and I recognized him from a picture, I wouldn't scream, 'That's my child' and grab him and run off. I'd just say how cute he is and polite stuff.

"I hope someday we can get together. I guess it will depend on how my life is then, and if it's better, then I wouldn't mind if he got in touch with me. But I wouldn't pursue him, I'd wait for him to pursue me first."

Here are several comments from a married birthmother.

"I placed my child with the state because it was my own decision to give that child a better life.

"My husband protested vocally but when it came time to signing the paper, he did. We weren't fit to be married, we were just kids.

"I think you can either give your children what you can or in some cases you can do better. I'm sure my daughter is getting an education and has a busy life that's not centered on the streets.

"I had a therapist then who told me that when you see mothers who are poor and drag their kids around in a terrible environment, they think they're so wonderful because they have their children with them.

"But the only reason they have those children is because *they* can't bear to part with them. I knew that if you're just one of the masses, then your child will be just one of the masses too.

"Everybody was mad at me and thought it was a disgrace for a married woman to give a child up for adoption.

"I think people who are adopting children must have a terrible fear that someday this person is going to creep into their lives. That was one reason I made sure when I did this, there was no turning back. I didn't want someone to take really good care of my child and then turn around and be screwed on account of it.

"I felt if they were going to take my child and raise her and give her a good home, then the least I could do was step aside.

"I won't seek her out. If she finds me one day, that is another thing. But I will not go to any length to find her."

Most of the interviewees were convinced they had done the right thing. The only ones with regrets were the birthmothers who placed their children fifteen or twenty years ago. Several felt they were forced into it. Some of these women are still working through their anxiety. Some have searched for and found their children, while others hope their children will someday seek them.

One birthmother who had found her adult daughter said she was worried about the adoptive parents of her daughter. Why? "Because she is spending so much time with me, and not enough with them!"

she said. When I asked why she should care, she said with irritation, "They're the ones who raised her, they're her parents!" (More information on the "Search" aspect is covered briefly in the last chapter.)

One other intriguing aspect about the birthmothers was that they *all* have children now. Some have four or five! In fact, one birthmother who was unable to have children later in life adopted a child—very symmetrical!

Motivations of Adoptive Parents

If you ask someone *why* she or he adopted, you'll probably be told "we couldn't have children, so we decided to adopt." But why did they adopt? You don't have to have children to survive. There must be something more to it. And there is.

Some parents have wanted to adopt since they were children themselves, and are fulfilling a lifelong dream.

"Ever since I was a little girl, I wanted to adopt a child," relfects an adoptive mother in New Hampshire. "I don't know why, but I always knew I wanted to adopt. My uncles and aunts would ask me if I would love an adopted child the same as I would one of my own, and I answered very confidently, 'Yes!' And I was right."

Another adoptive mother decided to adopt when she was ten years old and read an article in Reader's Digest about the Holt adoption agency.

"So I grew up with the idea of adopting an Amerasian," she explains. She later adopted an Indian infant.

Another adoptive Mom explains the motivations of many very simply, "It was the only way we were going to have children. We felt by not having children, there would be something missing in our lives and we would regret it later."

A Maryland nurse and her family decided to adopt to create their family and ultimately adopted a special needs baby. "We just started looking at adoption. As we were looking, we saw kids with problems, and thought, oh, that wouldn't be any big deal," she explains. This family adopted an infant with respiratory problems which the child is overcoming with age.

One adoptive parent found his family's infertility particularly painful. Because he was an adoptee, and, as he put it, "I had no biological link backwards, so I really wanted one forwards." It wasn't to be.

His story has a happy ending, however. Having been raised in a home he describes as warm and loving, he knew adoption could work. He and his wife adopted an infant from Mexico, and someday hope to adopt again.

Why do parents adopt internationally? Sometimes it's because they think it will take too long to adopt an American baby. Maybe private adoption is not legal in their state and the agencies all have long waiting lists, or perhaps they don't wish to apply to an out-of-state agency.

Others feel that there's plenty of demand for healthy American newborns, but South American, Indian, and other foreign babies are languishing in orphanages, in need of loving parents. (See the chapter on international adoption for further information on this topic.)

Profile of Adoptive Parents

Although most states do not provide statistical information on birthparents, some do analyze adoptive parents.

For example, acording to the Vital Records Division of the South Carolina Department of Health and Environmental Records, 54% of the mothers who adopted children ages newborn to eleven months were themselves between the ages of 25 and 34. Another 41% were between the ages of 35 and 44.

According to a report produced by the state of California, in 33% of all adoptions the adoptive mother was between 31 and 35 years old, and in 57% of the adoptions, the adoptive mother was over 35. (Unfortunately, this data did not break out the age of the children adopted; but, not all of the adopted children were infants and toddlers.)

California also analyzed the educational achievement levels of adoptive mothers and fathers. Over 57% of the mothers had some college or were college graduates, and over 59% of the fathers fell into the same category.

About 20% of the adoptive fathers and 28% of the adoptive mothers were only high school graduates. (Fourteen percent of the adoptive fathers and 6% of the adoptive mothers were not accounted for by educational achievement.)

As a result, it appears that most adoptive parents are mature and have a good education behind them. It's probably logical to assume that most are infertile. They're probably older than the birthparents by at least ten years, and they have sufficient income to raise a child.

Reactions of Friends and Family

When you and your husband—or you alone, if you're single—announce to your friends and family that you plan to adopt, are reactions always positive?

No, they're not. My father-in-law was baffled as to why we wanted to adopt a baby. It was inconceivable to him and he warned against it. Now he's our son's biggest fan and probably does not remember any objections he had. In fact, he recently told me he couldn't understand why people hired surrogate mothers. "Why don't they adopt like you did?" he said.

When a parent decides to adopt a child from another country or one of a different race, there may be some initial opposition from the family—but it almost always evaporates at or soon after the child's arrival.

"It takes a pretty cold-hearted person to shun a cute little baby," reassures a Florida mom.

One mother reports that her mom was turned off by the idea of foreign adoption because she was worried the baby would come with lice or scabies—or something worse. "I told her this is what we were going to do and we were committed," says the adoptive mom.

And now? "Well, as soon as she gets through the door, it's 'Where's the baby?' Forget about saying hi to me!" she laughs. Another mother was furious with her brother for not visiting her new son. She didn't see him until several months later when she went to *his* house to see his newborn son.

"He came rushing out to the car and apologized for not coming over," she recalls. "I was pretty mad at him, but maybe it was just an oversight on his part." She forgave him and the two families visit on a regular basis.

But what if all your best efforts fail and for some reason your parents can't warm up to your child? It occasionally happens and is very sad.

"My dad is seventy-five and set in his ways," sighs an adoptive father. He adds with increasing anger, "He acts like I've failed because we haven't borne him a grandchild. Well, we couldn't do it! And he treats our delightful daughter like a stranger!"

In such unusual cases, the parents must learn to live with a relative's reactions if he refuses to change, and may have to curtail visits to avoid upsetting the child.

Reactions of Strangers

Even if you are perfectly happy with the attitudes of your friends and family, you'll have to occasionally contend with the general public. This is especially true if you adopt a child who looks different from you, and you can expect stares and comments in the supermarket, stores, etc.

One blue-eyed blonde parent became so irritated by strangers' questions about her brown-skinned son, that when asked about him, she'd reply, "I don't have any idea who his father is!"

I can't say I recommend this response, but the parent was very satisfied by the reactions she evoked.

"I transferred the embarrassment back to them," she said with great satisfaction. "They'll blush, stammer and back away."

A spillover of prejudice onto other siblings can sometimes occur. One family with a biological daughter decided to adopt two biracial Black/White children.

One day the little girl came home crying from her kindergarten class, because several parents had ordered their children to avoid her because she had Black brothers.

In another case, a parent with her Korean-born baby daughter in the shopping cart at the local supermarket noticed a woman staring hostilely at them both.

At the checkout counter, the woman rudely slammed her cart into the parent's cart, almost knocking the baby out. Note: such extreme reactions are very rare, and parents shouldn't worry about them.

Why do people act this way? Probably a combination of stupidity, prejudice, racism, and who knows what else. It would be a better world if people could be more loving, but there are some people who just seem to want to be nasty.

Even if you adopt a child who *does* resemble you in skin coloring, hair coloring, etc., you will face surprising reactions from strangers, especially right after you receive your baby.

The most amusing are the people who stare at you, stare at your stomach, and then back at your face in perplexity. If they get up the nerve, they'll say, "Were you pregnant? I never realized!"

Other questions are less innocuous. Some people will ask you such questions as: "Were his parents married?" or "How much did it cost?" or "How long did you wait?" or maybe "Are you going to help him find his mother when he grows up," and ad nauseum.

Answer what you feel comfortable answering, but don't feel you have to explain every personal detail about your child to the world.

"When strangers say, 'Oh, what a cute baby! Who does she get her red hair from?' I just say, 'It runs in the family,' " says an adoptive mother.

She continues, "I'm very open about our adoption but don't feel I have to tell every single person about it. It's up to me and my husband to decide who to tell and what to tell them."

One approach is a Miss Manners-type approach for those questions you don't feel like answering, and say, "Thank you so much for your interest in Susie. We are very happy we were able to become her parents." If they persist, you just keep saying the same thing, over and over.

One parent laughed at the truly strange questions people have asked her. For example, when she brought home her 2 1/2 month old Indian child, a woman at the supermarket asked, "Does he understand English?"

She adds, "We have friends who adopted babies from South America, and people have said to them, 'Isn't it wonderful to have bilingual children?' But they were adopted when they were three months old, they don't speak a word of Spanish!"

Another irritating reaction comes from the people who think you are so wonderful to take in this poor little waif, especially if the child is from a foreign country.

"It makes me nauseous when people come up and say, 'Oh, aren't you wonderful, look what you've done for these poor little beggars!' "

She continues, "Adopt selfishly! Adopt because you want to, not because you need to make a statement for a cause. Because, if you're doing it for a cause, then you're doing your children a great disservice—you can't live with that kind of cause for twenty years!"

Said another parent, "We just like children. We're not Super Mom and Super Dad, and we get at least as much enjoyment and love out of it as they do—maybe even more!"

Raising Adopted Children by adoptive parent Lois Melina is a comprehensive book dedicated to a whole array of adoption issues from infancy to adulthood, and is extremely helpful to adoptive parents and prospective adoptive parents. (Harper & Row, Publishers, 1986.)

The positive reactions of most people will far outweigh the negative. "My mother wears a Tee shirt that says, I'm the Best Grandma in the Whole World," laughs an adoptive mother in Virginia.

You may even find yourself accidentally "converting" others to adoption. "We adopted a child after meeting a couple who had adopted. They seemed so happy that we decided to check into it, and now we have two kids!" says a Connecticut father.

Most friends and family members will be very supportive of your adoption, and the few who are not so thrilled will usually come around. And who cares about the rest of the world? Your family and its happiness is the most important issue here.

CHAPTER 4
Domestic Agency Adoption

This is what the average American sees as the "right" way to adopt: you apply to an adoption agency and they evaluate your potential fitness as parents. If you're approved, then at some future point you will receive your bouncing baby boy or girl.

And this is the way numerous happy Americans *do* adopt their infants. Today there are hundreds of adoption agencies in the United States, a diverse group with a variety of orientations, placing babies throughout the nation.

There are agencies mainly interested in your religious background, agencies which concentrate on "special needs" kids, agencies which allow birthmothers to choose the adoptive parents, and agencies with other areas of specialization. There are also agencies which concentrate on international adoptions, and that topic is covered at length in another chapter.

Where Do You Begin to Search for the Agency That's Right for You?

This chapter covers the pros and cons of domestic agency adoption and offers helpful hints on finding the agency for your family. Should you apply to more than one agency? What kind of parents are they looking for? What is this going to cost you? And much more.

A brief section on "identified adoption" is also included. Now legal in Connecticut and Massachusetts, this is a quasi-independent form of adoption which is strictly regulated.

Other states consider identified adoption as falling under the category of independent adoption, so be sure to read that chapter, too.

In addition, a section on Adoption Services is included. These are organizations which charge a fee to prospective adoptive parents and maintain resumes on adoptive couples which are shown to birthparents.

The birthparent—usually the birthmother—selects the couple she prefers. Some services also offer extensive counseling for both birthparents and adoptive parents. These agencies appear to straddle the line between agency adoption and independent adoption.

Pros and Cons of Agency Adoptions

A good agency will provide counseling to birthparents and adoptive parents, and social workers will do their utmost to ensure making an adoption plan for the child is what the birthparents really want. They'll also carefully screen the adopting parents to determine that they are ready to adopt, and suitable people to adopt.

Even when agencies offer openness in adoption, and leave the choice of adoptive parents up to the birthparents, agency social workers still screen prospective adoptive parents in the course of the home study. Then people who "pass" the home study are those who are considered as parents and usually receive a child.

Many agencies offer individual and group counseling based on a wealth of experience which social workers can share with adopting parents and birthparents. This educational aspect is another advantage of agency adoption.

Adoptive parents generally do not know they have been matched to a particular birthmother—although they'll know if the adoption is open to the extent of meeting the birthmother. If she's eight months pregnant, it's apparent!

As a result, if they *don't* know a birthmother has been matched to them or they are next on the list, then they won't spend sleepless nights the last month of her pregnancy, wondering if she'll change her mind and keep the baby after all. Instead, they are not told about the baby until the mother has signed a consent form. Agency social workers see this as a major advantage to agency adoptions.

Which leads to one of the disadvantages of agency adoptions. Many agencies give adoptive parents about 24 hours notice to come pick up their baby. If the agency has a policy that one parent must take off time from work—and some agencies require at least one parent to take off three months or more from work—this could make for a very unhappy employer, when told you're leaving effective immediately for three months.

Even if your employer knows you've applied to adopt a child, a one-day notice is usually very inconvenient. However, social workers insist that most employers are understanding. (If they aren't, the parents apparently don't notify the social worker of any problem.) Of course, you probably won't get paid for this time off, so you may face a financial pinch as well.

Another time related disadvantage of agency adoptions is the waiting list. Sometimes you actually have to go on a waiting list to get on the waiting list! After a couple has gone through the trauma of learning they're infertile, they want a baby *now* and don't want to wait two or three years; or even one year.

Studies have revealed that waiting for a home study is more anxiety provoking than actually undergoing the study itself. But when you are finally studied, you know that once you "pass," you are in the running for a child.

So couples must do their homework to find the agencies with the shortest waiting lists or no waiting lists. They should also sign on with the agencies with the five-year waiting lists for a home study. Who knows? You may want to adopt another child five years from now!

Before plunging any further into meaty practical issues, I'd like to make several *major* points here.

Several Major Points

Are you ready? Here's Major Point Number One: you don't have to restrict yourself to agencies inside your state or your four or five state region! Really!

An Ohio woman adopted from Virginia. People in Connecticut adopted through an agency in Texas; Texas Cradle Society. And according to Anna Belle Illien, owner of Illien Adoptions International in Atlanta, Georgia, most of her domestic placements are out-of-state.

The Edna Gladney Home in Fort Worth, Texas places infants in Texas, Arkansas, Oklahoma, Louisiana, Connecticut, New York, New Jersey, and Pennsylvania. Chosen Children Adoption Services in Louisville, Kentucky places infants in Kentucky, Indiana, New Jersey, Connecticut, Tennessee, and New York. And other agencies place infants out of state as well—too many to list here.

Many people seeking to adopt will restrict themselves to agencies advertising in the Yellow Pages of their local phone directory. Although your ideal adoption agency may well be listed within those pages, it also may *not* be in there.

So don't think you must limit yourself to the boundaries of your state! Most states follow the Interstate Compact for the Placement of Children, a sort of "treaty" between the states which governs interstate adoption. It may take a little longer to adopt from another state, but it is probably worth that wait!

Major Point Number Two: many agencies which specialize in international adoptions also handle domestic adoptions. Some prefer to place their domestic babies within the state while others will place out of state as well. So DO consider an international adoption agency as a possible resource for a domestic adoption.

And Major Point Number Three: don't ignore religious adoption agencies, thinking you could never qualify because you're a different religion from the name of the agency. For example, you may not have to be Catholic to adopt from Catholic Social Services. And the same is true of other religious-based agencies. It IS true, however, that they may expect you to be a member of some organized religion, and probably would not want applicants who are atheists or agnostics.

In fact, a Catholic family asked Jewish Social Services, which happened to be the nearest adoption agency, to perform their home study for an out-of-state agency. They agreed, and the family now has their baby.

So before you reject a local religious adoption agency, check with them on their criteria: you may be pleasantly surprised.

The State Social Services Department

For many people, the first source which comes to mind when considering adoption is the state social services office. This is also generally the place which has the least number of infants; for example, according to state responses to a questionnaire I sent out in early 1987, the state of Utah placed only 11 children under the age of 2 in 1986, Alabama placed 55, Oregon placed 58, etc.

Yet although the state social worker will undoubtedly be *very* discouraging about your chances for adopting a child under age two, there is always a small chance you might succeed in adopting an infant or toddler through your state. And your chances increase if you are Black, biracial, or another racial minority.

Most of the children in the care of your state will be there because they've been abused, neglected, or abandoned. Or they may be handicapped or fall into another "special needs" category.

The state usually puts such children in foster care for up to 18 months, while the social worker actively seeks to find a way to reunite the child with its mother. If this is impossible after an extended period, parental rights are terminated and the child is freed for adoption. As a result of this system, most children available for adoption through the state are over age two.

The advantage to a state adoption is that the cost will be very low, and may encompass legal fees only. In fact, there may be subsidies available to you if you adopt a special needs child from the state. (Check with your social worker.)

The disadvantage is that the wait could be very long and state social workers have so many older children, they may strongly urge you to consider adopting one of them.

For those interested in adopting a child from the state social services department: first, find out if anyone in your support group has adopted a small child this way and what the circumstances were. Was the infant disabled temporarily or permanently?

Next, sign up for an orientation meeting with the state social services department and learn to read between the lines. Is there *no* chance of adopting a small child, or just a slim chance?

Adopting through the state is one possible route, but I strongly recommend you use it as only one source and apply elsewhere as well.

Religious Adoption Agencies

Religious-based agencies represent a significant percentage of the total picture.

Most readers have probably heard of Jewish Social Services or Catholic Social Services, and other mainstream religious adoption agencies. There are also many smaller agencies you might consider.

For example, if you are a very faithful churchgoer, you should consider one of the lesser known religious adoption agencies; for example, the LIGHT House in Kansas City Missouri, Gentle Shepherd in Olathe, Kansas, or others.

These agencies *will* place infants out of state if families meet their requirements for age, religious commitment, and other criteria. (Gentle Shepherd also prefers non-smokers.)

You should be a member of a church or synagogue if you wish to adopt through a religious agency. And that means *now*, not twenty or more years ago when your parents dragged you there.

Gentle Shepherd will accept pre-applications for healthy White infants in December of each year, from strong, practicing Christians throughout the United States. Parents must be under age 41 at the time the pre-application is received. In the past year, it has taken 18 months or less for approved parents to receive their baby through Gentle Shepherd.

Gaye Rundberg, program director for Gentle Shepherd, says the agency also places year-round for their small Samoan and biracial program, and both couples and singles may apply for these infants. Some religious groups have a very strong pro-life orientation. For example, The LIGHT House in Kansas City, Missouri is a pro-life group which seeks individuals committed to their philosophy. Shepherd Care Ministries in Hollywood, Florida, part of the larger organization of Bethany Christian Services, is similarly committed to pro-life. (Shepherd Care is interested in Florida residents only.)

Says Leigh Ann Johnson, Director of Adoptions for Shepherd Care, "We seek born-again Christians of any denomination—Catholics can be born again, Methodists can be born again. We're looking at a couple's personal spiritual commitment and the way they have acted it out in their daily lives."

If religion is very important to the adoption agency, it will be apparent immediately from the questions they ask you over the phone or from the informational literature they send you. If the brochure is liberally sprinkled with Bibical references, it's obvious they want strongly religious applicants. Other religious agencies may be satisfied if you regularly attend services.

Compared to the other criteria of age, financial status, etc. which most adoption agencies look at, religious agencies will take a very hard look at your religious commitment, and will ask you to answer written and verbal questions on religion. (More information is provided in the Home Study chapter on types of questions religious agencies ask.)

The good news is that many religious agencies do have children to place, and if you can meet their criteria, you CAN adopt a baby—sometimes in less than a year.

Other Types of Agencies

There are hundreds of private non-profit adoption agencies to whom your religious commitment is not of paramount importance. Instead they concentrate primarily or solely on your potential as a parent.

Most agencies are very upfront about what their requirements are for adopting parents, and can quickly tell you whether or not you could be considered for a home study.

Says Dorothy Barkley, executive director of the Texas Cradle Society in San Antonio, Texas, (which places infants, primarily in Texas and New Jersey), "Basically we're looking at couples between 25-38 years old who are citizens of the U.S., have been married three years or more, have no more than one other child, and have had studies done to show why they cannot create a pregnancy or carry it to full-term."

Others are more flexible in their requirements. Says Anna Belle Illien, Director of Illien Adoptions International, Ltd. in Atlanta, "We do not limit on the basis of age or number of children already in the home; instead, we take everybody on an individual basis. Arbitrarily saying you shouldn't adopt a baby at age 45 doesn't make a whole lot of sense—it's just easier to weed out applicants."

But even if your standards are more flexible, there still *are* some criteria, and there will be a home study before any placements occur. Says Illien, "We look for whether or not that home is a loving home to place a child."

The Edna Gladney Home in Fort Worth, Texas is very successful at infant adoptions, and placed 258 infants in 1986. According to Marilyn Anderson, director of adoptive placement for Gladney, applicants must be married at least three years, be between 24-39 years of age, have a medical reason why they cannot or should not have biological children, and have no more than one child in the home already. In addition, they may not have more than one previous marriage each.

"Our strength is that we offer very good services for all the people involved in what's called the adoption 'triangle' of birthparents, adoptive parents, and adoptees," says Anderson.

She explains further, "We offer very good medical service to the birthmothers and a lot of counseling. We also counsel the birthfathers if they want to be involved.

"We offer the adoptive parents a comprehensive education, teaching them how to talk to the child over the years about adoption and addressing many other issues. And we also offer services to the adoptees as they grow up to adults and will always give them non-identifying social and medical information."

She concludes, "Our services do not end at the time the adoption is finalized."

Dr. Lorraine Boisselle, a psychologist with over 16 years experience in adoption who currently directs The Adoption Centre in Maitland, Florida, says it's important for agencies and adoptive parents to understand that you don't have to be perfect to adopt.

She says, "When the social worker goes out to the home with a pad and pencil in her lap and starts asking questions, sometimes parents get the idea that you must be perfect and that makes you be a lot more rigid in terms of showing your feelings. Parents don't want to share how they feel, because it might be 'wrong' and therefore they won't get approved."

Concludes Boisselle, "I think the whole message we as adoption agencies should give to adoptive parents is that we're not looking for perfection. We're looking for a few good people who can be good parents."

Open Adoption: A Few Comments

Although I have dedicated an entire chapter to openness in adoption, I think it's important to talk here about agencies who are pursuing this philosophy, because it appears to be an increasing trend in adoption today.

Openness means the birthparents have an input into who adopts their child—ranging from specifying a particular religion they want, all the way to actually selecting the adoptive parents. "Our birthparents choose the adoptive parents based on biographies," explains Rundberg of Gentle Shepherd.

What do birthparents want in adoptive parents? "Birthparents want adoptive parents to be young, beautiful, and rich!" jokes Bryce Hatch, director of the Southwest Maternity Center of the Methodist Mission Home in San Antonio, Texas.

But what birthparents actually look for in adopting parents is often the same thing most agencies seek. Explains Hatch seriously, "What they really want is a stable home and a good marriage." Birthparents choose adoptive parents from applicants to the Southwest Maternity Center, based on information provided in an autobiography.

The Adoption Agency, a new agency in Ardmore, Pennsylvania which places children in Pennsylvania and New Jersey, allows birthparents to choose adoptive parents from non-identifying resumes.

"We don't have a lot of restrictions because the birthparents choose," says Maxine Chalker, Director of the agency.

"So if they want a family with five kids, that's fine with us. And if they want a family with no kids, that's fine too." (She says there *are* some limits; for example, the agency would disapprove of people in their sixties adopting newborns.)

James Timmens, Director of Placements for Adoption Services Associates in San Antonio, Texas provides resumes for birthmothers to choose from, if they wish. His agency does placements in Texas, New York, New Jersey, and Connecticut, and in 1986 they placed over 120 White and Hispanic infants.

"I will review about ten families with a birthmother and she will tell me which family she likes. I feel honor-bound to go along with her choice," he says seriously.

Occasionally Timmens sees "repeater" birthmothers coming back a year later to place another child. "The birthmother will say to me, 'Is it possible that you could place this child with the child I placed last year?' "

In such a case, he'll contact the adoptive parents to ascertain if they'd be interested in adopting the sibling of their child, and he says it has worked out on four separate occasions. (I also interviewed several adoptive parents who later adopted siblings of their adopted children. It's not a daily occurrence, but it does happen.)

Mardell Groth, Director of Florence Crittendon Services, a division of Child Services and Family Counseling in Atlanta, also allows birthmothers to select adoptive parents, and says she is frequently surprised by their choices.

For example, a couple in their late 40's applied to adopt, and she cautioned them it was unlikely they would be picked. "Darned if we didn't have a girl who *wanted* an older couple," she said. In another case, a birthmother reviewing several resumes immediately selected a family who already had a son. "The caseworker didn't know it, but it turned out this girl had a very good relationship with an older brother when she was growing up. She wanted that for her child," said Groth.

She concluded, "They're after something which can surprise you but yet makes perfect sense. It's fine line stuff, not broad brush at all."

It's important to understand that if a resume is prepared for birthparents to review, it should not be similar to the detached and factual resume one might submit to be considered for a job. Instead it should be descriptive and emotional, and explain *why* the family wants to adopt a baby.

And if a photo is needed, make sure it's the best possible picture! Don't submit a candid of you and your spouse at your last cook-out. Jokes Timmens, "Avoid using the photo of Dad lounging in his dirty tee shirt holding a beer can!"

Instead, seriously consider hiring a professional photographer so you can appear at your best and are more likely to be selected by a birthmother—or at least, not rejected out of hand.

(More information on this subject is provided in the chapter on openness in adoption.)

An Overview of Adoptive Parents Criteria

I asked every agency director and social worker I interviewed what traits they were seeking in adoptive parents—what kind of people did they perceive would make good parents? Several responses were discussed earlier, but I'll summarize the common denominators.

The most popular prospective parents are the younger and older "yuppies"—ages 25-40, affluent or middle class, childless and healthy, albeit infertile. But if you *don't* fit these criteria, do not despair, because there are agencies who will place with people over 40, with children, etc.

Here's a summary of some basic requirements some but not all agencies have:

- married at least three years
- at least a high school graduate
- both parents currently in good health
- one parent employed. (Usually the father. They may ask the mother to stay home with the child for the first year or some similar timeframe.)
- both United States citizens
- ages 25-40. (This is highly variable depending on the agency!)
- childless or only one child in the home already. (This is also variable.)
- infertile or believe you are infertile. People under 30 may be asked to provide proof of infertility from a doctor.
- no criminal record.
- adequate income to support the child.

Often last year's income tax is reviewed by the social worker, along with current pay stubs. Many agencies use a sliding scale to determine the fee you will pay, and the lower your income, the less the fee.

There are often additional requirements for various agencies; for example, a requirement to take a parenting class or attend special seminars. Some agencies even have maximum weight requirements.

It's worth mentioning here that, very often, "all bets are off" when it comes to adopting a special needs child, and the whole array of age criteria, number of children already in the home, etc., may be considerably loosened. A separate chapter is dedicated to this subject. In addition, fees are frequently slashed for families interested in adopting a special needs child.

Which leads me to costs. How much does it cost to adopt a baby today?

Costs to Adopt

Based on interviews with agency directors and adoptive parents nationwide, it appears that the average cost to adopt a baby through a private non-profit agency—one not supported by United Way funds—is about $11,000, plus or minus several thousand dollars. If you go through a religious agency, costs may be significantly lower but will usually still run in the thousands of dollars rather than hundreds of dollars.

Costs *do* vary greatly depending on which part of the country you live in, whether you live in a rural or urban area, and other factors. As a result, total adoption costs in your area for a private agency may be $8,000 or less, or over $12,000.

For example, according to Timmens of Adoption Services Associates, his agency's fee for out of state residents is currently $11,000, which includes medical and legal costs of the adoption.

In 1986, his agency placed about 120 "Anglo" and Hispanic children primarily in Connecticut, New York, New Jersey, and Texas and he expects 1987 to be about the same.

If you live in the states of Washington, Utah, or Alaska, you can apply to the Adoption Services of Western Association of Concerned Adoptive Parents (WACAP) for your child. They placed about 100 infants in 1986 and fees as of January 1987 were about $8,000.

The first fees you'll pay are application fees of about $20-$50 and home study fees which could be anywhere from $500-$1,000. Placement fees are paid when you receive your child, but you must be financially able to pay when you originally apply, and your financial status will be carefully reviewed.

Do these fees sound like a lot? Medical expenses are high today, and if you paid for the birth of your biological child it would also be expensive.

People who've decided the expense was more than made up by the joy of having a child were able to raise the money—some took second mortgages on their homes. Said one parent, "We took out a home improvement loan and improved our home by adopting a child."

Others cash in IRAs or savings, or borrow from the credit union or their family. To be somewhat crass, when you think of the price of a new car, the expenses to adopt an infant aren't so unreasonably high. If there's no chance that you could come up with $8,000 or $10,000 in the next year to five years, don't despair. There are agencies with lower fees. For example, some agencies charge a flat fee and add on any medical expenses the birthmother may have. If she has health insurance, there is no add-on.

If you must keep expenses down, seek out an agency which will not charge a large flat fee, but take into consideration whether the birthmother has medical insurance.

Some agencies charge lower fees for healthy Black or biracial babies because they receive subsidies for such infants. For example, the placement fee for a White infant is $3,000 at Gentle Shepherd and is $2,000 for a biracial child and $500 for a Black child. (This does not include medical fees and other expenses.)

Be sure to get an upfront reading on agency fees when you sign up. And find out what these include. Are they subject to change after a year or two, or are you locked into the amount you initially agreed upon? It's no fun to think about the cost angle of adoption, but this is not a case of "if you have to ask, you can't afford it." Find the agency right for your pocketbook.

Agency fees are obviously subject to change. And if you read this book three years after it's written, it's very likely the fees will be higher than they are in 1987. But I *do* want you to realize that adoption is affordable. About a year ago, a woman wrote an anguished letter to People Magazine saying that it was so unfair that you had to be rich to adopt. Well, I'm here to tell you that you do *not* have to be extremely affluent. Middle class people adopt, blue collar people and white collar people adopt. End of lecture on costs.

The Agency With Your Baby!

How can you select the agency which is right for you and then impress the agency that you are right for them?

The first step is to find out *what* agencies are out there before narrowing yourself down.

Do your homework! Start by checking the yellow pages under "adoption" for the older established agencies. Go to the library and look at the Yellow Pages for adoption agencies in other parts of the state.

A truly ambitious person will also check Yellow Pages for other states and write letters to those agencies, asking if they accept out-of-state applicants. Or you could call and request information. When they hear you're in another state, they'll usually tell you if you may apply to their agency.

Important: ask your support group for suggestions and ask, particularly, about any new agencies which have just opened their doors and don't have a waiting list. Call or write to other support groups in your state and ask about agencies in their area. Tell them you're a member of the XYZ Support Group and they'll relate to you better as a "brother" or "sister."

In fact, tell everyone you know, again and again, that you're interested in adopting and you're making a list of all possible adoption agencies.

Read this book thoroughly, and check the appendix. It provides a broad sampling of agencies which was compiled from my research and information the various states gave me.

Ask your state social services department if they have a listing of adoption agencies in your state. They license agencies and may have an updated list they can send you.

Follow every lead, no matter how small! If a friend of a friend tells you about a new agency, check it out!

Before Calling an Agency

Before you make that first call to ask for an application, there are a few things you need to do. First, have you had a fertility workup? Many adoption agencies require information on the nature of your infertility, who the physician was, etc.

There's a good reason for this. Said Timmens of Adoption Services Associates in San Antonio, Texas, "I had a couple apply who really wanted to adopt and when I asked them about their infertility, they said they had gone to a general practitioner who told them it looked like they weren't going to have kids."

No diagnostic tests had occurred, no fertility workup. Timmens told the couple to come back after they'd had a fertility workup. "They called me about six weeks later and said the doctor thought they had a chance."

You can probably guess what happened next. "They called me six months later and said they were pregnant!" exclaimed Timmens. He reflects, "I feel like I was instrumental in getting them on the track."

Assuming you *have* had infertility testing or know you are infertile, the next step is to determine what kind of baby you want. Do you want a biracial baby? A healthy White infant? A Black toddler? Exactly what type of child are you seeking?

If you want a biracial child, then fine. Don't worry that some agencies will disapprove if you happen to be White and want to adopt a Black/White child. (Transracial adoption is covered more fully in the chapter on special needs.)

If you want a healthy White infant, then say so. You can expect more than a few discouraging words, because some agencies actually "test" you to see how bad you want to adopt. If you give up easily, then they assume you weren't really committed.

It's important to know *before* you call the agency what type of child you want, because when you tell the person who answers that you'd like an application, there may be a preliminary screening over the phone.

Do you want a girl or boy? Surprisingly, most adoptive parents prefer girls, as much as two or three to one. So, if you want a boy, or you don't care what the sex of your child is, then you will usually receive a faster placement. This is also true in international adoptions.

Says Dr. Boisselle, "We have a real hard time with people who have this fantasy of little girls in frilly dresses and patent leather shoes and dancing lessons. What I try to tell people is if you have a baby, you're not going to get a choice."

It's very likely they'll ask you what type of child you seek to adopt. If the person on the other end tells you they *rarely* or almost *never* place the baby you want, don't worry—be patient and polite, and tell her that you understand but you'd still like to apply anyway.

You may be asked how long you've been married, what religion you are, whether or not you own a home, and how old you are. Answer each question politely and simply. Don't elaborate on your answer—save any extended explanations for the social worker. Try to be as charming as possible, and yet not overly so.

The person on the other end of the phone may be more interested in asking you questions than in answering your questions. Or they may wish to send you some written material which only answers commonly-asked questions.

You're not the first person who ever called about adoption, so don't be discouraged if the person you speak to sounds somewhat jaded and lacks your excitement about your *Quest.*

People at adoption agencies are like everyone else: they have their good days and their bad days. And adoption may be just business-as-usual, not a terrifying and thrilling adventure, as it is for you.

One suggestion based on years of interviewing experience: don't call on Mondays. Many people are "down" on Mondays and don't feel like working. If you *must* call on a Monday, at least wait until they've had their morning coffee.

Occasionally the person at the other end of the phone call will ask you if you want to speak to a social worker, but more frequently the social worker will be too busy.

If it's offered, I'd advise you to enthusiastically agree to speak with her or him, even though it's a scary prospect. Tell the social worker you're very serious about adopting an infant, you realize how hard it is today (they love to hear that), and you'd just like to have a broad idea of what their criteria are and what your chances are of having a home study in the next year or two.

Remember: social workers are usually very pessimistic when it comes to time. If you ask the social worker how long it will take to adopt a baby, she will almost invariably inflate the time. The rationale is that you won't be terribly disappointed if they tell you it's a two-year wait and then it takes two and a half years. And conversely, if the adoption is finalized sooner, you're ecstatic and the social worker is a hero.

For example, several agency directors told me they could place a child in about a year—but they didn't want that to appear in print. "What if we have less children next year, or more applicants?" they said with great consternation.

So a good way to find out how long it really takes is the indirect approach: ask approximately how long it might take to get a home study. If it takes about a year to get a study, then you will probably be placed with a child in under two years. Because they don't start a home study unless they are serious about you and also because a home study is usually only "good" for a year before it needs updating.

For example, a mother in New Jersey applied to the Golden Cradle adoption agency in Pennsylvania in mid-1985. Her home study started in January 1986 and she and her husband received their child in July 1986.

Most adoptive parents who adopted through a variety of other agencies agreed that they received their children in under a year after the home study was completed.

Says Anderson of Gladney, "Once we complete the study of a family, they can have a baby within a year at this point."

So the operative question is *not* "How long 'til we could adopt a baby", but "About how long would it take for us to have a home study?"

Should You Apply to More Than One Agency?

Maybe your search reveals two or three agencies which sound very very good. Should you apply to one and wait until that one comes in for you?

My attitude is when you apply for a job, you don't usually go for one interview at one place and then sit and wait until they offer you the job, or reject you. You look for other jobs in other places and go with the best offer.

Isn't looking for a child as important as finding a job? Consequently, you should apply to more than one agency unless you're utterly convinced that you've found the right and only one for you. Sure, most agencies will ask you to send in $20 or $30 with your application—but that's a small price to pay in your strategy to find your child.

Says Anderson of Gladney, "It's like putting all your eggs in one basket if you put your name on only one agency waiting list," and she recommends applicants place their name at other agencies if at all possible.

Many applications will ask you if you've applied elsewhere. Should you lie? Personally, I would have trouble doing so, but some parents advise that if you list other agencies where you've put your name, then this agency won't take you seriously. So this one is a judgement call.

One way out might be to add a sentence explaining that you want a child so intensely that you're seeking every option available—although you are *very* interested in their agency.

If the agency accepts your preliminary application and actually wants to do a home study on you, it's usually best to stick with that one agency. Because when they want to study you, that means they're serious about a possible placement.

It would also be expensive to be studied by more than one agency: costs can run $500 or more for a study. If for any reason you decide *not* to pursue the home study, then it's very likely you will lose all or part of the home study fee.

Another reason to stick with one agency doing a home study is that the logistics of talking to more than one agency and social worker could be mind-boggling! And most social workers would look askance at you and question your commitment if you were involved with several home studies concurrently.

Mary Ann Curran is Adoption Program Coordinator for Adoption Services of WACAP in Seattle, Washington. She feels strongly that an adoptive couple should undergo only one home study at a time.

"If they want to apply to several agencies at once to see how they're received, that's one thing. But to actively pursue a child in more than one agency is really unethical! It's a lot of wasted work on our part."

Concludes Curran, "We ask people to terminate any applications elsewhere once they've committed to our program."

Anna Belle Illien of Illien Adoptions International, Ltd. says she would not be upset about a family trying other means to find their child and says, "I think they should actively pursue anything that works. If I'm working with a family and they get a child from somewhere else, I'm delighted for them. That same child who might have been theirs will go to another family, the child is not a loss."

Dealing With Your Agency

After receiving information on a variety of agencies, and determining you've found one or more which seem right for you, should you merely fill out the application forms and then wait until you're called?

Adoptive parents and social workers agree that you should check in periodically with the agency. "We found out later that every single call had been logged in," said a New Hampshire mother. "It was clearly a positive factor."

So be pleasantly assertive and check in at least once every other month until you're accepted for a home study. Then you're "in the game" and have a very good chance of achieving your goal.

Always be polite. Remember, they have the power and you don't. "Our social worker said she didn't want to play God," said one parent. "But she was the one who decided if we could be parents and who we could be parents to!" Most social workers do not act overbearing and power-mad. Some do. Treat all with equal courtesy, but never act groveling or submissive. You are worthy of respect and so are they.

How Do Social Workers Match Birthmothers to Adoptive Couples?

Once you've actually been approved, how do social workers decide who gets which baby?

Some agencies merely go by first-come, first-served, and match a birthmother who has just given birth to the next approved family on the list. But many agencies attempt to do matching, whether by physical appearance, socioeconomic status, religion, or other criteria.

"We look for a family that could, in a sense, bond with the birthmother," says Johnson of Shepherd Care Ministries.

She explains further, "For example, if the girl is from an upper middle class family and she's going on to college, usually she's only going to be happy with a professional family for her baby, and would be unhappy with a blue collar family."

Johnson also takes temperament into account. "I would be real leery of putting a child from a very non-structured type famiy situation into an adoptive family who was somewhat perfectionistic. You would want an adoptive family to be easy going for that type of child, because you don't want the child to feel inferior."

If a birthmother has musical or artistic talents, agencies may seek families who have common interests. They don't want to deprive a child who is a potential concert pianist of a family who would develop or encourage that talent!

Says Anderson of Gladney, "We look at physical matching, certainly, but many of our adoptive parents tell us that it's not important to them. Because in all families, there are people who don't look alike."

Other agencies take into account height, weight, characteristics that stand out—such as high cheekbones, red hair, and others.

Identified Adoption

Massachusetts and Connecticut now allow "identified adoption," which means adopting parents may find a birthmother and adopt her baby after it is born, if many terms and conditions are met.

"Identified" means the birthmother, and in some cases, the birthfather as well, know by name who the adopting parents are. (And vice versa.)

An agency home study is required by law. If the birthparents change their mind about the adoption and decide to keep the baby, the adoptive parents will lose any money they have spent on medical expenses, legal fees, home study fees, etc.

The advantage to such an adoption is the extensive counseling received by all parties. In addition, everything is spelled out clearly; for example, in Connecticut, if a pregnant woman making an adoption plan wishes to receive living expenses, she may not receive more than what a woman on AFDC would receive, and living expenses may only be paid for two months.

All monies are channeled through the agency. The birthmother's medical expenses are usually paid and other expenses may be covered, such as prescription vitamins, etc.

A Novel Approach

I interviewed several parents who, through their own efforts, found birthparents interested in placing their babies for adoption. But the adopting parents were not comfortable with independent adoption through an attorney and really wanted agency involvement. So they called a local agency and requested complete counseling services.

And they got it. Was it independent? Was it agency? It was independent in the sense that they found their own birthmothers and were matched to those women.

It was independent in the sense that they took the financial risk involved with independent adoption: the woman could have the child and then change her mind about placement. It is difficult/impossible to regain that money because most birthparents are in dire financial straits.

It was agency in the sense that it was umbrellaed under the agency as far as counseling services. The agency received their fee and, as much as possible, provided the same services they would offer their "regular" adoptive parents.

Is this method fair? An interesting question: after all, the adopting parents advertised for the birthmother or found her through other resourceful means. They screened her over the phone and she screened them. On the other hand, what about all those other people waiting on the agency list? They paid their money, they had their home studies and filled in all the squares.

The problem with many agencies is they don't advertise. They think a listing in the Yellow Pages is enough and some restrict themselves to the White Pages. That's it for recruiting birthmothers who might want to place their children for adoption.

Said one social worker, "We're the XYZ Adoption Agency, WE don't advertise!" Sure, everyone knows you exist, right? Well, maybe all birthmothers *don't* know you're out there.

So, sometimes parents aggressively get the word out and they *do* find a birthparent who wants to place her child.

Yet there are many problems with this approach. "I think the couple who does this is trying to have their cake and eat it too!" says Johnson of Shepherd Care Ministries.

She is convinced that this method of adoption is putting the proverbial cart before the horse, and feels strongly that counseling and discussing key issues such as infertility, the type of child you want to adopt, and many other topics cannot be fully explored if you've already found the birthmother. Instead, you're just going through the motions.

In addition, there's no matching of your family with a birthmother—you found her or she found you and it's one for one. Maybe you're right for each other. And maybe not.

Finally, you'll have the additional expense of agency fees added on to the expenses incurred in an independent adoption: medical bills, legal fees, etc.

Timmens of Adoption Services Associates *does* think it's okay for parents to advertise to find a birthmother—once they've already completed their home study and been approved.

"After approval, they can go the traditional route and sit and wait for the agency to find a birthmother and make an appropriate match. That's the old-fashioned traditional way," says Timmens.

He continues, "Or they can aggressively go out on their own and advertise. Recruiting by using the mass media, they will reach the birthmothers that the agency won't reach. Then, once the birthmother makes contact with them by phone, the agency steps in and sorts things out."

Timmens says the agency must make it clear that they reserve the right to disapprove this match, and he warns that the birthmother may change her mind and the whole thing can fall through.

But the advantage of this tactic is speed. "When you put an ad in the paper and Susie Smith answers the ad, that gal is already at least three months pregnant. So you know if all goes well, you'll be a parent in six months!" exclaims Timmens.

Timmens says the agency has also placed ads, but received a disappointing response in comparison to the response prospective parents receive. This baffled him until he asked several birthmothers why they would call a total stranger to discuss placing their child over a reputable adoption agency.

"They tell me, 'I want to talk to these people myself, I want to hear their story and make up my mind. I want to have something to say about my own destiny and my child's destiny," he says.

He continues, "Some agencies are so bureaucratic, if a birthmother walks in, they'll say to her, 'Oh, sorry, we do intakes on Thursday and this is Friday. Come back next week.'"

In contrast, Timmens says if a birthmother calls, "we'll meet her anytime, anywhere, and provide transportation to and from the agency."

He concludes, "You've got to keep up with the times! Maybe someday we'll be making videos of adopting parents and showing them to birthmothers instead of resumes. We'll show her ten videos and she'll say, 'I really liked Number One.' "

Charlotte Little supervises adoptions for the Department of Social Services in Colorado, and she takes a middle-of-the-road approach on this issue. Although she still prefers traditional agency adoptions, she's coming around to seeing some value in this quasi-agency adoption route, which she calls "designated adoption."

Says Little, "At first I was sort of jaundiced by the whole idea. But at least with designated adoptions you do have counseling and agency involvement, and that's very important."

Little says designated adoption is growing in Colorado because it's humane and safer than private adoption as a result of the counseling aspect, and she feels it's important that this aspect of designated adoption be explained to birthparents and adopting parents. She says birthparents will feel more secure knowing that adoptive parents have been studied and are really okay.

Any disadvantage to this option? Primarily, there's just the additional cost of the home study and counseling, added on to legal and medical fees. Advocates insist it's "cost-effective" because it will give the birthmother a stronger feeling of security about the adoption and will also educate adoptive parents, who often receive no counseling or advice about adoption issues when they adopt privately.

Note: if you think combining agency counseling and assistance with your own active search to find a birthmother sounds ideal for you, your local agencies may or may not share your enthusiasm.

Many social workers resist veering away from the tried and true. In addition, many social workers take a dim view of independent adoption, and want to control the entire adoption process themselves.

Yet assuming you follow Timmens' guideline of first undergoing a home study, it may be a viable route to your child—if you can convince your agency.

It would probably be a good idea when "selling" this concept to your social worker to tell him or her that you want and need the counseling aspect of adoption and yet you also want some modicum of control yourself. You desire a child so much that you feel you can't sit on the sidelines but need to be an active part. I don't know if that would "play in Peoria," but it certainly is worth a try.

Here's another side-benefit of this approach which you could soft-sell. If you place an ad and three birthmothers contact you, you would obviously refer them all to the agency. You adopt one baby and two other families on the agency waiting list have a chance to adopt the other two babies.

Adoption Services

There's a new breed of quasi-agencies appearing on the horizon. In trend-setting California, some social workers and counselors have banded together to form adoption services for the purpose of assisting birthparents and adoptive parents interested in independent adoption. Check your state laws to verify that using such a service would be okay before pursuing this option.

These groups *do* think it's fine and dandy if you find a birthmother and they will actively encourage you to do so.

Here's a sampling of several California organizations: the Independent Adoption Center in Pleasant Hill, California, the New Beginning Consulting Service, Inc. in Santa Ana, Ellen Curtis Adoption Counseling in San Anselmo. These and other services fill a link missing in most independent adoptions: counseling.

They assist prospective parents in resume writing and they assist birthparents in selecting the ideal couple for their child. (All independent adoptions in California are open and identified.)

Many of these services will help adoptive parents from other states, although you can often count on at least one trip to California. "That's no hardship tour!" said one parent.

Dr. Bruce Rappaport is Executive Director of the Independent Adoption Center, and he says his service helps about 80 birthmothers find adoptive parents for their children each year.

Adoptive parents are from all parts of the country where independent adoption is lawful, and Rappaport says about 40% of his adoptions are out-of-state. Prospective parents pay the fees for the service.

"They pay us a blanket fee which pays for all the counseling and support," says Rappaport. Fees at present are $1600, although they may be greater at a later date.

"About 1/3 of the money goes to outreach, which is how we get most of our leads, about 40% goes to counseling, and the rest is administrative costs," he explains.

Rappaport says it takes six months to a year for the average adoptive couple to be selected. His service assists adopting parents with resume writing and also places the resume in their files. About 60% of the adoptive parents are chosen by birthmothers reviewing these files.

"We do a lot of coaching," says Rappaport. He jokes, "It's like taking English 101: we red-pencil their letters and they go through four or five or six drafts and may take a hundred photos."

Rappaport says the most common mistake made by people writing a family resume is they make it sound too much like a job resume. "They should make it emotional and explain why they want a child," he says.

He says that when a letter sticks mainly to facts, birthmothers wonder why the family wants to adopt and is less likely to choose them. "The mothers say, 'They have a wonderful home, a great life. So why do they want a kid?' "

The Center doesn't limit itself to people under 40, married x numbers of years, etc. "If a birthmother wants a couple in their twenties, fine. If she wants a couple where he's 60 and his wife is 54, that's fine too. It's a subjective decision, but one which should be made by the mother of the child."

He does have some limits, however. "Obviously we don't let drug addicts or alcoholics use our service," emphasizes Rappaport, "or people who hate each other and seem on the verge of divorce."

The birthmother and, if possible, the birthfather travel to the Center to meet the prospective parents and undergo counseling, and sometimes they come together from three different parts of the country.

Open identified adoptions are the rule at the Independent Adoption Center. "We're giving women what they want and have a perfect right to," says Rappaport.

"Most agencies still don't want to let go, but non-identifying stuff still reeks of somebody being ashamed of something, that these women are second rate and not to be trusted. That's crazy because they are exceptional people and should be given a lot of credit."

The Independent Adoption Center has branches throughout California and Rappaport hopes a Center will be opened in Chicago and other parts of the country.

Ellen Curtis is an adoptive parent who assists about one hundred adoptive couples and birthparents per year, and she says most couples receive their children in about three to six months.

Curtis charges $550, including a $400 fee and $150 for extensive reading materials she provides. She assists couples and singles.

"I'm also agency-affiliated," says Curtis. "I currently work with five agencies, including Jewish Family Services, Partners for Adoption, and three agencies in the Midwest."

Curtis "Ellen-izes" her adopting parents by teaching them how to write effective resumes and by insisting they undergo an extensive self-education process. She requires attendance at local adoption classes, and adoptive parents must send out a mass mailing of about a thousand resumes to physicians nationwide.

"If you're really a go-getter, you can do everything in a couple of months, depending on how much you will read and how fast you can do the mass mailing," she says. Curtis will also show your resume to birthparents—but not until you've completed the required workload.

Conclusion

An agency adoption is often the ideal way to adopt a child. Both the adopting parents and the birthparents receive counseling, and leave the adoption process knowing they've fully explored many issues.

They understand that it's not all over when the adoption is finalized; the child will raise questions as he or she grows, and particular and adoption in general.

A good agency will give adoptive parents an education on the various issues and will prepare the birthparents for what lies ahead for them. In fact, many agencies provide vocational training or strongly encourage their birthmothers to pursue their G.E.D. (A high school diploma equivalency.)

This is valuable because it will help them orient to the future, rather than stewing about the past and regretting mistakes, worrying constantly about the baby, etc.

Educate yourself about agencies in your area and out of your area. Research may not be "fun" for you like it is for me, but it's worth it! DO YOUR HOMEWORK!

It'll pay off when you adopt your baby.

CHAPTER 5

The Home Study: What Do They Want to Know About You?

Okay, you've found your agency and they're ready to begin the home study. What do they really want to know about you? And is it generally recommended to steam-clean your carpets the day before the social worker comes?

"No!" says Judith Nichols, director of Small Miracles, an adoption agency in Midwest City, Oklahoma which places Black and biracial infants nationwide. "But they still do it anyway. They'll wash down the baseboards and clean areas of their house that normally don't get touched!"

Most social workers and agency directors would say I'm getting ahead of myself here. Because the actual home visit is only a small part of the home study process, and there are many other aspects to determine whether you should be approved as an adopting parent.

There will be apparent reams of paperwork to fill out providing detailed information about you and your spouse. In addition, you'll often be asked to provide a copy of last year's income tax, your marriage certificate, birth certificates, verification from your employers on gross wages, and much more.

In fact, some agencies may require certified copies of such documents as birth and marriage certificates. And divorce decrees, if you've been married before.

You'll usually need a current physical and certification from your doctor that your expected life span is normal. You'll also need references, and here are a few pointers on that topic.

References

Your references might only be contacted by phone by the social worker, but often an adoption agency will require a written reference which is sent directly to the agency. Some agencies will allow references from both family and friends, while others are very specific that one reference must be from your employer, one from your clergyman, one from a friend, etc.

Important: when you ask someone to give you a reference, make it clear to that person that if they'd rather not do it, it's okay! And ALWAYS ask permission FIRST before listing a reference!

It's far better to have all glowing testimonials than to have one watered-down reference from a reluctant person who maybe doesn't believe in adoption—for whatever reason. Most people would be thrilled to be asked to be listed as a reference for an adoption, but not everyone is.

Explain to your references what is basically needed. The adoption agency is interested in your high moral character as well as your outstanding ability to parent an infant. Ask your references to be specific and provide examples of why you are a good candidate for adoption.

For example, one family's reference cited the couple's obvious love of children. She also stated that she and her husband trusted this couple so much that they had listed them in their wills as the ones they wanted to care for their children if they both died while their children were still dependents!

One reference was so positive about the adoption that she sent the reference to the social worker via overnight mail! This is rarely necessary, but probably did impress the social worker!

Be sure your references get their letters in on time. To be safe, give them a deadline so they won't forget!

Don't tell your references what to say, but instead explain to them WHY you want to adopt, your basic motivations. Tell them you hope to adopt a baby, as opposed to an older child, so they can better key into what is needed. And be sure to thank them profusely!

Other Requirements

Many adoption agencies ask you to answer questions in an essay style. "Why do you want to adopt a child?" is a popular question and should be answered very thoughtfully and completely.

If you are infertile, obviously you can't have children. But other couples opt for a "childfree" lifestyle: why do you feel children would be important to your lives?

What experiences have you had with children? One professional single woman related that she loved to babysit the neighbor's kids, and explained why.

If you are affluent, don't dwell on it, because it'll turn off most social workers. "We earn over $100,000 a year and can provide every advantage to this child" is a mistake if that's your main argument for yourselves as adopting parents.

More importantly, will you love this child and pay attention to him or her? Besides, the agency already knows how much money you make, that's in the earnings section of your application.

Says Dr. Lorraine Boisselle of The Adoption Centre in Maitland, Florida, "Sometimes people think, 'We would be good adoptive parents because we have this beautiful home and so much money in the bank,' and so forth. But we've turned down people who were affluent, because they had a poor attitude about adoption or hadn't resolved feelings about infertility."

She continues, "Some of them felt that if they had enough money, it would be just a matter of signing some papers and paying some money, and then the agency owes them a baby. But they didn't want to go through the educational process. I pride myself on having a democratic agency, and you can't influence us with money."

Religious agencies will often ask you questions about your commitment to religion; for example, "Do you consider yourself a Christian, and if so, why?"

Here's a "wrong" answer, according to one religious adoption agency director.

"I am a practicing Catholic who believes you have to live a good and upstanding life here on Earth in order to enjoy the benefits of the hereafter." This person was rejected because his answer sounded selfish and very uninspired.

A person who *was* accepted was one who wrote a fairly lengthy description of her background and liberally quoted Scriptures. Don't fake it! Sure, anyone can look up Biblical verses, but you'll be found out if you're not sincere!

Here's another potentially tough question from a Christian agency: "In what way do you think Christianity is different from other religions that also encourage good deeds, moral conduct, and brotherly love?"

Writing an Autobiography

The majority of agencies ask prospective parents to write an autobiography. What in the world should you put in there? Should you only describe the high points—the awards you won in high school, your triumphs in college or on the job?

"Everyone who has lived has faced problems," says an adoptive parent in New Hampshire. "I don't think the social worker expects that you've skipped through life and everything has been just perfect. Instead, they want to know about the rough spots and how you've resolved the tough situations."

Keep the autobiography to under ten pages if at all possible, even if you've lead an utterly fascinating life! Remember, social workers have to read more than one of these, and you don't want things held up because the caseworker is wading through your life story.

Describe your childhood and life growing up. What family activities did you enjoy? What were your parents like? What was school like for you?

You should also discuss how you met your spouse. What attracted you to him or her? What was your "courtship" like, how long before you decided to get married?

Your current job is important, as well as your future career goals. What do you like best about your field?

If you have children in the home now, how do they feel about adopting a child? What changes will they need to adjust to after the baby arrives in the home?

Reiterate your motivations for adopting, even if that question is asked elsewhere in the application form.

Families Adopting Children Everywhere (F.A.C.E.) is a support group based in Baltimore, Maryland, and their coursebook on the adoption autobiography also recommends you describe your most important personal achievement, current goals, and the greatest influence in your life.

You can also discuss your infertility and feelings about it, but you will hopefully have worked out your anxiety and frustrations and accepted the infertility. The social worker wants you to realize that your adopted child will not be a "clone" of the child you might have had biologically, were you fertile.

F.A.C.E. also recommends you enclose directions to your home with a sketched map so the social worker can find you without spending needless extra time in search of your house.

Orientation and Group Meetings

A group educational process is important to many agencies. Says Dorothy Barkley of the Texas Cradle Society, "If we decide to work with a couple, we'll invite them in for a seminar, with a panel of birthparents and sometimes girls who have released their children several months or several years ago—as well as girls who are now pregnant and looking at adoption."

Prospective adoptive parents appreciate the chance to talk to people who've been involved in adoption.

Said an adoptive mother, "A birthmother came and spoke to us and it was very interesting to meet a flesh and blood birthmother! After that session, there wasn't a dry eye in the room. There also wasn't any fear left about the faceless person looking over your shoulder. It really gave us a different perspective."

Barkley also includes adult adoptees and adoptive parents of teenage children whenever possible at her seminars. "I want to give them a feel of what it's like to raise a child who's adopted, because it's different from raising one you gave birth to," she explains.

Sometimes group meetings occur once a week for six to eight weeks and prospective parents discuss a myriad of issues related to adoption. Social workers report that couples who go through the process together very often become friends, and see each other socially for years afterwards.

After the seminar, Barkley's couples are interviewed as a couple and also separately. Many agencies interview couples separately to make sure each person is committed to the adoption, and it's not just one person pressuring the other. Often one parent is more eager to adopt than the other—usually the wife—but both should want this adoption.

Interviews With Your Social Worker

You'll generally make at least one trip to your social worker's office, although one adoptive parent who lived hours away from her agency found a very understanding social worker: her interviews were held in a Burger King halfway between the office and her home! (Of course, the social worker made an actual home visit as well.)

Every agency has its own methodology, but there are certain common denominators: interviews with the prospective adoptive parents and that home visit.

Your social worker will want to know who will be the primary caretaker of the child, and agencies may expect the Mommy to stay home and take care of Baby for some period of time.

The social worker will usually be interested in your marital relationship if you are married. She doesn't want to give a baby to someone on the brink of a divorce!

What activities do you enjoy together and alone? She may ask you when you had your last argument. How do you react when you're angry or upset? Excited and happy? If you could change one thing about your spouse, what would it be? And other questions related to how you two get along.

And you may well get sick of all these questions. "There were times when we hated the social worker and thought we'd never get our baby," recalls an adoptive mom.

She recommends one way she resolved her feelings. "We kept a journal and wrote down how we felt. It was a kind of a therapy for us and helped us vent our frustration."

The journal has a side benefit. "Now we won't forget anything important when it's time to tell our son about the adoption!"

Other Issues

If you plan to adopt a biracial child, an international child or a special needs child, there will be other questions to cover. How will your lily-white community react to a biracial child? Your family?

Will you be prepared for stares in the supermarket if you're adopting a Korean child? A Black family adopted a Korean toddler and found themselves denouced because they had not adopted a Black child.

During an airplane trip when the adoptive father found himself sitting next to an affluent Black businessman, the attack became particularly heated. Finally, the parent became disgusted and ended the argument this way: "How many Black children have YOU adopted?"

Your openness and flexibility as a family is especially important if you adopt transracially. (See the chapter on special needs, which includes information on transracial adoptions, disabled children and other categories of special needs.)

Social workers want to make sure you know what you're getting into when you adopt across racial lines.

A social worker considering a White family for a Black baby told the adopting mother to visit a Black beauty parlor, to see how she would react and to expose her to being a minority. Your social worker may or may not request a similar exercise, but will expect issues to be carefully considered.

The Home Visit

No matter *what* I or any social workers tell prospective parents about the home visit, unless they've adopted before, they'll still spend hours cleaning and hours worrying about the home visit. Although the house should be neat and clean, the social worker will actually be looking for other elements you really can't control for. Consequently, it's somewhat like an aptitude test: you either have it or you don't.

Although the social worker *will* walk around your home for a cursory check, she won't check under the bed for dustballs or search for cobwebs in corners. One couple was mortified because when the social worker came they were in the middle of remodeling. "She had to come into the house through the back, it was a mess outside!" recalls the adoptive mom. Everything went smoothly, and they did adopt their child.

"But I still sent her a picture of the house after it was finished," said the mother.

The main issue to most social workers regarding your home itself is, is it a clean, safe home? After that, it's more questions about your family.

"We want to see how the couple relates to each other in their home," says Maxine Chalker, Director of The Adoption Agency in Ardmore, Pennsylvania.

"People act differently at home than they do out in public. Are they relaxed, do they seem to get along well?" Remember: a stable marriage is very important to social workers.

There are many questions and issues the social worker may address during her home visit—or possibly at her office. Here's the classic one again: why do you want to adopt a baby? If you're infertile, have you worked through any conflicts you may have or disappointment about your own inability to bear a child as a couple?

Many social workers want to know if you've actually envisioned your life with a new baby. As a result, it's probably a good idea to describe in writing how you think this child will change your life, both positively and negatively.

For example, when you have a baby in tow, you'll need to lug around a bagful of diapers, bottles, extra clothes, and other accoutrements wherever you go. There'll be dirty diapers, midnight wakeups, getting thrown up on if the baby is sick, and struggling to figure out what the baby needs.

On the plus side, you'll have the joy of the first smile and the first word, and watching your efforts in caring for this child flower as he or she matures.

Many agencies are concerned with how you think you'll feel about the birthparents of your child. "We tell them if you don't have a special place in your heart for the birthmother, then go to another agency," says James Williams, Director of Adoptions for The LIGHT House in Kansas City, Missouri.

Do you intend to tell your child he or she is adopted later on in life? The "right" answer is "yes": today, most experts feel it is extremely inadvisable to lie to the child about being his biological parents. Said one adoptive mother, "If you lie about that and they later find out, they think, 'What else did you lie to me about?' It's much better to be open and honest."

If you've been divorced in the past, why did that marriage break up? How do you feel about your ex-spouse? Did you have any children by this marriage and if so, what is your current relationship?

What are your hobbies and interests? Are you more the stay-at-home type or the outgoing physically adept person?

Your attitudes towards and expectations of your future child are very important. How will you discipline the child for incorrect or unacceptable behavior? Do you think you can be flexible and not perfectionistic when it comes to a child?

In addition to the psychological angle, there are practical considerations to the home visit. Do you have a place for the baby to sleep? It may not be decorated and ready now, but is there an available room or do you at least have a plan for where baby will spend many of his or her sleeping and waking hours?

If you already have children, the social worker will take a look at them. Do they appear happy and well-adjusted? How do they feel about a new baby coming into your home?

If they are school-age children, the social worker will often interview them separately from you. If your child(ren) appear(s) confused about or opposed to the adoption, the social worker may require family counseling before approval.

Don't be afraid to ask your social worker questions—it shouldn't be a one-way street. For example, about how long does she think the entire home study process will take? And once you are approved, about how long until your child is placed?

Keep in mind that when it comes to talking about the time to receive your child, social workers are often very conservative. Even if she knows a child who would be right for you and who she could place the day after you're approved, she won't tell you. She wants to make *sure* everything is in order first.

What if Your Agency Is in Another State?

As mentioned in the chapter on agencies, and worth repeating, you are not usually limited to only agencies available within the boundaries of your state. An Ohio family adopted from an agency in Virginia. An Oregon family adopted from an agency in Atlanta.

So how in the world is a home study done if your agency is a thousand miles away? Your agency may require you to fly or drive to their office for a preliminary meeting. After that, they may agree to allow a licensed agency in your state to perform the study.

Adoption Services of WACAP offers a domestic program called Options in Pregnancy. This agency places over 100 mostly White infants per year in Alaska, Washington, and Utah.

"I really would like you to make it known that it is possible to adopt a healthy baby," said Mary Ann Curran, WACAP's Adoption Coordinator in an interview with me. "The word doesn't seem to be getting out. It may not be a Caucasian baby—although in our area they are certainly available."

WACAP's home study is comprised of two orientation meetings held in the homes of adoptive parents. "It's a non-threatening way to start," she explains. "Then they meet individually with counselors—sometimes counselors fly in and live with the family for a day or two!"

"We're looking for flexible loving people who do not have rigid expectations of what the child should be like," says Curran.

"We go into how they were brought up, how they would do things differently from how they were raised, how they think a child would change their lives—for the good and for the bad. We want to see how a family has solved and surmounted problems in the past," explains Curran.

Dorothy Barkley of the Texas Cradle Society in San Antonio, Texas, says her agency places Hispanic and Anglo children in New Jersey and biracial infants elsewhere in the U.S. "Our New Jersey families are all processed in terms of their acceptance of the full Hispanic," she says. "We also do seminars there to help them to stay in touch with the Hispanic culture."

The Gentle Shepherd agency in Olathe, Kansas places a limited number of healthy White infants with active Christians. This agency requires the couple to travel to Kansas twice: once so they can meet the couple and the second time to pick up their child. The home study will be done in the couple's state by an agency approved in advance by Gentle Shepherd.

The Southwest Maternity Center in San Antonio, Texas does White placements in New Mexico and Texas, and Mexican placements in Colorado and Louisiana. Biracial babies are placed nationwide. Hatch says his agency places between 60-85 infants per year.

"We do all the home studies here," says Hatch. "They fly here for a half-day orientation meeting to make sure they understand our procedures and our philosophy and the adoption process."

If the couple decides to continue, they are brought back for a second all-day meeting. "During that second meeting, we have a panel of birthparents, adult adoptees who talk about what it's like to grow up as an adopted child, and a newly-constituted adoptive family. We can tell them all this information ourselves, but to hear it directly from people who are experiencing it, drives it home."

If the couple still wishes to pursue the adoption—and the agency wants to continue with them—they are brought back for couple and individual meetings. Home visits are also accomplished by approved social workers.

Some newer and smaller agencies may come to you; for example, the James Kirby Read Child Placing Agency in Texas will send a social worker to your state and your home to interview you, at your expense.

"We do a lot of placements in Connecticut, as well as other states," says Beth Parsons of this agency. "If it's a long distance home study, and they usually are, we receive written information from the prospective parents which is quite lengthy. Then we perform a home study in a concentrated form."

Sometimes Parson does the post-placement supervision as well, while other times another recognized agency will handle this task. Sometimes other agencies will perform the entire home study. "We've established relationships with some agencies in Connecticut, California, Alaska and Hawaii who do the work for us," says Parsons.

Parson says her agency placed about twenty Hispanic and Anglo infants in 1986.

The LIGHT House, in Missouri, will also do out of state placements. After a preliminary screening through a pre-application, the agency invites prospective parents to the office for an information meeting. They placed 33 infants in 1986, mostly White.

"We explain details of the adoption process and give them a formal application which is about ten pages long," says James Williams, director of adoptions.

The formal application includes an autobiography, references, answers to questions, copies of income tax returns, and other data. "I do the initial reviewing of the family and then I pass it on to my executive coordinator and he reviews it," says Williams. "If there's a question about health, our physician will also review it. Then if we approve the formal application, we go ahead and do a home study."

If the family is in Missouri, LIGHT House social workers will study the family. At this writing, it's expected that the agency will also have a branch in Kansas soon.

If the family is out of state, then they must find a licensed agency to do the study, and it's always wise to ask the main agency if the agency you've found to do your home study is acceptable before you proceed.

Did You "Pass?"

After the social worker has completed all interviews and home visits, the results are written up and approval or disapproval is recommended. You may think this is the hardest part—but every adoptive parent interviewed agreed that The Wait for your child is the toughest aspect of the whole adoption process. Even if The Wait is in terms of mere months!

Once you've been approved, when you actually receive your child depends entirely on the agency. Some are very careful about matching with adoptive parents of similar weight, hair color, etc. of the birthparents. Others go merely in order of application. And still others allow the birthparents to choose—which means the length of your wait is extremely difficult to predict.

But one day you'll receive The Call. If The Wait should be capitalized, then THE CALL is certainly worthy of all caps!

Be ready! Adoptive parents usually don't receive much time at all when they're called and told their child is here! The agency has all relinquishment papers signed and sealed before they notify the adoptive parents of the happy event.

Copies of Your Home Study

Betsy Burch is a Massachusetts single adoptive mom who is director of Single Parents Adopting Children Everywhere (SPACE). She has valuable advice for both couples and singles: ask for a copy of your home study.

"Let the agency know upfront you would like a copy when it's completed," she says. Why would you want copies, other than an unbearable curiosity about what the social worker said about you?

Explains Burch, "It's the aggressive parents who are successful in adopting. And if you find out about a child in another state who you'd like to adopt, the agency will need a copy of your home study."

Or perhaps you might see a photo of a toddler from a foreign country in a parents magazine and you'll call up and find out if that child is still available. You can immediately send off your home study to the social worker if so.

Of course you could ask your agency social worker to forward the report to the other social worker. "But you might call the agency and find out she just went on vacation for two weeks," says Burch. "Timing is important."

In addition, it would be annoying if you found three or four or more "sources" and asked your social worker everytime to send off your study. "Your social worker will be doing post-placement work and you don't want to cause her extra trouble," says Burch.

What if you tell the agency upfront that you will want a copy of your home study when it's done, and they tell you to forget it, it's against their policy?

If you feel that you've found the agency that you want to work with and that they *do* have infants available for adoption within a reasonable time, then you may want to go with this agency. Otherwise, you may want to consider finding a more open agency.

When Will You Take Baby Home?

This varies from agency to agency. Because of the recognition of the importance of early bonding, many agencies try hard to place the baby as soon as possible after birth. In fact, some agencies make a ritual of the birthparent handing the child over to the adoptive parents.

In other cases, the infant will be placed in a foster home until all the bureaucratic red tape is resolved and the social worker is convinced the birthparents are committed to their decision to place.

This delay can sometimes cause the infant temporary anxiety. An adoptive mother in Ohio describes the sadness she felt at the emotional pain of her two month old infant that first night in her home.

"He cried all night," she said. "Everytime he'd look at me and seem startled, like I wasn't the person who was supposed to be there. His crying sounded like a wounded animal." Her son rapidly adjusted to his new mother—however, it seems likely an earlier bonding would have been much easier on the child.

Some Do's and Don'ts in Your Home Study

1. Don't lie to your social worker about something in your past. For example, if you were charged with smoking marijuana at a youthful 18, and now you're 35 years old and you've treaded the straight and narrow ever since, explain what happened.

   Won't such previous mistakes be reasons to reject you? Says Nichols, "If we find out you lied to us, we'll reject you. But if you tell us about mistakes you've made and how you've overcome them, you won't automatically be rejected." Since most agencies run checks with local police and sometimes the FBI, they WILL find out if you have any kind of a record.

2. Be pleasantly assertive. Call the agency once a month or so to see how things are going. Or every other month. Make it brief and very positive. "After our home study was completed, we found out the agency had logged in every call," said an adoptive parent. "They were impressed at our persistence."

3. Don't always have the same person call the agency—often, it's the wife who makes the calls. "They seemed quite impressed when my husband called them," explained an adoptive mom. "I guess they kind of expected it from me, but when he called too, they knew we were both very serious."

4. Most adoptive parents want a girl. If you don't care whether your child is a boy or a girl, be sure to say so in your application! This should help speed up placement. On the other hand, if your heart is set on adopting a girl, and the agency will give you a choice, (some don't), then say so and know that the wait could be longer.

5. If you have a personality conflict or other problem with your social worker, ask the agency director to assign you a different worker. Not just because you don't like her or him that much—I'm talking serious conflict here.

This advice comes from both adoptive parents *and* agency directors, although both agree that the need rarely arises to change social workers.

"Complain to the director of the agency," advises Anna Belle Illien, director of Illien Adoptions International, Ltd. in Atlanta, Georgia. "It rarely happens but occasionally does occur."

Adoptive parents agree. Said one mother, "The social worker made me nervous—I don't think he liked doing home studies or maybe he was inexperienced. If he hadn't been suddenly transferred, I would have definitely asked for someone else."

Finalizing the Adoption

Every state has its own rules and regulations on how long before your adoption will be finalized in court. When that day comes, a judge will review your paperwork and your social worker may or may not appear.

The judge may swear you in and ask you several questions, and often in an hour or less, the child will be legally recognized as yours. "Baby Boy" or "Baby Girl" on the original birth certificate now has an official name.

The state will eventually create a second birth certificate, usually sealing the original birth certificate, which means no one gets to see the original without a court order. The adoptive parents will be listed as the parents of the child.

One couple nearly didn't make it to court in time! "We didn't know there were two courthouses!" said the adoptive mother. "We had a two o'clock appointment, and it was ten minutes of two when we suddenly realized something was wrong! No social worker, no lawyer, nobody we knew was there!"

So they asked someone at the courthouse who said, "Oh, adoption is at the other courthouse!" The family rushed like mad to the courthouse, arriving twenty minutes late.

"The social worker said, 'I was so worried!' and the judge looked very very serious." Although they were terrified their lateness would be held against them and the judge would refuse to allow such a scatterbrained couple to adopt, their explanation satisfied the judge, and the adoption was finalized.

Conclusion

The bottom line is that prospective adopting parents can and do survive the home study in virtually all cases.

"In retrospect, the home study wasn't too bad," says an adoptive parent from New Hampshire. "It was mostly fear of the unknown, and you felt like the social worker is coming along and standing between you and the thing you want the most. But she was actually very nice."

Is it *fair* to study adopting couples so completely—it's a question most adoptive couples ask themselves. After all, if you were fertile and could choose to have a child, who would "test" you? On the other hand, if you were in charge of placing babies for adoption, wouldn't you think a thorough investigation of the adopting parents was in order? I would!

My view is that although the home study is hard work and can be a very intense experience, your baby is worth it. I've never met an adoptive couple who would disagree.

CHAPTER 6
International Adoption

Sometimes they travel halfway around the globe to their "forever families," flying in from Korea, Hong Kong, Thailand, El Salvador, the Philippines, and many other countries. Other times their new families come to them to bring them back to their new homes in the United States from Chile, Ecuador, Guatemala, and other nations. Who are they?

They're children adopted from foreign lands, and over 9,000 "international" children emigrated to the United States to their new adoptive families in 1986. The overwhelming majority were infants and toddlers, some only a few months old.

Numerous adoption agencies specializing in foreign adoption are ready and eager to help prospective parents. Some are religiously-based while others are non-sectarian.

In some cases, parents prefer to arrange their own adoption independently and many agencies will perform the home study and assist with questions regarding parent-initiated adoptions.

Some Countries Where Children Need Parents

Here's a listing of some of the countries where infants and toddlers wait in orphanages and foster homes for parents, and where your child may wait for you.

Belize	Bolivia	Brazil
Chile	Columbia	Costa Rica
Dominican Rep.	Ecuador	El Salvador
Guatemala	Hong Kong	Honduras
India	Japan	Korea
Mexico	Panama	Paraguay
Peru	Philippines	Samoa
Taiwan	Thailand	

Where Do You Start?

The first step is to educate yourself, by talking to others experienced in foreign adoption and asking numerous questions.

"Learn as much as you can about adoption!" advises a Florida adoptive mother. "Join a support group because this will give you a chance to talk to people who have adopted."

Probably the largest support group in the United States is OURS, Organization for a United Response. Located in Minneapolis, Minnesota, OURS has over 10,000 members nationwide.

Most of them join because of the outstanding bi-monthly magazine, which is packed with informative articles written by other parents. Parent/authors often include their home phone numbers and addresses, and are very willing and eager to talk to prospective parents.

The magazine also includes factual articles on child rearing, special needs kids, and a host of topics. In addition, "waiting children" from a variety of agencies are featured, complete with photos and descriptions. United States membership in the organization is $16 per year, as of this writing.

OURS has parent support chapters throughout the United States, and anyone interested in international adoption should contact them for further information. (OURS, Inc. 3307 HWy 100 North, Ste. 203, Minneapolis, MN 55422.)

There are also many other valuable local support groups, such as F.A.C.E. in Virginia, the Open Door Society of Massachusetts, and more. (See the appendix for a listing of groups.)

Another very good source of information is the *Report on Foreign Adoption,* published by the International Concerns Committee for Children (ICCC), a non-profit charitable organization based in Boulder, Colorado. (Not an adoption agency.)

Report on Foreign Adoption is an annual listing of agencies, countries they deal with, fees, information about children, articles on parent-initiated adoption, adjustment of your child, etc. Names, addresses, and phone numbers of nearly 150 adoption agencies are provided.

If you order the book, you'll also receive monthly updates of the latest agencies, fees, etc. This is very important because the international adoption scene is constantly changing, and the way things are in January will probably change by the time July rolls around. (Current charge for the Report and updates is $15.)

Here's a sample listing for an agency which does placements in Guatemala, extracted from the *Report on Foreign Adoption* for 1987:

FAMILIES FOR INTERNATIONAL ADOPTIONS

AVAILABLE: infants only, Indian appearance. Very few siblings.

COST: $5,000, including transportation.

TIME: betweeen 8 and 10 months, less for boys.

FACTS: no religious restrictions. Singles, yes. Travel is not required. Parent(s) will be between 25 and 55. If married, at least two years is preferable."

Pros of International Adoption

There are numerous advantages to adopting an infant or toddler from a foreign land. One advantage is that many agencies will accept families over age 40; in fact, some agencies will accept parents as old as 60!

Another advantage is that you generally need not go on a "waiting list" for a year or more before you can have your home study done.

Many agencies will begin processing your home study as soon as they receive your paperwork, and in a few months you may be approved and waiting for a child to be referred. Your baby could be available for adoption in from six months to a year, and this speed is a definite plus.

Because they may need parents and are very eager to help children abroad, agencies which assist parents with international adoptions often seem to take an attitude that it's a partnership between adopting parents and the agency.

This does *not* mean it's easier to adopt from a foreign country, nor does it mean the home study is a rubber stamp. It's not—yet there seems to be a subtle difference in the international adoption agency's attitude towards parents, as compared to the attitude domestic agencies sometimes evince.

Perhaps it's because social workers for international adoption agencies know that children in foreign countries reside in orphanages and need parents right away. Some are sickly and American medical care could rapidly bring them around. In contrast, most American-born infants can be quickly placed in an adoptive home.

Says Cheryl Stevens, Executive Director of Homes for Children in Atlanta, Georgia, "When you are considering children who would starve to death if they were not placed for adoption, then you want to work with as many families as you can to help these children!"

Many agencies will allow parents to adopt more than one child, either siblings now, or another child later on. Some international families have adopted five or more children! In contrast, most American adoption agencies limit the number of children you can adopt to one or two.

Another advantage is that a foreign adoption makes a family more aware of the world. Many families learn about the customs of their child's native land, in an attempt to preserve the child's cultural heritage.

"Everytime we heard or read anything about Chile, we paid attention!" said one adoptive mom. "That's where our daughter is from, so whatever happens there is important to us, too."

Traveling to Your Child

Many South and Latin American countries have a travel requirement for adopting parents. Some parents consider the travel requirement to be an advantage rather than a problem. "I really enjoyed my trip to Honduras, it was very exciting and not scary at all!" says a single adoptive mom.

Another adoptive father, whose baby came through an attorney, said his trip to Mexico was like a nice vacation and he and his wife did a lot of sightseeing while simultaneously getting used to their new baby.

Others were less enamored of their trip abroad. "Our hotel looked like a Hilton plunked down in the middle of Bogota," said one adoptive mother. "But it was really filthy!"

She liked the fact that there were many Americans there and she and her husband didn't have to struggle with their elementary knowledge of Spanish. But the lack of cleanliness probably contributed to the fact that the couple came down with a severe case of salmonella.

It's also probably a good idea to bring over-the-counter stomach and anti-diarrhea medications with you on your trip, because a change in water and diet can often cause your stomach to revolt. Who wants to spend all your time in the bathroom when you could be hugging your baby?

You may also want to avoid iced drinks and consume warm cola, or hot tea or coffee instead. Ask your doctor for any other precautions to take.

Before traveling overseas, it is a *very* good idea to talk to couples who've already been there. Tourist brochures simply do NOT tell all—they're advertisements, after all. The agency should be able to give you ideas on where to stay, but other couples will be more candid about conditions.

For example, one agency director told me you could rent a room at the orphanage where your child was coming from. Before committing to that arrangement, it would be wise to talk to other adoptive parents. It might be cleaner or dirtier than the hotels, and they will tell you. Try to find adoptive parents who have been there recently, not five or six years ago when things may have been entirely different.

A few Spanish lessons, ahead of time, might also be a good idea, if you will travel to a Spanish-speaking country for your child.

Disadvantages of Foreign Adoption

There are also a few problems related to adopting your child from a foreign land. The travel requirement, previously discussed, can be seen as either a plus or minus, depending on your viewpoint.

The bureaucratic red tape of a foreign adoption is formidable, and some parents may become disgusted and disgruntled when dealing with agency requirements, requirements of the foreign country, United States Immigration regulations, and the changing nature of the whole thing.

Staying in a foreign country for more than a few weeks can also be very stressful, especially if you don't know anyone, don't speak the language, and are unfamiliar with the customs of the area. In addition, the time you are spending down there is eating up your vacation time from your job.

Time is another factor over which you have little or no control. Of course, domestic adoption agencies tell you that for an American child you must wait one year, two years, whatever. But although the wait may be shorter for a foreign child, there is plenty of potential for mistakes and changes.

Says Anna Belle Illien, Director of Illien Adoptions International, Ltd. in Atlanta, "It's very hard for Americans to deal with time they can't control. And yet in an adoption, you just can't control the length of time it will take. You can say, 'I want to adopt a baby in a year,' and that's true, you *do* want to. But it doesn't always mean you *can* do it in that timeframe."

Illien pauses and adds, "So if you apply to an agency and ask how long it will take, and they give you an estimated time, it's really hard for a family to accept that that timeframe is not etched in stone.

"Every case is different and in international adoptions there are constant changes, delays, and constant frustrations. A person must have considerable patience to go through this process," she concludes.

Stevens of Homes for Children agrees. Stevens' agency places children from Peru, Ecuador, El Salvador, and Honduras.

She says, "Americans like to be in control and responsibility is important. If you have a problem here in the U.S., you can call your Congressman or speak to the supervisor of whatever. But down there in Latin America, you are not in control."

Don't Be an "Ugly American"

According to Stevens, Americans who plan to adopt children from Peru must travel there for the initial processing, and one or both of the parents must stay throughout the four to six week long processing or return later on for another two weeks.

She says, "When you take a person who has never been out of the United States and drop them in a society where they don't even speak the language, they're at a disadvantage. I haven't had anyone with serious problems, but I think that's something that really hits them when they get down there—the culture shock and the lack of control."

Revealing personal aspects of your life to strangers both here and abroad can also be stressful.

"You have to open your life up to lawyers and judges and social workers and that can be unsettling," says Stevens. (She agrees that people who adopt domestically must also open up their lives to social workers and/or attorneys.)

Stevens thinks it's also important to note that people in Latin America are more relaxed, which sometimes aggravates North Americans. (They consider themselves Americans too! They're "South" Americans!)

"If you go in to get something signed and the person who is supposed to sign isn't there, nobody worries about it," says Stevens. "She'll probably be there tomorrow. Or the next day."

Gaye Rundberg of Gentle Shepherd in Olathe, Kansas has a small adoption program for infants from Samoa, and she agrees that it's tough for Americans to wait. "It's the waiting part they get crazy over!" she says.

"You hear about the child and then it could be two to five months before you ever get the child. So the kids are ranging from about six months to fifteen months by the time they get here."

Americans abroad can sometimes create problems if they are too impatient. "If you are pushy, by their standards, a person can take offense and think that you are not respecting them," explains Stevens.

As a result, most agencies try to prepare traveling adoptive parents to be flexible and very very patient.

Parents considering international adoption should also take a very hard look at themselves.

Says Stevens, "If they're very rigid in their requirements, they don't need to go international. For example, if they want a baby girl who is under six months old, has no medical problems, is light-skinned, and other requirements, they should not apply. Because the children who need to be adopted are not going to fit these perfect ideals."

Betty Laning, an adoptive parent and Board member of the ICCC and the Open Door Society of Massachusetts, agrees and says, "Flexibility is the key. If someone is real uptight and wants a 100% healthy kid who looks like them and is going to grow up and go to Harvard—that's just not realistic.

Sometimes international adoptions fall through. One mother carried around a picture of her child from El Salvador for a year. But it never happened. She doesn't know whether it was the agency's fault, or the social worker, or something with the bureaucracy of the country itself. So she opted to adopt a domestic infant.

"It was a painful experience to mentally give her up," she says. "I had her room all decorated and ready. But she never came and I don't know what happened to her. I couldn't find out."

Agencies may be very competent and still have problems. They must comply with the laws of the other country, as well as with United States immigration laws. Laws in foreign lands change, judges change, and an adoption which may be acceptable to a country today could be very unacceptable next month.

The Agencies

There are agencies which concentrate on prospective parents in their state or region, agencies which seek Christian couples nationwide, agencies which need parents for special needs foreign kids and agencies which pretty much span the entire nation.

The pathfinder of international adoption agencies is Holt International. Founded by Bertha Holt some thirty years ago, this agency concentrates largely on adoptions of children from Korea, with programs also in Latin America and Asian countries such as Hong Kong and Thailand.

"We placed 1,116 children in the U.S. in 1986!" says John Aeby, Public Relations Director for Holt and an adoptive father.

"About 75% were infants and children under the age of two, and about 83% of all the children we placed were from Korea."

According to Aeby, the home study takes six to eighteen months, depending on which state you live in. Holt covers Oregon, Iowa, California, Kentucky, Nebraska, New Jersey, Tennessee, South Dakota, Mississippi, and Arkansas. Other states have agencies which deal directly with Holt's sister agency in Korea.

"Once the home study is completed, it takes four to six months to receive a Korean child," says Aeby.

How is it decided which country a family will adopt from? Aeby says that decision is left up to the adopting parents.

"We certainly might make a recommendation if a parents wanted a child through us from Brazil and we already had families in the works for this small program," he says.

"But usually parents make the decision on a particular country, because a family may have had a previous association with the country. Perhaps they were in the military. Others don't have a particular preference and decide based on how long they think it will take and where the children are available."

Betty Laning says many factors influence a family's desire to adopt a child from a given country.

"Some people think it will be easier to adopt a Latin American child because they look vaguely Southern Italian," she says.

"Others take into account fees, and it's usually less expensive to adopt an Asian child than to adopt a child where you have to travel to that country."

She adds, "Sometimes there's just an affinity to a child. They may look at pictures and fall in love with a child from India, and that's it for them."

Some agencies are small and cater to a clientele only within their state or a certain radius, while others virtually span the United States.

A large agency which specializes mostly in Latin American children is Los Ninos International, based in Austin, Texas. The agency is run by Jean and Heimo Erichsen, adoptive parents and authors, and also places Texas-born children in other states. (You must apply for a foreign adoption to be considered for a domestic adoption.)

Los Ninos sells a detailed handbook on their programs, as well as books on international adoption, and even a charming and informative videotape.

Adoption Services of WACAP is an agency in Seattle, Washington, which places children from Korea, India, Columbia, and Thailand.

Only families they have directly studied can have Korean children placed with them, but families studied by other agencies within their own states may receive children from the other countries WACAP works with.

"If a family sees a photo of one of our children in the OURS magazine and falls in love with the child, they call us and ask if the child is still available," says Mary Ann Curran, Adoption Program Coordinator.

She continues, "Our main question is, do you have a home study? Because the home study is the first step and sometimes a long and difficult one to take." And if they don't yet have a home study completed?

"Then we'll usually tell them that it's very doubtful this chlld will still be available by the time your home study is done. But we try to tell them if there are other children of that age and sex available."

Who can do the home study? According to Curran, the home study may be performed by any adoption agency licensed by your state or by the state social services department itself.

"In some areas, people have their home studies done by private social workers, and that isn't as desirable," she says.

"Because some countries feel if you run into any problems, there's no agency available to give you support." She concludes, "We prefer home studies from agencies, but for some people, there's no alternative but a private social worker."

What if you *have had* a home study completed—can you adopt that adorable toddler from Thailand?

"In that case, we talk to them briefly and see if they fit basic requirements of age, numbers of children already in the family, and whether or not they're willing to travel. Every program is different and we have information packets available covering each country we deal with," says Curran.

Anna Belle Illien says her agency concentrates on the adoption of children from India, although she also places children from El Salvador and Costa Rica, and does domestic placements as well—as do most of the international agencies.

"I set up our program in India," says Illien. "I go over there two or three times a year and work with everyone. It's a good source for infants and they're healthy."

Will parents travel to India to pick up their child? "No, we can escort the child over to the U.S.," she says.

Illien says waiting for their child is the hardest part for adoptive couples or single people who are adopting.

"We explain all the steps, but it is frustrating and slow sometimes," she says. "There are a lot of bureaucratic steps to international adoption."

Medical Problems

Children from third world countries often do come with minor, and sometimes major, medical problems. Scabies, lice and parasites are typical, as well as ear infections, malnutrition, and other ailments.

As a result, BEFORE your child arrives, you should find a pediatrician who understands, or is at least willing to learn about, ailments which are rare in the United States.

Birth weights and growth of a foreign-born child may be at a much slower pace than the average American; consequently, physicians should not worry if the child doesn't track to an American growth chart.

Sometimes, physicians may be alarmed by the shape of a new baby's head when the child is from South America.

Says Judith Nichols, Director of Small Miracles in Oklahoma, "The head shape is different for Guatemalan babies because the kids are laid on their back instead of their tummies. So their heads are more flat than we're used to and pediatricians have gotten upset because they thought the child's brain wasn't growing. That wasn't a problem at all!"

Physicians may also wish to reperform all childhood immunizations, not knowing if or when they were administered, and probably not trusting any medical records that are available.

According to the *Report on Foreign Adoption* for 1987, parents should also ask the doctor to analyze stool samples for up to six months, to rule out any parasites. The *Report* also recommends testing for venereal diseases, particularly if the child was abandoned.

It's important to realize that medical information will never be as good as what one might expect from an American doctor. Some parents have felt that their child was a lot sicker than they were lead to believe.

"My son had had pneumonia several times and they didn't think he was going to make it!" says a single mom, who is also a pediatric nurse. She didn't learn about the seriousness of his condition until she actually arrived in Bogota. Fortunately, she has been able to "nurse" him back to health.

"He's still small for his age, but he hasn't had any ear infections or respiratory problems for quite a while," she says. "As he gets older, a lot of his medical problems seem to be clearing up." Whether or not the child is likely to have health problems is dependent on a myriad of factors: which country he comes from, whether he lives in an orphanage or a foster home, how old he is, and much more.

Adoptive Parents Speak

A Florida mom, who adopted Korean twins and also has a biological son and an adopted daughter from the United States, sees adoption as a very positive experience, and relates one reason why.

"My husband is Scottish and he wears kilts to celebrate special occasions," she explains. "And we also do Korean things and German things—because my youngest daughter is of German ancestry, so we celebrate Oktoberfest!"

She was touched by her oldest son's comment one day. "He said to me, 'Mommy, I'm Scottish because Daddy is Scottish and the twins are Scottish because they're my sisters. And I'm part Korean and I'm part German, too, because the baby is German!"

Concludes his mom, "It made perfect sense. The way he was looking at it was we were all one family and all a little bit of what everyone else was."

She says that when her family decided to adopt five years ago, the process didn't take long. "About five and a half months from the time we first called the agency," she recalls. "The twins were just under four months when they arrived."

The whole family went to her Korean-born daughters naturalization. "They said we didn't have to bring the girls, only my husband and I had to come. I said we'd all be there and we took everybody— even my sister who was here on vacation!"

Another adopting mom and dad decided to adopt from the Philippines. "When we first looked into adoption, I called several agencies and they said, forget it, you have two children and you can't get on our list."

But she and her husband were determined to have more children. "I had three miscarriages and couldn't try anymore. So we found out we could adopt from the Philippines. My husband had been there in the military and he loved the people and the country." Was adjusting to a baby who was older than a newborn hard? "For me, the first night was like, what am I doing? But after that, he was my son." This mother adopted her third son from the Philippines about a month ago, a healthy toddler.

Additional Requirements

Because they must comply with the laws of the country they're dealing with, as well as United States laws and immigration requirements, an international adoption agency may have a sort of multitiered rules system.

For example, since some countries don't want parents to be over 40 and they don't want anyone previously married, this requirement would apply to people adopting from that country. But the agency may also deal with other countries which allow adoption as old as 55, and don't mind a previous divorce, children already in the home, etc.

Another requirement in international adoption is fingerprinting: you will have to have your fingerprints taken, and your local police department may be able to help you out with this.

This is to ensure that criminals don't adopt children from abroad. Ask your nearest Immigration office for the fingerprint forms and any other forms they require for an international adoption.

You may also have to obtain a letter from your local police chief saying that you've been a good upstanding citizen. If they've never heard of you, your police can probably assume you *are* among the good guys. But asking for this letter might embarrass some people.

One woman ran into trouble when she asked her bank for a letter stating she was in good financial standing as far as the bank knew.

"That was one of the toughest requirements—they said they didn't do that for anyone!" she said. Finally, she drove to the bank's headquarters in another city and demanded to see someone in authority. She got her letter.

"But you felt like they were checking you over and kind of evaluating you, too," she reflects. "As if, since they were giving you this letter, they should have a stake in determining whether you were good enough to adopt."

The international agency may also require photos of your home. "They wanted pictures of me in every room in my house!" said a Tennessee adoptive mother. "Of course, theoretically, I could've gone to somebody else's home and had the pictures taken, although I didn't."

If you travel to another country to get your child, you'll need a passport, so be sure to arrange for that ahead of time. You *can* get one-day service at regional passport offices, but the nearest office may be very distant from your home.

The foreign country may require a physical by one of their doctors—even though you've had a physical at home.

An adoptive mom traveled to Honduras and encountered this requirement. But she said it was no big deal.

"They just listened to my heart and gave me a real quick once-over," she said. "It wasn't anything like our complete physicals."

Selecting an Agency

Many parents opt to adopt through an agency, although others prefer "parent initiated adoptions," which are similar to United States independent adoptions.

If you do decide to go through an agency, how do you know which one to choose? First, find out which agencies are available in your state and region, and request their brochures. Read them carefully.

Adoptive parent Jan Capello, also active in the Open Door Society of Massachusetts, advises parents to call every agency in the state and ask for information packages.

In addition, while you have them on the phone, ask a few quick questions. "Ask them if they have an informational meeting you can attend," she advises. "Often those are free and you can get a good idea of their policies and procedures."

She also recommends you ask the agency about how long it will take before your home study can be done. You don't want to be caught in a backlog at Agency A when Agency B is dying for parents to apply.

Fee structures should also be closely monitored. "If one agency charges thousands of dollars less than another agency, are they including everything in that price?" says Capello.

For example, do they charge a flat fee per country, which includes everything. Or is it "cost plus" for telephone calls, telegrams, or other expenses?

Some agencies also require you to post a bond of $5,000 or more, in case of extraordinary legal problems, which means you must pay several hundred dollars more.

Find out if anyone in your support group has adopted through them. Will the agency recommend a parent who has adopted through them?

Read very carefully and if you don't understand something, ask questions. Do not sign up for a home study until you're confident this agency is right for you.

Costs of Foreign Adoption

International adoption can be as low as several thousand dollars and as high as $10,000 or more.

Most agencies require a registration or pre-application fee and, once you pass the initial screening, you'll pay an application fee. Then there's a home study fee, and that could run $800 or more. The bulk of the entire amount is often required at or near placement time.

One of the biggest expenses involved in international adoption is completely out of the control of adoption agencies: airfare. Because even if you don't have to fly to pick up your child, you'll still have to contribute to paying for an escort to travel to wherever your child is; although, an escort may bring back more than one child, thus reducing your costs.

And airfares can run high. For example, as of this writing, the round trip airfare from New York City to Lima, Peru on Eastern Airlines is $1441 coach. Multiply this by two, if both you and a spouse must travel there, and remember, you may not have enough advance warning to qualify for any of the special fares.

So, be sure to add in airfare, hotel, etc. when you consider all expenses involved, to be sure you're financially ready.

Parent-Initiated Adoption

Not all foreign adoptions are agency adoptions, and parents may also adopt independently, through an attorney or orphanage. A home study by a licensed agency is still required, but the parent takes charge of the adoption.

Some parents feel they can move faster with the adoption if they handle it themselves. Others want to adopt from countries which agencies have not yet become involved in. And still others want to adopt children younger than the agencies can generally place; for example, a New York adoptive father and his wife adopted a four-day old infant from Mexico, through an attorney. Their home study completed before the child's birth, the attorney contacted them on a Monday to notify them of the child's birth, and on Thursday they flew to Mexico. Two weeks later, they returned home with their newborn son.

Parents who have succeeded with parent-initiated adoptions— and made mistakes—provide valuable advice on the do's and don'ts.

For example, the first step is probably to get a home study, right? Wrong!

Jane Moss, Executive Director of Adoptions Unlimited in Montclair, California, did a parent-initiated adoption of her daughter from Taiwan.

Explains Moss, "In most cases, your home study is only valid for a year. So, if you get your home study done and then it takes you six months to find a source and six months to get a referral, your year is aleady up and you're going to have to pay for an update. And some agencies insist on redoing the whole study!"

The first step for any parent contemplating a parent-initiated adoption is to learn what your state laws are. For example, if your state bans independent adoption, will they allow you to do a direct placement from a foreign country?

If your support group doesn't have this information, write or call your state social services department to find out what the laws are. Or you could check a local law library, usually at a courthouse, You should also contact the nearest Immigration office to find out what their requirements are, and verify that you would be eligible to adopt.

Once you've determined it *can* be done lawfully, you can start the process of finding your child.

Moss recommends that you prepare a letter/resume about your family first, no more than two pages long and with a photo of yourselves attached.

Make it look as nice as possible, and describe your family, why you want to adopt, etc. (This should be similar to the letters written for domestic adoptions when the birthmother selects the adoptive family.)

"Show as much stability as possible," advises Moss. For example, if the prospective father has been employed by the same firm for ten or fifteen years, say so. If you've owned your home for eight years, tell them that, too.

Also tell them the name of the agency that has agreed to do your home study—even though you haven't started a study, you should find an agency willing to work with you.

Attach a translation of your letter into the language of the country, whether it's Portugese for Brazil, Spanish for Columbia, etc.

Where do you send these letters? If, for example, you want to adopt a child from Guatemala, send the letter to the American Consulate for Guatemala at the nearest large metropolitan city and to the American Embassy in Guatemala. (Ask your reference librarian or your Congressman for these addresses.)

Realize that not everyone you write to will reply, but you should receive some responses. They may send you a list of attorneys or orphanages. You may also receive a copy of the rules and regulations of the country—in fact, it's a good idea to specifically request it, explaining that you want to understand their country's laws, so you can fully comply.

Write to the orphanages or attorneys, sending them your nice letter and photos. Then when you've received replies, start screening them.

"If you deal with an attorney, ask him how many adoptions he's done," says Moss. "Is he going to find the child or will you need to have someone else do that?"

In addition, where is he going to put the child until you can adopt—in a foster home? What information can he provide about that home? What kind of references can he give? Will he meet you at the airport? Readers can probably think of many other questions to ask as well.

Ask him what the fees are and GET IT IN WRITING. If he wants the entire amount up front, say $5,000, do not give it to him. He's entitled to some fees for child care and expenses, but it would be foolish to pay the entire amount for the adoption beforehand.

If you are dealing with an orphanage, ask them what the fees are, what is covered, how long will it take, etc. Ask very specific questions.

Remember: you should not get down to the nitty gritty in your first letter to them. Wait until they show some interest in your proposal before you get down to facts, figures, and timeframes.

The ideal case is to have personal contacts abroad. One parent had a friend living in Honduras who actually fostered her infant son until the adoption was final. As a result, she knew the child was very well taken care of.

Make *sure* you also receive a birth certificate and a release form for the child, and these should be notarized in the child's country of birth. (The ICCC's *Report on Foreign Adoption* provides further information for those interested in parent-initiated adoptions.)

Whatever the reason, it's important to take extra care with a parent initiated adoption. If independent adoption in the United States is risky, then independent adoption overseas has even greater potential for fraud, abuse, and heartbreak. Yet the parents who have successfully adopted in this manner are very happy with their choice.

American adoption agencies frequently deal with overseas attorneys; and, if they are experienced and adept at dealing with foreign cultures, they may be better able to cope with the process than you.

Receiving a Referral

Once your home study is completed, you will be considered for the children in the country or countries you've specified. And eventually you'll receive word on a child.

It may be in the form of a phone call or a telegram and you may not have much time—a day or two—to decide whether or not this is the child for you. Sometimes you may also receive the child's photograph and some biographical material.

"Did you ever see a sonogram?" said one parent. "Well, that's about the quality of the photo they send you! You can't tell anything!" It may be a photocopy of a photocopy.

If you do have any doubts and think this child may *not* be right for your family, do some research. If it's medical problems you're worried about, talk to your doctor and ask him to refer you to another doctor. Yes, it is often hard to get through to doctors fast, but when you explain your predicament and the urgency of the situation, you should be able to break through.

Talk to your social worker and talk to other adoptive parents. You can talk to your own parents and siblings, but they probably won't be much help, unless they're experienced in international adoption.

You Meet Your Child

If you adopt a child who is escorted to this country, say a Korean or El Salvadoran child, then you'll anxiously await your baby's arrival at the airport with many other excited parents. When will they ever get here?

Or you may travel to the foreign country and see your child at the orphanage for the first time. Or an attorney may bring the child to you.

Many moms—and dads—are so thrilled to meet their child for the first time that the tears are free-flowing. Can this really be happening? Or is it a dream?

All this work and it finally paid off! You've got your child and you're ecstatic! And yet, sometimes parents are so exhausted and nervous that they wonder why they ever did this thing! That's the normal jitters, similar to the kind you feel the day before you get married or make another really big decision.

You should understand that it may not always be love at first sight from your child's point of view, especially if she's eight or nine months old and going through the "fear of strangers" stage. She doesn't know you're her parents!

On the other hand, one mom relates that her toddler son came right over to his new parents, leaving his Filipino foster mom and never looking back.

"He was very quiet, but there was never any holding back," she says. "The bonding was right away."

Sometimes the long plane ride home can be an ordeal. The child may be sick or just plain scared. Even if the ride is uneventful, you'll both be tremendously relieved when it's over.

Experts recommend that you give yourself time to adjust to each other and get to know each other before you throw a big party and invite all your friends, neighbors, and relatives over.

After the Adoption

Eventually, you'll settle into a routine, you'll handle the paperwork to get your child naturalized, and life will become relatively "normal" again.

Jane Moss strongly suggests that you then send a photo of your child and maybe a letter to the attorney or orphanage from which you received your child. Why? To reassure them.

According to Moss, some foreign citizens have pretty bizarre ideas about why Americans want to adopt, and she read me a translated article in a Guatemalan newspaper explaining that this is what "really" happens to the babies: their bodies are stuffed with cocaine and brought into the United States. According to the reporter, the children are then sold to hospitals, at great profits, for medical experiments. Or worse.

Read Moss, " 'The children are being escorted out of Guatemala like ripe bananas or avocadoes to unknown destinations.' The journalist could offer no other explanation why Americans would want malnourished and illegitimate children."

She says, "They don't understand we just want to love them as our own children." As a result, if adoptive parents *do* send photos and letters, these ridiculous rumors can be disspelled. These pictures could potentially be used to prove that the kids are okay, both to birthmothers, judges,—and of course, sensationalistic journalists.

And of course, sending a photo or a letter would be a nice thing to do even if they *don't* see Americans as Bad Guys.

Is International Adoption for You?

If you are intrigued by foreign adoption, don't stop here! Call or write some or all of the agencies listed in the appendix, and find more to contact. Read their brochures, analyze their literature.

Perhaps your child is waiting for you in some faraway country even now, as you read.

CHAPTER 7

Independent Adoption:
A Path Many Have Chosen

Thousands of prospective parents are thrilled to find they can rapidly adopt the healthy infant they yearn for. Waiting periods for these adoptive couples average six months to a year, and before they know it, they're assembling the crib and hanging up a mobile of duckies and bunnies!

I'm talking about independent or "private" non-agency adoption, legal in every state except Connecticut, Delaware, Massachusetts, Michigan, Minnesota, and North Dakota. At least 50% of all infant adoptions of American babies are independent, and most adoptive parents range in age from their twenties to their forties.

It's not all a bed of roses, and there are numerous serious disadvantages to independent adoption, which I'll detail later in the chapter. The people who select this route to adoption must be willing to do plenty of hard work and also be able to suffer the roller coaster ins and outs of the whole process. But those who have succeeded swear by this option.

Many social workers have a strong aversion to and suspicion of independent adoption, which they perceive takes babies away from agencies. Many label it "gray market", a tawdry-sounding name which hints of illegality. (There *are* people doing illegal things out there too! But those cases are "black market.")

"We see serious risks with independent adoption," says Jeff Rosenberg, Director of Public Policy for the National Committee for Adoption, a Washington D.C.-based organization representing about 135 adoption agencies nationwide.

He continues, "It's not set up to serve the best interests of the children or the birthparents, but instead is set up to find babies for infertile couples who are aggressive enough and quite often who can pay enough."

Independent adoption can be expensive, and attorneys estimate costs run from $7,000 to about $10,000 for a normal delivery, including legal fees and medical expenses—although costs may be lower or higher, depending on individual circumstances. In addition, about 20% of all births are Caesarean sections, which can drive the costs up thousands of dollars.

Birthparents can change their mind before or just after the delivery, and any money already spent is usually lost forever by the adoptive parents. (Although in some states such as Illinois, medical expenses are not paid until after placement.)

Yet even with the inherent risks and the high costs, private adoption is very popular, primarily because of the relative speed of a placement.

"If prospective parents do all the work I ask them to do, they could find a birthmother in about six months," says John Hirschfeld, a Champaign, Illinois attorney who handles about 250 infant adoptions each year and has also assisted in rewriting many of the adoption statutes of his state. In addition, he testifies for or against proposed changes in legislation. Less active clients, says Hirschfeld, will need more time to find their birthmother.

This dedicated professional says his adoptive parents may find their birthmother in one day or three years, depending on individual situations and their degree of commitment.

Other adoption attorneys agree that placements by the birthmother can occur rapidly. "I'd say it takes about as long as it does for the stork to come!" says David Keene Leavitt, a Los Angeles attorney who oversees 200-300 infant adoptions per year. (And who has overseen approximately 7,000 adoptions over the past 26 years.)

I interviewed adoptive parents throughout the country who adopted their infants privately, and most succeeded in six months or less of beginning efforts to adopt. Sometimes a "situation" fell through, but after several months they'd start over again. This strong commitment is imperative to success.

Independent adoption is also the choice of thousands of birth-parents, convinced an adoptive placement is right for both them and their child.

A Texas birthmother explains, "I wanted the control of a private adoption, but the agency wouldn't let me have any input whatsoever on what kind of parents would receive my baby. That was important to me, so I placed my baby independently."

This birthmother was able to choose the adoptive parents from resumes. Many agencies today allow birthparents far more information and choice regarding placement than they were offered only a few years ago. In addition, some attorneys favor "open adoption" and allowing birthparents to choose the adoptive parents, while others prefer confidentiality. (See the chapter on open adoption for more information.)

Sometimes birthmothers choose independent adoption because a private placement may allow them to receive support during the latter part of their pregnancy. This money can be spent on an apartment and food, and as a result, there'll be no need to go on Food Stamps or other welfare programs. They can still afford to stay in their apartments, rather than being financially forced to live in a group home for unwed mothers—which some consider a degrading experience. (Support money is not lawful in every state.)

In addition, the birthmother can generally select her obstetrician, and need not rely on the lowest cost option, which an agency might select. Adoptive parents generally pay prenatal fees and the hospital costs, unless the birthmother is on Medicaid or has health insurance.

How does a private adoption basically work? When the baby is born, the birthmother—and in many states, the birthfather as well—will sign consent papers relinquishing the child to your lawyer, who, in turn, relinquishes the child to you. In some states, the birth-parents relinquish the child directly to the adoptive parents.

The actual process varies from state to state. For example, the state of Illinois actually requires the baby to be "served" by the Sheriff's Department, by touching the child with the appropriate documents. But generally the birthparents sign consent and then you take the baby home.

Most states require the consent of the birthfather. If he is unknown, then notice is usually advertised and if he does not respond, the adoption can go through.

According to Lake Oswego, Oregon attorney Larry Spiegel, who is currently researching a law book on independent adoption, the state of Oregon has a registry for birthfathers, although few other states use this method. Consequently, if fathers do not register, or pay support, or have never attempted to pay support, and have never lived with the child and do not claim paternity, then paternal rights can be terminated by the state.

After a waiting period of days, weeks, or as much as a year, depending on which state you live in, the adoption will be finalized in court by a judge. And "Baby Boy" will officially become "John Jones" or whatever name you've chosen, which will also be reflected on his new birth certificate.

Who Adopts Independently

What kind of people opt for private adoption? They're very often people who would be attractive to agencies: childless, mid-thirties and making enough money to support a child. But they don't want to wait a long time to adopt their baby, especially after years of frustrating infertility testing. "After you've undergone all those tests and decide to adopt, you want to adopt now!" said an adoptive parent.

It's also true that the decision to adopt independently is a choice for some adoptive parents who *don't* quite fit an agency profile for the ideal candidate. With the "ideal" generally being someone who's childless, under 40, married a certain number of years, and other criteria.

Said an adoptive parent from Illinois, "We were both just over 40 and none of the agencies would accept our application unless we wanted a handicapped child. We really wanted a BABY, so we decided to adopt independently." They successfully adopted a healthy infant son.

Another mother already had a "biological" child, but then discovered she had cancer. The doctors told her a year later she was cured. But she should never become pregnant again, because pregnancy could make her cancer recur and would probably kill her and the child, too.

Torn with an intense desire to have another baby, she sought to adopt, applying to an agency that put her on its waiting list. Then she heard from an attorney who knew of a pregnant woman who wanted to place her baby.

"That was in April, and the baby was due in July," she said. The week before the baby was due, the birthmother changed her mind. "We were terribly upset, and I had to take a leave of absence from work because I was so emotionally drained," she said.

But this story has a happy ending: within a year, she was contacted by another attorney about a birthmother. Almost literally holding their breaths, she and her husband agreed to adopt the baby.

This time it really happened. "The attorney carried the baby out of the hospital and when he gave him to me, I just melted!" she said. "There was no adjustment period—it was exactly the same way I felt with my first child."

When the agency finally called her to find out if she still wanted to adopt, her child was 2 1/2. Hearing she now had two children, they told her she was ineligible. If she ever adopts again, she says she'll adopt independently or adopt a foreign-born child.

Advantages of Independent Adoption

Some families are so successful at private adoption that they pursue it more than once: a Florida woman has adopted independently six times over about twelve years! (Probably a record!)

In my own case, my husband and I adopted independently and our birthmother delivered several months after we saw our attorney. The "road" to finding the attorney was a process of under a year's research. (We found our attorney through networking—a friend told us of an attorney who handled adoptions on a part-time basis and was extremely competent and ethical. She lived up to her billing!)

In addition to the relative speed of an independent adoption, you don't have to meet rigid agency criteria to adopt independently, although in most states you must be able to "pass" a home study investigation of your family.

For example, most agencies will not allow you to adopt if you already have "biological" children, even if you are now infertile and even if you have only one child. This is an important point, because the same agency which allowed you to adopt several years earlier may turn you down flat when you decide you don't want to raise an only child.

Said an adoptive mother of one in Ohio, "We wanted to adopt another baby, but the social worker told us one child is enough and too many people have problems when they adopt another child!" Incensed, this adoptive mother decided to adopt her second child privately.

If you have two or more children, it's a rare agency that will allow you to adopt a healthy infant, although some do exist. While some lawyers will only help childless couples, that's a personal policy, not a general rule.

Another *big* advantage of a private adoption is that you'll usually receive your baby right from the hospital and can begin an immediate bonding process. In fact, some adoptive parents go to the hospital when the birthmother is in labor, in the case of an open adoption. In a traditional "closed" adoption, the lawyer may bring the child to you.

Contrast that experience to the policy of many agencies, which require the child to go to a foster home for weeks or even months while papers are pushed, depriving you of the joy of your newborn child. However, more agencies are aware of this problem, and some are doing their utmost to ensure placement within days of birth.

"I wanted my child to have that immediate bonding," said a 20-year old birthmother. "I knew he'd have to go to foster care if I placed through an agency locally, and I definitely did *not* want that! So I went through an attorney."

Costs of Independent Adoption

A key disadvantage to the independent route to adoption is cost, which can runs into thousands of dollars: as previously mentioned, you could spend as much as $7,000 to $10,000 or even more when all medical expenses and legal fees are paid.

"Costs can also be lower," says Fort Lauderdale attorney Leonard Feiner. "I've got one now where the mother is in another county and will receive Medicaid benefits from the hospital."

But you can't assume the final cost will be low—even if it appears so. Warns Feiner, "Make sure you have the financial ability to meet the costs that might be involved. Because sometimes you go into an adoption with one set of figures in mind and things change, whether because of complications in the delivery or because the baby has some problems. The adoptive couple needs to know what their financial limitations are." (Feiner is an adoption attorney and also a member of the Adoption Advisory Council in Florida, a newly-formed agency which will make recommendations to the state of Florida on adoption laws and policies.)

Some couples save their money for years before beginning a search for a birthmother, while others take out a personal loan. Sometimes doctors will be understanding if medical bills are inordinately high, for example, in a delivery with complications. "We send a certain amount of money each month to the doctors," said an adoptive mother in New York.

But although it is true that the "entry fee" for a private adoption can run as high as $10,000, it should also be noted that private agencies charge $10,000 and more for a healthy infant.

The key advantage to an agency adoption, as far as costs run, is that if the birthmother changes her mind you don't lose any monies paid and have to begin at "Start" again. This is a real plus in states where adoptive parents pay medical fees before placement.

It's also important to note that increasing numbers of health insurance companies will cover part of the hospital costs in an adoptive placement. Be sure to investigate this possibility, you may be pleasantly surprised!

Still, you stand to lose a considerable investment if your birth-mother decides to keep her baby; for example, if you've paid upfront for your birthmother's OB bill, you could lose all your money if she changes her mind after the baby is born. In fact, the state of Florida requires adoptive parents to sign an affidavit stating they understand that any payments made do *not* guarantee they will receive a child.

Conversely, in an agency adoption, if a birthmother changes her mind you are *not* responsible for her medical bills, and you'll often go in the queue for the next available baby.

One adoptive couple actually went through *two* cases when birth-mothers changed their mind and medical payments had been paid in advance. Yet they tried again. "We knew it was the only way for us to adopt a baby, and it was worth the risk," said the adoptive mother. And on her third try, the baby did come home. (And stayed there!)

What Expenses Are Allowable?

Most states allow payment of a birthmother's medical expenses such as OB care, and the actual delivery. Some states also allow payment of support for the woman during the period she cannot work, and some will allow expenditures for maternity clothes.

Says Oregon attorney Spiegel, "I recently had a birthmother who had five children she was supporting alone. Even though it was only a couple of months of support she needed, because of so many children, it came out to $3500. It was on the high side, but when I filed the petition, I included an explanation to the court." (Check with an attorney for allowable expenses in your state.)

Feiner recommends adoptive parents ask their attorney *how* any money will be disbursed: will it be given directly to the birthmother or will payments be made to the hospital, obstetrician, etc.?

"I would always recommend that payments be made directly to the providers of services, whether it's a hospital bill, rent bill, utility bill, or other," he says. "The only thing I give to the natural mother directly is a weekly food allowance."

Why should providers be paid rather than the birthmother? "Because you may find she spent the money on something else and now her rent is past due," says Feiner. He continues, "If the mother spends money for maternity clothes or vitamins, I tell her to send me receipts and I will reimburse for that."

Disadvantages of Independent Adoption

In addition to the relatively high costs of independent adoption, there are other disadvantages which should be carefully considered by an adoptive couple.

For example, there may be little or no counseling for the birthparents and adoptive parents. Most states require a home study to ensure the adoptive couple would make suitable parents, yet in many states this study is done *after* placement. And some states require no study, or only mandate a study if the court orders one.

Counseling for the birthparents may be non-existent as well. Although the social worker will try to verify the birthparents are aware of their rights and are acting freely, it's unlikely that many hours of counseling will occur.

Some adoptive parents will pay for the birthmother to be counseled, but I know of no state which requires such counseling. Ask your support group what they recommend; some advise that counseling is worth the extra expense, while others disagree.

Trend-setting Californians have found a way around this dilemma of non-agency and no counseling: a non-profit group called the Independent Adoption Center based in Pleasant Hill, offers counseling and assistance to both adoptive parents and birthparents, and will help both Californians and non-Californians who are seeking to adopt in an open adoption which includes meeting the birthmother. (Be sure to read the chapter on open adoption for more information on this topic.)

According to a November 1986 issue of the Marin Independent Journal, the center helps families hoping to adopt, and one family adopted two children through birthparents who chose their letters from files maintained by the Independent Adoption Center.

The article says costs for each adoption were $3,500 and $4,500, including fees for the Center, medical expenses, and legal fees. What about the time involved? According to the article, their letter was chosen within a month by a birthmother who selected them. The second time they went back to the Center, it took a little longer: eight months.

As far as the general public is concerned, probably the greatest disadvantage involved in a private adoption situation is the fact that the birthmother can change her mind. Although a birthmother can change her mind in an agency adoption, the agency usually won't tell you about the child until consent is signed.

An adoptive parent in Arizona sorrowfully recalls the birthmother who decided to illegally abort her child in the seventh month of pregnancy. "What happened to our baby, Mommy?" said her 4-year old adopted son, and she struggled to find the words to explain. (She later successfully adopted again.)

Said Attorney David Keene Leavitt, "The main disadvantage of an independent adoption is if you're dealing with a girl who IS really ambivalent and she really isn't sure she wants her baby adopted, then an independent adoption will blow up in your face and it'll hurt you." According to Leavitt, 1 in 150 of his birthmothers changes her mind. If he feels a birthmother is "ambivalent" about her decision, then he sends her to an agency.

Note: not all adoptive couples suffer anxiety and frustration waiting to hear "does she or doesn't she" on signing the consent: Hirschfeld says his policy is to inform the adoptive couples after consent is signed. Of course, if they've advertised, they may know that pregnant women have responded to their ad, but nothing is definite until consent is signed. This policy is similar to how agencies handle adoption.

Because of these reasons and others, it's critically important to find a good lawyer. Even if you're in a state which requires *you* to find the birthmother, a lawyer generally performs the paperwork for you. And if your lawyer is actively assisting you with the adoption, it's essential you find an attorney you can trust. Guidelines on finding an attorney are offered later in this chapter. Be aware, even the most honorable attorney can agree to handle the case of a birthmother who ultimately decides to keep her baby, since lawyers don't read minds or see into the future. But a bad lawyer can botch up an otherwise easy adoption.

As a result, adoptive parents must face that very real possibility that a change of heart on a birthparent's part could happen to them— no matter how certain the birthmother appeared prior to the child's birth. (It's interesting to note that studies have revealed the birthmothers most likely to opt for adoption generally are those whose own mothers agree with their decision. In addition, their peers are not raising babies.)

Attorney Leavitt challenges the popular assumption that most birthmothers will change their minds, insisting that this belief relies on some wrong assumptions.

"A girl gives her baby up because it's absolutely clear to her that bringing that child home would be a terrible catastrophe," says Leavitt.

He continues, "She perceives that separating from the child is the only reasonable way her baby can have the kind of life she feels it should have, and she can get her future restored to her. The girl who is safe for independent adoption sees this with tremendous clarity."

He concludes, "The girl I see and who goes safely through an adoption is relieved and thankful that she was able to find a couple to 'marry' her child and love it and keep it safe. They're like the cavalry coming down the mountainside while the Indians are surrounding the wagon train!" Leavitt sees a successful adoption as a "win-win" situation, and says, "To her the ability to make this adoption is a source of great happiness."

Hirschfeld agrees and says, "I see seven to ten unwed mothers each month, and they range in age from ten to their forties, including some married couples who've already raised a family and want to place their child for adoption." Their common denominator? "They all seek good homes for their babies."

Other Disadvantages

In an independent adoption, where you're working with one particular birthmother, you can't choose the sex of your child. This is an important factor to some adoptive couples. Every agency director I interviewed agreed that most adoptive parents prefer to adopt girls.

In rare cases when a family already has children—for example, all boys—and wants a girl, an attorney will agree to sign up two families, one who wants a girl and one who wants a boy.

Then, if the newborn child *is* female, the family with the boys finally gets a daughter and the other couple gets their money back, which has been held in escrow for the medical expenses.

If you are *very* adamant about the sex of your child, ask your attorney if he or she will consider this possibility, but ask him or her in person rather than over the phone before you've met.

Incidentally, this was not an isolated case: I heard of couples using this strategy in more than one part of the country when they really wanted a girl or a boy. Of course, you may have to find the other couple, but if it's important to you, then it's probably worth the extra work.

Far more disturbing is the possibility the baby may have a birth defect or a medical problem—will you want the child in that event? It's unlikely, but something to consider very seriously.

Adoptive parents are given health information about the birthparents—but even apparently healthy people can have children with medical problems. Many physicians order ultrasound testing of pregnant women, which may detect a serious birth defect or problem pregnancy. In our family's case, we decided to deal with whatever problem came up. Fortunately, our son was normal.

Some parents feel they can't tell their friends and relatives about the adoption, because it may fall through. So they deny themselves the social support other mothers receive—baby showers, excited shopping sprees, etc. until the day when they get The Call. And then they scurry around like mad amassing everything. And of course other fearless couples tell everyone about the pending arrival of their baby.

Societal attitudes toward independent adoption are another negative, albeit, a relatively minor aspect to consider. Because most people believe that you must go on a "waiting list" for at least three or four years, they'll ask you how long you waited for your child. If the answer is "six months," you'll often get some strange looks. Some people may ask you if that's legal, and the ones who don't ask will probably think it.

A defensive person could become upset about the appearance of impropriety—however, it's easy enough to announce that private adoptions are perfectly legal in your state.

Whether you adopt independently or through an agency, people are bound to ask you about adoption. (After all, now you're an "expert", since you've done it!) Some hope to adopt too, others are merely curious, and still others fall into the category of annoyance questions. (For example, "How did you know he wouldn't have bad genes?"). These reactions are covered more fully in a previous chapter, but are worth mentioning again here.

Says attorney Feiner, "You should feel confident that you can cope with the questions the child and others will have on adoption. Even though you'll treat the child as if he were your natural child, questions may come up."

Another negative aspect of independent adoption is that it's hard work! Whether you opt to find your child through networking, resumes, advertising, or a combination of these methods, identifying your birthmother takes time and commitment. "It was very draining on us emotionally, although it was well-worth it," said an adoptive parent.

Says Hirschfeld, "I have people who come in and say 'I'm not going to go to an agency because I don't like social workers, and I'm not going to tell my friends and relatives I want to adopt, it's too embarrassing. I'm not going to advertise because I think that's cheap. How soon can I get a baby?' My answer is NEVER: they're not willing to do the work."

Baby Buying—Don't Do It!

One very frightening risk of independent adoption is that even the most honest and upright citizens may find themselves offered a black market baby adoption.

"Quite often things of value may be exchanged in an independent adoption, sometimes money, sometimes cars," says Rosenberg of the National Committee for Adoption. He continues, "It's illegal, but is hard to catch because you have this totally unregulated independent adoption market."

Says Oregon attorney Spiegel, "The most flagrant case I've seen was a birthmother who came in with a father and wanted $1700 a month for nine months of pregnancy and several months afterwards. I said no way would I handle that case!"

Baby selling is illegal in the United States and if someone offers to sell you her baby for $50,000—or even 50 cents—or for a college education or a cruise to the Bahamas, it's unlawful. No matter how desperate you are, no matter how long you've waited for a child, do NOT allow yourself to become involved in a black market adoption.

"You're better off going through life childless than having a baby for four or five years and then having that baby yanked—and it happens in black market adoptions!" says attorney Hirschfeld.

Hirschfeld says he can tell in "two minutes" if a situation is black market or legitimate. And when he's confronted with a baby seller, he tries to convince them to obey the law. "Sometimes when they're told it's illegal and why, they'll revert back to a normal placement," he explains.

How would an evil baby seller find a nice normal and upstanding citizen like you? Advertising often brings them out, and even though advertising can be extremely successful, as one adoptive parent put it, "every crank in the area" may also be attracted.

So, if you think you may have fallen into a black market situation, notify your lawyer, immediately, and follow his or her advice.

Do Birthmothers Change Their Minds After Placement?

In the early stages of adoption, many adoptive and prospective adoptive parents fear that their child's birthmother will change her mind and demand the return of the baby. Does this fear have any basis in reality? Very rarely does this worst nightmare of an adoptive parent come true.

Unfortunately, it has happened. In San Mateo, California, adoptive parents cared for a baby girl from the time she was two days old. The birthmother never signed a final consent, and when the child was eight months old, the birthmother demanded the child be returned to her.

"The judge listened to the facts for fifteen minutes before ordering us to give her the baby," said the embittered adoptive father. The determined adoptive parent wouldn't give up without a fight, and he and his wife appealed the decision. A higher court decreed the adoptive parents could keep the child until a ruling could be made later on whether or not the birthmother had "abandoned" the child.

"If she wanted the baby back, why didn't she tell us when she was two weeks old or two months old?" said the adoptive father. "To wait until she was eight months old and so attached to us!"

It's been an ordeal for this family. They fired their first attorney, when at the initial hearing he said, "Well, I guess we'll have to get you another kid." He talked as if children were replaceable, like dolls.

For months, the adoptive father has spent at least four hours a day researching the law and learning as much as possible in an effort to help his case. He hired an attorney he trusted. As of this writing, the case is still pending.

What about *after* finalization—do you ever have to worry that the birthmother is going to someday show up on your doorstep or maybe at the schoolyard? "I've done 7,000 adoptions and have yet to have a girl stand outside the schoolyard or knock on anybody's door," says Leavitt. "Such behavior would make sense if you postulate she's not a normal girl with normal ethics. But she IS an ordinary girl with normal ethics and won't do it."

The scary stories make it to the media but they're the exceptions. We rarely read about the thousands of happy and successful placements. Says Hirschfeld, "I've never had an adoption that has gone sour after placement in 5,000 adoptions."

What if You Change YOUR Mind?

This will probably be very difficult for my readers to believe—it was for me. But there are actually cases when prospective parents back down on an adoption. One attorney advises his clients to carefully consider their commitment because he doesn't want a repeat of an earlier experience: an adoptive couple changed their mind after the baby was born, and, although he could have easily placed the child elsewhere, the birthmother took this as a sign from God that she should keep her baby.

Leavitt has even had a few cases where the parents have rejected a child *after* placement. "They had the baby six weeks and said they just couldn't 'relate' to it," said Leavitt with apparent disgust. He placed the child with another ecstatic couple.

One adoptive mother was very happy to adopt a baby that "no one wanted" because he was of foreign-born Caucasian parents. "He was born right here in the U.S.!" the mother says. "But so many people said, 'If I wanted a foreign child, I'd adopt internationally." Their loss was her gain.

Other adoptive parents speculate that sometimes childless couples assume they have a right to a "perfect" child, like the one they believe they would have had if they had been fertile. Anything less than perfect, even down to eye color and other traits, is unacceptable.

One couple rejected a newborn because it had one blue eye and one brown eye. "They could buy him a contact lens when he's twelve years old!" says Hirschfeld. Wanting only a "perfect" child, they refused the baby. Another family was happy to adopt this child.

Another couple turned down a baby who had red hair because they said red-headed girls get teased in school. But so do thin kids, fat kids, unathletic kids, kids who wear glasses, kids who wear braces, etc. Nobody is perfect!

Spiegel recently had a problem with an "open" adoption. Although he is in favor of it as an option, and about half of his birthmothers want to meet the adoptive parents, one case went very sour.

"An adoptive couple was committed to a particular birthmother," he explains. "They were two mental health professionals—you'd think they'd be able to sort out their feelings!" The two wanted to meet the birthmother and did.

"All of a sudden, they threw a bombshell that they were getting too close to her, and therefore they didn't want to continue with her. She was devastated! She really wanted them to adopt her baby." Fortunately, another happy family adopted the child.

Says Feiner, "People can back down for various reasons. For example, if it were determined by the obstetrician that the birthmother had been using drugs recently, even though she told me she didn't use drugs. Another reason is that the baby turns out to be biracial, and that was not anticipated. I also had one set of adoptive parents who backed out for financial reasons before the baby was born."

Making Your Own Private Adoption Gameplan

Okay, let's say you've taken all the benefits and risks of independent adoption into consideration, and you're ready to start. What should you do first?

"Get a copy of your state's adoption laws," advises a Florida adoptive parent. She says reading the law *before* seeing an attorney will give you knowledge and a calibration point so you can evaluate your attorney.

"You want to make sure your attorney or agency is not in violation of the law—don't assume the law will be impossible to understand," she says.

Albany Attorney Barry Gold handles adoptions on a part-time basis. He agrees, and says, "Be an intelligent consumer of legal services. Do some research in advance on questions such as what constitutes a valid consent, and if there are time periods within which natural parents can retract their consent. Those questions should be asked when the client knows the answer ahead of time in order to find out how familiar the lawyer is with the adoption process."

Armed with this information, the next step should be to find an attorney. In some states, you must find the birthmother yourself, and the attorney legalizes your agreement with her. In other states, the attorney is more actively involved with assisting you. It's probably a good idea to find a good attorney in either case, because if you suddenly locate a birthmother and things start to click, you won't want to waste precious time searching for an attorney. So I'll address that issue next.

Finding an Attorney

In an earlier chapter, I strongly recommended that you join an adoptive parents support group, and again, I urge you to take that step. A support group may well know of a good attorney, expert in adoptions. They will also know of attorneys who've botched cases in the past, and warn you away from them.

What if your support group can't advise you: should you pick up the phone book and let your fingers do the walking?

"Don't look in the Yellow Pages for your attorney!" warns Hirschfeld, who says he personally knows of attorneys who list themselves under the heading "Adoptions" and yet have done few or none. (Hirschfeld says he's willing to recommend adoption lawyers in other states.)

Advises Attorney Feiner, "You could contact the local branch of the state office handling adoptions and ask them who they've dealt with on independent adoptions. And your bar association may have a listing of attorneys who specialize in adoptions."

Find out how many unrelated adoptions the attorney performs in a year. (Many attorneys handle stepparent adoptions, which are usually easy and uneventful.) Not all adoption attorneys handle the caseload of Hirschfeld or Leavitt—but they should probably administer at least ten or twenty adoptions a year, and have several years experience. You don't want them learning on you!

Finding Your Birthmother

Okay, your lawyer is in place. Now what's the next step? You have several alternatives; get on attorneys' waiting lists, network, send out resumes, or advertise. (Advertising your intention to adopt a baby is *not* legal in all states, so make sure it is in yours before proceeding with that step!)

Attorney Waiting Lists

Some attorneys will maintain waiting lists of adoptive parents, and some will place babies in the order in which the parents applied, while others will try to match the desires of the birthmother. Even if you're not Number One on an attorney's list, it's still a valuable resource. One adoptive mother recalls receiving a call from an attorney who told her, "You're not number one, two, or three on my list, but I can't find any of them. Would you be interested in this baby?" She was!

Networking

I personally think networking is extremely effective, and when I say "networking," I mean telling everyone and anyone that you want to adopt. "Some couples are embarrassed and don't want to tell people," says Hirschfeld, who feels this reticence will definitely inhibit their chances for success.

He says, "When you go to a party and someone says, 'How are you doing?', you should respond, 'Not that well. We're trying to adopt a baby. If you know of anyone who might want to place their child for adoption, could you contact our lawyer?' " Then you give that person the lawyer's business card, from a sheaf in your wallet.

An adoptive mother in Vermont used this method: at a party she heard someone ask another person if they were still interested in adopting a baby. They weren't. She rushed over and said, "I'm interested!" and she ultimately got that baby.

Networking works, and sometimes from the most unusual sources. One woman told her endocrinologist she was going to give up infertility testing after two years. No cause for infertility had been found in her or her husband—but they weren't having babies either. The doctor told her sometimes he heard of women who wanted to place babies for adoption.

He meant it. Six months later, his secretary called and asked if she was still interested in adoption. Yes! Today she has a son from that contact.

Another adoptive parent called her doctor and asked him to let her know if he heard of anyone interested in placing their baby. He said, "I never get any of those cases." Two weeks later, he called her back, and said, "You're not going to believe this, but a 16-year old girl just walked into my office, and her baby is due in three weeks! Do you want this baby?" She did!

In another case, a couple seeking to adopt put their name on every attorney's list, and then successfully adopted through an agency. "Congratulations!" said the attorney when he called the adoptive mother. "Your baby is due in six weeks!" But she was no longer interested.

She remembered that a woman in her support group really wanted to adopt, so she contacted her. The rest is history: the friend, her husband, and the lawyer got together and eight weeks later (the baby was two weeks late!) the baby arrived and was adopted by the ecstatic couple.

It may be the cousin of a friend of a friend that you hear about—but continually telling people of your desire to adopt often pays off.

Resumes

Another technique many people, and some agencies, use is creating a family resume.

"Don't make it sound too businesslike!" warns one adoptive parent who succeeded. "It should be very warm and friendly, and include emotionally appealing information about you and your husband."

This lady included a photograph of herself and her husband, and was contacted by several birthmothers. "They said the first thing they noticed was the way my husband and I looked at each other, and the love they could see in our faces," reflects the mother. She later met the birthmother, and speculated that they look so much alike, they could be sisters, perhaps another reason the birthmother chose her.

Some prospective parents do a mass mailing of as many as 1500 resumes to doctors and abortion clinics nationwide. (Women who go in for abortions may be too far along in their pregnancy to safely or legally abort. Others change their mind.)

Leavitt favors the use of resumes. (Advertising for a baby is illegal in California.) He says, "You can at least direct them into respectable channels. Instead of just relying on talk—because people forget who you are by the next day—you put together a resume and send it off to doctors, maternity homes, right-to-life committees, or preachers. Then they can put it in a box and if a woman walks in who wants her baby adopted, they can reach into that box and have some information in a usable form."

Hirschfeld sees a mass mailing of resumes as a waste of time. "Doctors are preoccupied with malpractice and liability and are unlikely to contact an unknown person," he explains. Instead, Hirschfeld recommends you inform your *own* doctor or doctors of your intention to adopt, because if he or she discovers a "situation," they'd prefer to recommend a placement with someone "safe" like you.

Dawn Smith-Plinor, founder of Friends in Adoption, a support group for adoptive parents based in Pawlet, Vermont, offers valuable do's and don'ts for readers who want to prepare a family resume:

- Do keep your resume to one page, and keep it neat.
- Do provide a color photo of your family, and include any children you may already have. Some birthmothers like the idea of their baby having a brother or sister. Or both! "If you have an old family dog, get him in the picture too!" says Smith-Plinor.
- Do attach the photo permanently to the resume, staple it, glue it, or affix it somehow so it'll stay on. No paper clips.
- Don't dwell on your infertility. Try to be positive: it would be much better if the pregnant woman sees you as a potential solution to *her* problem.
- Do give facts about yourself: you love camping, gardening, travel, etc. Your parents can't wait until the baby comes, they're so excited about becoming grandparents. Make it warm and personal.
- Do provide positive and general information about your area; for example, if you live in a town with good schools, say so. Or if you're proud that you live in the country with fresh air, or in the city with many cultural advantages, mention it.
- Don't brag about your wealth if you are affluent. Instead, concentrate on the love and caring you can give a child. If you must, you can give some clues to your social status, but don't make a big deal out of it.
- Don't give your age. If she wants to know it, she'll ask you.
- Don't list your height, weight, eye color, etc. She can see what you look like from the picture.
- Do put your religion in if religion plays an important role in your life. Otherwise, omit it.
- Do provide two phone numbers and put those numbers right on top of your resume so they jump out at you and don't have to be searched for. And give phone numbers where someone is generally available.

"Birthmothers become so frustrated when they try and try calling, and no one is home!" says Smith-Plinor. "It takes a lot of courage for her to make that call, and then you're not there! If you provide two numbers, she has a much better chance of reaching you." She recommends the second number be your support group, your minister, or someone else you can trust. Of course you should clear that with them first.

Smith-Plinor recommends an initial distribution of about 100 resumes to all your friends and acquaintances, as well as doctors, clergymen, and others who know you. "They're far less likely to throw your resume in the trash than a complete stranger is," she says. "And this method is extremely effective."

If the first hundred don't get you anywhere, then Smith-Plinor recommends you broaden your search. Imagine throwing a rock in a lake, and watching the ever-broadening ripples. You start small and then move out to larger and larger concentric circles until you meet with success.

Advertising for a baby is another practice on the rise, and is both important and controversial. So, I'll devote my next section to this practice.

How to Advertise

Let's assume you've researched whether it's legal to advertise for a baby in your state, and it is. (If not, skip this section or move to one of those states!)

Advertising can be very effective, and Hirschfeld estimates about 75% of the private adoptions he administers came from ads. The other 25% come from friends, relatives, and acquaintances.

He says, "Advertising is really the key. In fact, so far today I've received three responses from ads adoptive parents have placed, and I need to return those calls."

Attorney Gold says he sees numerous ads in New York. "A week
doesn't go by without an ad in the classified of major newspapers
or some of the small suburban weeklies, containing pleas from people who'd like to be parents," he says. (Note: I once saw an ad
placed by a birthmother in a magazine! She was a genius who
wanted her child adopted by a fellow Mensan.)

Although he hasn't placed ads for clients, Gold sees advantages
to using this technique, and says, "You can get some kind of feel
for what's going on through ads, and you can gain some direct contact over the phone."

Feiner generally disapproves of advertising because he thinks
you get too many unsatisfactory responses. He adds, "Many newspapers will not accept your advertisement—it depends on their internal policy."

For those willing to take the inherent risks of advertising, here
are some guidelines to follow, based on interviews with people who
have succeeded using this method.

Step One for many prospective parents is to obtain an unlisted
phone number so that any responses to your ad will come in only
on this line. (Smith-Plinor thinks an extra line is a waste of money
and advises her support group members to use their home phone.)

Next, you'll begin planning the ad. Understand that even if advertising is perfectly legal, some newspapers in your state may refuse
to run the ad. Or they may ask for a letter from your attorney, stating
that you intend to comply with the law. Hirschfeld advises that you
be very careful with the wording of your advertisement, and show
it to your attorney before running it, because you don't want to
inadvertently offer or imply anything that would violate state laws.

Here's a sample ad which Hirschfeld recommends in Illinois:
"My husband and I are interested in adopting an infant. If you know
of anyone who is considering placing a child for adoption, please
call collect." You can add "after 6 P.M. or on weekends" if you
both work full-time.

Smith-Plinor says advertising is *very* popular among her support
group members, and most locate their babies in less than a year.
She advises against an ad like this: "Loving couple wishes to adopt

healthy white infant". Why? "It's been overdone!" she says. Instead, Smith-Plinor recommends you write an ad you create yourself, not one that's a clone of what everyone else is doing.

"Obviously you want to adopt and hopefully one could expect you'd be loving and caring. I prefer ads that give a little bit more information or at least are more thoughtful," she says. She also recommends you provide two numbers where you can be reached, even if one is an answering machine.

Where should you place the ad? One possibility is the daily newspaper, and Hirschfeld recommends running the ad from Wednesday through Sunday, the big circulation days. Run it for a week, and if you don't get a response, wait a month and then run it again.

Weekly shoppers are considered an outstanding place to advertise by all my sources. One adoptive mother rapidly found a birthmother after she placed her ad. She was contacted by the birthfather, who said he'd been looking for a used car and saw her ad. He and his wife already had two children and didn't want anymore. After asking her several times if she was really serious, and determining she was, the birthfather contacted the lawyer she recommended. And several months later, her daughter arrived!

Another possible recipient of your ad is the college student newspaper. Says Hirschfeld, "Run your ad in the student newspaper in September, after the long hot summer; in December, after fall relationships have occurred; in February after they've gone home at semester break; and in late April or early May. Do not run your ad in a student newspaper during the summer, when attendance is way down.

Smith-Plinor's members even place hand-written ads on bulletin boards located in laundromats, department stores, college campuses, or health food stores.

What Do You Say to a Birthparent?

Before running your ad, you should plan ahead how you will respond to anyone who calls. You might try role-playing, and you could be the birthmother and your husband or a friend could play you. (And vice versa.) You'll never know exactly what a birthmother may say to you—but it doesn't hurt to try to anticipate possible questions with a little rehearsing.

In fact, to avoid the problem of forgetting yourself completely when the phone rings, why not write down a few of the basics that you want to be sure are covered: your eagerness to adopt, your lawyer's phone number, and other essentials. Tape that piece of paper to the phone and you'll be ready!

The first time that phone rings, especially if you have opted for a separate line and can assume this call is a response to your ad, your heartbeat will surge full-speed ahead! And if it's some salesperson calling you at random, you'll probably treat him less than kindly!

Don't be surprised if you get several calls from other people who want to become parents and are curious if this method works! Or who want to know if you've already found someone and have any extra birthmothers! (If you have committed to one birthmother and you hear from others, I recommend you refer those calls to your adoption lawyer or to your support group: they'll be happy to get the information and you'll help someone in your own organization.)

You should be prepared for a few crank calls too! Says one adoptive mother, "People called me to tell me they'd come over and help me make a baby!"

Smith-Plinor says you shouldn't worry about receiving a huge volume of crank calls. As president of her support group, her name is listed in various ads as an alternate number, and so far she's only suffered two minor crank calls. "I just hung up," she says.

Smith-Plinor does live in rural Vermont and a city dweller might conceivably receive a greater number of annoyance calls than she would, which is why some attorneys recommend all calls be routed directly to them. Most people won't shout obscene or insulting remarks after hearing "law office" on the other end of the phone line.

The tradeoff is that your lawyer's office is not always open, and a legitimate call might be missed. In addition, if you do take the calls at your home and ultimately receive a call from a real live birthmother, any stupid calls will fade away from memory.

But what do you do if you have a real birthmother or birthfather on the phone and not a crackpot? What in the world do you say to him or her?

Hirschfeld says, "It'll most likely be a female voice calling you, and she'll say she has a 'friend' who has a problem. You're probably speaking to the friend."

He recommends thanking the girl for calling you and telling her you are the people who placed the ad. Tell her you're very serious about your desire to adopt and ask her to call your attorney collect. (After clearing that with your attorney.)

If your attorney is handling adoptions for more than one family, how will he know this girl who calls has responded to your ad? Advance planning will take care of that: you tell the girl to either use a pseudonym—like Molly Pitcher or Nancy Reagan—one you've previously told your lawyer about. Or you could tell her to give him the phone number she called—and your lawyer should have that number written down in his office, so he'll know this is for you.

Or you could give *yourself* a code name, like Susie Sunshine, and tell the lawyer ahead of time that all Susie Sunshine calls were referred by you.

Smith-Plinor says often when you answer the phone you'll hear silence on the other end, and you must draw out the pregnant woman as empathetically as possible. Tell her you're the one who placed the ad and you're very interested in adoption. Try to make her comfortable.

She also thinks you should ask the girl for her phone number and says few people will refuse to give it to you. Then you won't have to worry about this person disappearing forever: you have a way to contact her too.

In some cases, the girl will want to know more about you, and in fact, some girls may call three or four families and actually "interview" them over the phone. Adoptive couples agree that it's okay to provide such information as the number of years married, and why you want to adopt, as well as your religion, if that's an important aspect of your life.

"Don't get so excited about the call that you tell her your name, address, and Social Security Number!" cautions the adoptive mother who adopted six times. "Keep your wits about you."

She adds, "Don't ask her if she's supporting herself, because then you're getting into money, and you should not do that over the phone. Leave those questions to your attorney."

Because Attorney Hirschfeld is simultaneously working with over a hundred adoptive couples, he advises his clients to refer all calls to him. "If the girl who calls you finds out you're not Catholic, and she really wanted a Catholic family, my clients tell her that I have many couples seeking to adopt and can very likely find a match for her needs," he says. Adds Hirschfeld, "With so many people advertising, it's very likely that a birthmother will call someone else and describe YOU."

Another caution: don't ask the person too many prying questions or you may scare her off. Says Smith-Plinor, "They're so worried you'll say something like, 'Oh, you *smoke*! Forget it, I don't want your baby!' " So be positive and friendly: try to put yourself in her place.

It's okay to ask when she's due and perhaps when—or if, she's seen a physician. Don't ask her what drugs she's taken, if she smokes, etc. That information can be gathered later.

Once you do refer a birthmother to your lawyer, maybe she'll call—and maybe not. In the meantime, you sweat bullets waiting to hear. And even if she does call the attorney, she may or may not go through with the adoption. Hirschfeld says that of the girls who change their mind, most do so right after delivery rather than while pregnant.

Nerves of steel help a lot, but few of us have them! Yet, although this is a definite nail-biter technique, if it works, then it's worth it!

Can You Adopt Privately from Another State?

Perhaps you don't want to limit your search to your home state—can you adopt privately from a neighboring state? Or even one far-away from you? As long as private adoption is legal in your state and the other state, and you follow state laws for each, you can often adopt from another area. However, some states, like Florida, ban infants from leaving the state in a private adoption. As one attorney put it to me, "Babies can come in, but they can't go out."

Says Leavitt, "About 30% of my adoptions involved people in more states than one—a baby entering California from another state or leaving California to be adopted in another state."

Hirschfeld says he has handled out-of-state adoptions, but prefers to limit the majority of his cases to Illinois. "There are plenty of babies right here," he says

The advantage of extending your search is that the potential for success is increased because there will be more birthmothers as you add states to your area of consideration. The disadvantages are that the cost increases because you must hire an attorney from the other state in addition to paying the attorney in your state: to ensure state laws are followed and ensure compliance with the Interstate Compact, which governs the interstate adoption of children.

Summary

Thousands of Americans have adopted babies privately. You can't always readily identify them because so often their children "blend in" with their families. But they're out there and this means of adoption might work for you too. Said parent after parent, "Don't give up! If you want a baby bad enough, and you work hard enough, you will get your baby!" A strong sense of self-confidence and determination, combined with the willingness to take risks and perform sometimes exhaustive and exhausting research, will often lead you to the ultimate goal: YOUR BABY.

CHAPTER 8
Special Needs

It takes special parents to adopt a "special needs" infant or toddler: people who are loving, flexible, and willing to accept the child just the way she/he is, whether the child has medical problems, is a member of a minority race, or whatever the reason is behind the child being labelled "special needs."

Yet these parents are not superhuman or saints, nor are they necessarily more loving or wonderful than you are. They're regular people who've decided to adopt children that many other people didn't think were perfect enough. And they're very glad they did.

They're people like a Maryland couple who adopted a one year old with severe respiratory problems, which finally abated a year later. Or a New Hampshire family who adopted a child with a stomach tube, possible liver disease, potential cataracts, and a host of other problems. Or an Oregon mom who adopted two Black infants from another state.

A special needs child is a child which an agency considers hard to place. Since they no longer like the phrase "hard to place," regarding it as too negative, they invented the term "special needs" to mean the same thing.

But one agency's hard-to-place child may be a "piece of cake" for another agency, and agencies within the same state, and even the same city, can vary drastically on what they perceive as "special."

There *are* a few common denominators in what most agencies consider special needs kids. She/he could be emotionally disturbed and/or suffering from parental abuse. Or he could have medical problems which are correctable; for example, a cleft palate or a hole in the heart.

Sometimes, there are problems of the intellect: everything from learning disabilities to severe retardation.

Special needs children may also be biracial, which usually means half Black and half White, although it could also refer to some other combination of races. Or they could be a brother and a sister of the same race, as siblings are frequently considered special needs, unless they're twins.

There's also a very wide "gray" area where specific agencies would consider healthy infants as special needs; for example, a child whose mother was a drug addict or a prostitute, or whose father was schizophrenic. Other agencies list such categories as "hyperactivity," "malformed external ears," "stuttering," and a host of others.

This chapter will cover adoption of several major categories of special needs children under the age of two: children with medical disabilities, abandoned or abused children, foster children who become available for adoption, and Black and biracial children.

But first, I'd like to go into some exploration of the kind of people who adopt special needs kids.

Parents of Special Needs Children

Research done in 1983 at the University of Texas in Austin compared and contrasted adoptive parents of special needs children to families who adopted healthy White infants.

The study revealed that both groups adopted because they wanted to create a family. (No big surprises here.) The differences were seen in how the subjects viewed themselves.

Parents in each group discussed what they felt were important traits in potential adopters, and the special needs adoptive parents placed greater emphasis on flexibility, patience, and motivation.

The healthy White infant adopters stressed spousal relationship, love of children and desire for parenthood as most important.

The special needs adoptive couples were also different in that they were older, had more education, and were married longer than the adoptive parents of the infants. Of course, this aspect could be a function of the fact that many agencies have age restrictions for applicants seeking babies.

Children with Disabilities

When you receive an application from virtually any adoption agency, you'll be asked if you'd consider a special needs child. Sometimes a variety of disabilities will be listed, and you are to check "yes," "no," or "maybe." Everything from diabetes and epilepsy to bed-wetting and much more is covered.

Consider saying "maybe," unless you're certain you're dead-set against a particular malady. For example, you might have trouble accepting a retarded child: in that case, you'd check "no" for Down's Syndrome. A mother's drug abuse, a child's premature birth, and many other ailments may not bother you, so check either "yes" or "maybe" for those.

"Go over the list carefully with your husband," suggests a Maryland mom. "Some disabilities which didn't bother me at all *did* bother my husband—you should both agree on what you can accept."

This adoptive mom was certain that she wanted a child who could be independent at adulthood, and she made this very clear to social workers. "They said we'd never get a baby or it would take a very very long time, and they delayed our home study," she recalls.

Despite the social workers' dire predictions, this adoptive couple *did* adopt within about eighteen months, and did adopt a child with breathing difficulties which are clearing up as she gets older.

Sometimes, social workers try to steer parents who are themselves disabled towards special needs kids. Two wheelchair-bound parents who taught at a school for disabled kids were immediately offered special needs children.

"We didn't want to be social workers off-duty," said the adoptive father. "And we didn't want to be offered a special needs kid just because they saw US as special needs adults." With persistence, this couple adopted a healthy child.

Another adoptive mom and her husband had two healthy biological children but yearned for more kids. They decided to adopt, and found a brand-new agency willing to accept their application.

For nearly a year after their home study, the agency sent them numerous photos and short biographies of children who needed homes. "I read every one carefully and called the social worker with questions," says this mother.

"I didn't think it would be fair to read just four paragraphs on a child's life and glance at a mimeographed picture, and then throw it away in the trash."

But none of the children worked out: either the active adoptive parents didn't think they could handle a child who would need a sedentary life, or the agency didn't think the parents were right. For example, they were interested in a little girl who had been sexually abused, but the social worker didn't want to place her in a home with brothers.

The family was persistent: they called the agency at least every other month to check on progress. And finally, one day, the agency called to ask them if they might be interested in a newborn girl. The childless family ahead of them on the waiting list had rejected her, because she was premature and had medical problems.

"I told my husband, and he said, 'ALL RIGHT!' " laughs the mother. Receiving careful instructions from her doctor, the parents took the little girl home and gave her plenty of TLC.

That was about a year ago. "She's still underweight, but all her problems have disappeared!" says her mother.

"I'd say she's as healthy as a horse! They thought she might have cataracts, but she's only slightly far-sighted, and other than that, she's fine."

Of course, you can't assume *all* children will make such a rapid turnaround. Each case must be evaluated on an individual basis.

A nurse in Maryland and her husband adopted a child with mild cerebral palsy and a chronic lung disorder. Her condition has improved considerably over the past year, and the prognosis is for a normal life.

The first year was tough, and one part of that was the adoptive mother's anger and resentment towards the birthmother.

"Her mother abused drugs and alcohol, and that's why she's had these severe medical problems!" she said. "She will outgrow them, fortunately, but she has suffered too much."

Another family adopted a newborn who was born with syphilis and contracted spinal meningitis at the age of six weeks. The syphilis was treated and cured, but doctors weren't sure if the meningitis would cause any learning disabilities later in life.

Said his mother, "Before we adopted him, we took his medical papers to our pediatrician, and he said, 'I can't believe this little guy made it, the blood workups were so bad! He must be quite a fighter!' "

Today, the child is five years old and his mother says he's very active and bright. "He's the one with all the tough questions!" she laughs. He is about a year behind in maturity, and will go to kindergarten when he's six instead of when he's five.

Says Gaye Rundberg, Program Director of Gentle Shepherd in Olathe, Kansas, "One of our little boys was born without an esophagus. The doctors tried to do corrective surgery right after he was born, but it didn't work."

She continues, "So, they had to wait until he was two and take part of his bowel and resection it into his esophagus. The family who adopted him was so neat! They said, 'We've never fed a baby a bottle, so to us, feeding him through a stomach tube is normal.' They wouldn't trade their experience with parenting this child for anything. And now his problem is corrected!"

When the special need is a medical or intellectual handicap, the agency will consider many families. When the special need is the child's race, it's a whole other ballgame.

Transracial Adoptions

In 1972, the National Association of Black Social Workers declared that Whites adopting Black children was an unacceptable policy and a form of racial "genocide."

As a result of these strong feelings and statements, most public welfare agencies stopped placing Black and even biracial children with White families. Today, in many states it is either an official or unofficial policy to do racial matching in adoptions.

Yet, an important study, performed and later updated by sociologist Rita Simon of the American University School of Justice, concluded that Black children raised in White homes did not suffer a loss of self-esteem and apparently did well in school and were well-adjusted.

Over 90% of the adopted children reported that they enjoyed family life and said their parents would stand by them if they had a problem. These are the same percentages found in the responses of White adopted and biological children!

Perhaps we can also conclude that the families who opt to adopt Black and biracial children are very sensitive and understanding people.

But even the most liberal-minded parent should search his and her soul before considering a transracial adoption, because any traces of racism will eventually emerge and hurt the child. If they can be recognized and exorcised, all the better.

"Our friends were thinking about adopting Black children, and someone told them that their White daughters would be more likely to marry Black men if they did that," said a very candid adoptive mom.

She continues, "It did take them aback for about a week, especially the girls' father who didn't know if he'd like Black sons-in-law too well." He decided he *could* handle it, and the adoptions went through.

Another family who adopted a biracial Black/White child was surprised to find they had some vestiges of prejudice. "My husband was brought up with prejudice, but he thought he'd overcome all that," says the adoptive mom.

She continues, "But it took him longer to bond to the baby than it did with our other adopted children. We had already adopted Korean children with no problem like that, so it was a surprise." Reactions from their families were not positive either. A cousin came to visit over Christmas and said, "Well, this little baby is cute, but you're going to have problems when she grows up. But you can straighten her hair and get her nose repaired when she's about sixteen, I guess."

The parents' response to such remarks? "We just look at them and say we like our children just the way they are."

This mother has been quite disturbed by one finding: White people have been far more negative than Black people. "When we go out to a mall or out in public, we hear terrible remarks behind our back from Whites and the stares are antagonistic. But the Black people just say, 'Oh how cute,' and they don't seem to be bothered by a White family raising a biracial child."

The mother has two biological children in high school, and she says, "Their friends say, 'You have a Black sister.' They never say a 'biracial sister,' I guess they only see her as Black."

She concludes, "The prejudice against biracial kids is not as subtle as it was towards the Korean kids. I think biracial children have a more difficult time of it."

Why would a White family want to adopt a Black or biracial child? One reason is that there are numerous Black and biracial babies in need of homes, and waits can be very short—sometimes a few months. If race is not an issue and parents only see that a child needs a home, then sometimes a White family wants to and does adopt transracially.

One reason for the availability of Black and biracial infants is that not enough Black families are applying to adopt Black or biracial children. Sometimes Blacks cannot afford private agency fees. Whatever the reason, if Black and biracial children are not adopted, they must enter—and will probably remain in—the foster care system.

There has been a recent backlash to policies prohibiting or preventing Whites from adopting across racial lines. Two Florida families recently sued their state adoption agency when they felt they would be denied the right to apply to adopt their biracial foster children.

One mother had actually brought the child home from the hospital as a newborn infant. But when he was freed for adoption about 18 months later, she was told he'd fit better in a Black family. She and her husband did not agree.

"I loved this little guy and so many people commented on how beautiful he was," says the child's foster mother. "But they told us at the beginning if he was biracial, then we couldn't have him."

Since the child's mother was White and the father was unknown, the foster mother decided to try to determine if maybe the child was Hispanic. But her pediatrician was unable to determine the child's race. "The state could never prove he was Black and we could never prove he wasn't," says the mother.

Terrified that the state would take the child away suddenly, the family initiated a class action suit on the grounds that their civil rights were violated. The state social services office gave in, and agreed to pay the $10,000 in legal fees for both families, who are undergoing home studies as of this writing, to adopt the children.

Other families have readily adopted Black or biracial children. An Oregon mom and dad decided to adopt two biracial children under the age of two. They sent out inquiry letters to forty different adoption agencies nationwide, explaining what type of children they wanted to adopt and why.

"Within a week, I got a call from an agency in Atlanta about two Black infants," said the adoptive mother. She and her husband had intensive discussions about whether their home would be appropriate for two Black infants—could they handle it? They decided they could, and called the agency back.

Because their home study had already been updated, within a month the two babies, ages two months and three months, were in their home.

Most agencies are very upfront about whether they will allow transracial adoptions or not. If you are Black, you are *always* welcome to adopt a Black or Black/White child. And if you are White, then it depends. The private agencies seem to be the most lenient on transracial adoptions.

It should be noted here that thousands of Americans have adopted infants and toddlers from Korea and other foreign countries, and yet that seems socially acceptable, even though those children are of another race. In addition, many children from other foreign countries are racially mixed.

Said Judith Nichols, director of the Small Miracles agency in Oklahoma, "My own adoptive kids are Asian and I am not Asian. So I would have a hard time saying you couldn't love and bond and take care of a kid who is of a different racial mix." As a result of her beliefs, she places Black and biracial infants throughout the United States.

Yet many social workers, even those who will "allow" biracial adoptions by Whites, have qualms about transracial adoptions.

Said one caseworker, "Everyone thinks babies are cute, Black or White. But what about when they get older or reach their teens and the Black features become very prominent? How will they feel then?" Apparently the families studied by Simon felt fine.

As a result of the restrictive policies of many state and private agencies against transracial adoptions, some parent groups are striking back. One example is a group called The National Coalition to End Racism in America's Child Care System.

Based in the Detroit suburb of Taylor, Michigan, the organization was founded in 1982 by "seven terrified foster parents" and has developed a mailing list of over 1200, nationwide.

Carol Coccia, President of the Coalition, says the motivating force was previous treatment received by Black infants in the Detroit area. She claims that healthy Black children languished in hospital beds, rather than being placed in White foster care or adoptive homes.

"There were extenders on some of those cribs, so these toddlers couldn't climb out!" she said. "The state was paying hundreds of dollars a day to confine these kids in cages, instead of placing them in homes."

She decided to take on the system and now reports on adoption issues and foster care issues, nationwide.

"The public is always supportive of people who want to love kids and they don't see all this color business," says Coccia.

She has also assisted Blacks; for example, a Black family recently complained to Coccia that a local adoption agency would not consider their application, so Coccia took their part and filed a complaint with the state.

Coccia cites a recent example of how silly social workers can get in searching for excuses to NOT place Blacks in White homes. She says a Black professor became furious when told the reasons why a White family was denied the chance to foster or adopt a Black child.

She recalls, "When he heard that the family was turned down because they couldn't teach the child Black English or how to walk, he nearly fell out of his chair and he got very very mad. He said he guessed HE couldn't foster or adopt a Black child either, because he didn't speak Black English and he had never noticed any difference in the way Blacks and Whites walk!"

Some adoption applications ask the applicant to describe what they think a Black diet consists of. "What are you supposed to say, fried chicken and watermelon, or chitlings or something! How racist can you get!" said one adoptive father.

"Maybe they were trying to find out if YOU are racist by your answer," said another parent.

Other parent groups are also actively concerned about transracial placements. Says Betty Laning, an adoptive parent who serves on the Boards of the Open Door Society of Massachusetts, the International Concerns Committee for Children, and several other organizations, "We receive calls constantly from states like Texas and Georgia, where they have healthy Black and biracial newborns! They're begging us to help them find homes for these kids so they don't have to get put into the foster care system."

One Massachusetts adoptive mom was thumbing through the MARE book, which is a listing of special needs children available for adoption. She was appalled by one listing for a Cape Verde child. "The first choice was for a family from Cape Verde—do you know how many of them are likely to be here, let alone interested in adoption!" she said angrily.

She continued, "The second choice was for a Black family. Whites can't enter this game: we're shut out. I wonder how long this kid will be in foster care?" she speculates.

The National Committee For Adoption has taken a stand on this controversial issue of transracial adoptions.

Says Jeffrey Rosenberg, Director of Public Policy, "Our position is quite simple: a racially matching family would always be the preference, if available. But if you don't have a racially matching family, you place that child in an appropriate non-racially matching family. You don't make kids wait."

Blacks and biracial children are not the only racial groups that social workers try to place solely with other Blacks. American Indians are also placed with other American Indians as a matter of federal law.

If an American Indian birthmother has a baby, she may not place that child with a White family unless she has the tribe's permission. It is generally preferred that the child be placed with another family of the same tribe.

If that is not possible, then the second choice is generally to place the child with another Indian tribe. This policy has also generated considerable controversy, beyond the scope of this book.

Concludes Coccia, "The general public doesn't worry about race. Instead they think kids need families."

Are Special Needs Children Easier to Adopt?

Since there are many special needs children needing parents, including special needs kids under the age of two, is it easier to adopt if you decide to go for a special needs baby?

Yes—and no. Although there are many children available, many social workers say they'll require an even closer screening of the adoptive parents, to make sure they can handle a special needs child.

"I think a special needs child needs a different type of family than the family needed by a newborn infant," says Joellen Williams, Adoption Worker with Catholic Social Services in Cocoa, Florida. "We look for very flexible people who have a need to give and to parent. They're not looking to the child to give them something, instead they want to share their lives with a child."

Because there *are* many special needs kids, and because applicants for them aren't beating down the social workers' doors, often criteria is eased up. For example, if the agency requires a parent to be under 40 for a healthy infant, they'll generally rethink that age requirement when it comes to a special needs child.

Some agencies charge lower fees for special needs children, in part because they receive financial assistance, but also because they want to facilitate placements.

In addition, adopting parents of special needs kids may be eligible for subsidy payments. Don't be embarrassed to ask your social worker about this.

Foster Parenting

Another way to adopt a toddler is to become a foster parent, and some states consider this category a "special needs" child. This way is fraught with peril, and most social workers would have a conniption fit if I recommended it as a "back door" to adoption.

Foster parents are supposed to give plenty of TLC to their foster kids, but yet somehow maintain an arms-length relationship.

This is because most social workers go to great lengths to reunite foster children with their biological parents. If nothing seems to work after 18 months of trying, then the social worker will reluctantly terminate parental rights and free the child for adoption.

Very often, at that point the foster parents will be asked if they want to adopt the child. If they do, they have "first dibs." If not, the child is placed elsewhere.

Foster parenting a toddler is just about the only way to have an American toddler placed in your home today. Why? Because it's easier to find a newborn or an older child than to find a one or two-year old. They're not available, because mothers either place their children at a very young age or they don't voluntarily place them.

The toddlers in the welfare system are generally there because the state removed them from their homes.

Newborn infants and toddlers ARE available from foster care systems nationwide. Yet to foster a child with the intention of ultimately adopting that child is a tremendous emotional risk. Maybe the child will be freed up, and maybe not. In the meantime, if you have your heart set on adoption, you'll be on an emotional roller coaster for those 18 months or longer.

Yet foster children ARE adopted, and according to Toshi Tatara, Director of the Research and Demonstration Department, of the Voluntary Cooperative System, of the American Public Welfare Association in Washington, D.C., about 20,000 foster children were adopted in 1984. (Most recent data available.)

Twenty-four states provided data on the ages of foster childen who were adopted. According to this information, 11% were under age one and 41% were between ages one and five.

Only fifteen states reported data on the percentage of foster parents adopting foster children, but the statistic is worth considering: 30% were adopted by former foster parents. (Sometimes foster parents are offered the option of adoption, but they don't wish to adopt.)

Some states have programs for parents interested in adopting "legal risk" children—children who probably will become available for adoption, but may not. Other states have programs which are a combination of the foster parent and adoptive programs.

Most adoptive parents do not recommend telling the foster parent social worker that you want to adopt "going in." Because she or he will most likely tell you that you're in the wrong program. (And remember how very important the reunification of the child with his biological parents is to the social worker.)

Bottom line: I cannot, in all conscience, tell you this is the easy way to go if you want to adopt a child through your state. It is an option, but there are many easier ways.

On the other hand, if you've never been a parent before and you think the experience would broaden your horizons, and if you think you can take it if that child is removed from your home, then maybe foster parenting would be right for you.

Ask your local parent support group for information before you pursue this course. In addition, find local foster parent support groups and talk to several of their members as well.

Other Categories of Special Needs Kids

Special needs kids can also be siblings, sexually abused, physically abused, or neglected. Don't assume that because a child is only two years old that he'll adjust easily and rapidly.

An adoptive mom adopted two "healthy" brothers, ages two and four. The older child seemed to adapt readily to his new home, but not the younger child.

"For the first few weeks, his only response was to throw himself down and he never smiled," says his mom. "We took him to see a psychiatrist and he said our son was delayed by about a year."

How much was a function of having been in several foster homes, and how much a function of being separated from his brother in the last home is uncertain. And how much was a function of living out of a car with his biological mom and dad before the state took the children away is also uncertain.

But he has made progress. "He is starting to talk a little and warm up, and I think he's going to make it," says his mom.

Previous sexual abuse can be a very tough problem to handle. A loving and affectionate father was saddened because his little toddler cringed every time he came near her. She thought it would be like the other times with her biological mother's boyfriend. (Yes, some people even abuse infants and toddlers sexually.)

Children may complain about sexual abuse in a previous foster home and disturb the adoptive parents by these reports.

Said one social worker, "Sometimes when a child blames a foster parent for abuse, we find it was really the natural parent who did the abusing. It took a long time for the child to remember and the memory was very distorted in coming back."

Parents who opt to adopt a child who was a victim of abuse should be willing to continue to receive advice and counseling for this child, which may be long-term. But such efforts are certainly well-worth it to turn around a child everyone thought was hopeless.

Conclusion

So, there are many infants and toddlers who do have "special" needs, and maybe you are the parent for one of these kids.

"She's a beautiful baby!" said an adoptive mother. "She's had a lot of medical problems, but it's all worth it, she's so wonderful!"

CHAPTER 9
Single Parent Adoptions

If the average person buys into the popular mythology that it's impossible to adopt an infant, then the idea of a single person seeking to adopt a baby must sound absolutely ludicrous. Yet today singles ARE successfully adopting infants and toddlers.

Many of them are female professionals with stable and steady jobs. Their lives are predictable and orderly, and they are self-confident about the future. And growing numbers of single women are deciding to adopt infants and toddlers, from both the United States and overseas.

How many singles are adopting? Statistics are hard to come by, but we can get a ballpark figure from an expert in the position to know.

Hope Marindin is Executive Director for the Committee for Single Adoptive Parents, a national parent support group for singles based in Chevy Chase, Maryland.

She identified 657 adoptions by singles from 1983 to 1986, and says about half were infant adoptions. (She estimates she hears of less than half of all single adoptions.)

Increasing numbers of single parent support groups are springing up throughout the United States, either spinning off from a main parent group or starting out on their own, another indication that interest in single parent adoptions is on the rise.

Who are the singles who are successful in adopting babies? A New York single mom who is an active member of Single Parents for Adoptions in Niagara Falls, New York adopted her child from India when the baby was just two months old.

Or a Tennessee single mom, a successful saleswoman who adopted her infant son from Honduras, and is an active member of Mid-South Families Through Adoption, her support group. "We really need the support group because we don't have a spouse to talk to," she reflects. Or a Florida mom who adopted her Floridian infant son independently, through an attorney. Or a Washington state mom who adopted her daughter independently.

What kind of careers are single adopters involved in? In 1986, the Committee for Single Adoptive Parents analyzed data received from single parents, and learned that 47% of the respondents were in such "helping" professions as teachers, nurses, social workers, ministers, child care workers, etc.

The Committee was surprised to learn that 36% were businesspeople, including entrepreneurs, attorneys, computer programmers, engineers, accountants, and others.

What about education and age of single adopters? Another impressive statistic: 84% were college graduates and 69% had gone on to graduate school. In fact, 9% of the respondents had Ph.D.s! As for age, most of the singles were in their thirties, with a few in their forties.

Motivations

Why would a single person covet the rarefied air of dirty diapers, the crying in the middle of the night, and the complete responsibility for an infant? And yes, the smiles, hugs, and all the pluses of parenthood. Pretty much for the same reasons as couples want to adopt babies: they love children and feel their lives would be greatly enhanced by parenthood.

"I think it's a reaction and a veering away from 'yuppiedom,' " says Hope Marindin. "The biological clock is ticking away and women have normal desires for children. They've had their trips abroad and all that material stuff and now they want kids."

Explained one single mom on her motivation in adopting, "I wanted to enjoy seeing the early growth and development of a child. Because of my background as a pediatric nurse, I've seen the important effect of parenting in the early years."

Some singles are infertile.

"I had a hysterectomy at the age of thirty-six. It's like, all those children you were thinking about having someday, well, you can't ever have them. It was a shock to me," said one single.

She continues "I don't consider myself an extremely religious person, but I said after that, 'God, you did this to me, and I really want kids. Show me what to do.' "

A neighbor suggested adoption. "I said, 'Singles can't adopt,' but she insisted I check into it." She's glad she did: about a year later she became a mother to her South American infant son.

Other singles don't know if they are or aren't fertile because they've never tried to conceive. One single who recently adopted a baby is now engaged to be married, and says, "I'm thirty-five years old now, and that is kind of old to have your first child. But we hope that maybe we'll have a biological child too after we're married." If not, they will probably adopt another child together.

Where Do You Start?

Most singles who decided to adopt started with the agencies. And some were extremely disappointed at the treatment they received.

"Some agencies refuse to work with you if you're single," says a forty year old divorced businesswoman.

"I guess they assume if two people adopt the child, that child will always be in a two parent home. Of course, that's not always true," she reflects.

Another single applied to her state social services department and was discouraged when they lost her paperwork several times and she felt she was getting the runaround. She was interested in a special needs child with a medical problem but couldn't seem to make any headway with social workers.

"They wouldn't give me any information and didn't return phone calls," she says.

Only a strong appeal to a supervisor finally worked to get her a home study. But she was never offered a child over the course of three years, so she finally decided to check into a private adoption agency.

Note: to be fair to the state social services agency, many states do not have a lot of physically handicapped babies available for adoption. Instead, they have older children, biracial children, abused children, etc. Still, the state agency should have been more upfront and fairer in their treatment of this single woman.

Getting back to our single mom story, the private agency she applied to *was* interested in her and was very positive. The state social services department told her she'd have to make a choice: stay on their list or go with the private agency. She went with the private agency and had another home study.

Ultimately this very persistent lady adopted her son from Columbia, through an agency in another state that accepted her second home study.

Another mother applied to a local adoption agency and says, "They told me I could adopt a twelve-year old girl or a handicapped pre-schooler. I didn't want an older child, and how could I handle a handicapped kid?" said the dismayed woman.

Adds another adoptive mom who is also a social worker, "It's so hard to convince a lot of social workers that they shouldn't give only the most difficult time-consuming children to the people who have the least amount of time and energy to cope with them."

She recommends, "Be assertive! Too many people are afraid that the agency won't give them what they want if they are assertive. Instead, they should be politely persevering and stay on the caseworker's back about what they can handle."

Yet even a very assertive woman may have a tough time with domestic adoption agencies. They have many couples applying, and social workers generally figure those families are better bets for the children they place.

As a result, many singles are opting for international adoption or independent adoption. (Although some domestic agencies will work with singles, and more information is provided in that chapter.)

Adopting a Foreign Child

Not all foreign countries are open to the idea of placing children with single applicants, but many will accept singles; for example, such countries as Columbia, Guatemala, El Salvador, India, and others will accept singles as parents, as of this writing. Singles are adopting infants as young as two months from India, South America, and other parts of the world.

Very often singles must travel to the country to pick up their child, just as couples do. Which means a leave of absence from work, and which also, unfortunately, cuts back on the amount of time the single can spend with the child once he or she arrives stateside.

Singles don't get a break on fees, which can be as high as $10,000 including agency fees, airfare, travel, etc. (See the chapter on international adoption for a comprehensive discussion of costs.)

The major benefit of international adoption is that there ARE many babies available who need homes, and once your home study is completed, a single person has a good chance for a placement.

Both the International Concerns Committee for Children (ICCC), and the Committee for Single Adoptive Parents maintain listings of adoption agencies that accept singles as prospective parents, so singles should be sure to order this valuable information. (See the appendix for addresses.)

Gaye Rundberg of Gentle Shepherd in Kansas says singles are welcome to apply for her racially mixed or Samoan program.

"We just placed a Samoan baby with a single woman in Wisconsin," says Rundberg. "That placement just worked so wonderfully that we bypassed a two-parent family because we felt she had so much to offer the child."

Jane Moss, Director of Adoptions Unlimited in Montclair, California, an agency which concentrates on foreign adoptions, says she'll "advocate" for singles, and about 25% of her parents are singles. The majority of her applicants are females, and she says most of her parents are teachers.

"A lot of our singles try to work out their timeframe so they can travel to the country in the summertime when they're off from school. That is frequently possible," she says.

Her agency opened in 1982, and says Moss, "Our first applicant was a single gal who received her Honduran baby three months after she applied to us!"

"We also assist singles in doing parent-initiated adoptions for many other countries as well," she adds.

Not Many Male Single Adopters

Many singles are happily adopting infants and toddlers—if they're women. Men are frequently shut out of both domestic and foreign infant adoption, and must really do their homework to find an agency willing to accept them.

According to a paper issued by the Committee for Single Adoptive Parents, foreign and domestic agencies often frown on single men as prospective parents of infants.

The reasoning behind this aversion to male applicants?

"One reason may be the fear that a man may sexually abuse the child placed with him. A separate problem seems to be doubt that a single father can cope with the emotional and practical needs of his child.

"A third reason was suggested by a social worker who has worked with adoptions from several Latin American countries: the alleged Latino belief that nurturing is not a proper role for a man, and that a man who takes an active role in parenting must therefore be a wimp".

International adoption agencies agree that male applicants face a harder road ahead of them than female applicants.

Says Mary Ann Curran, Adoption Program Coordinator for Adoption Services of WACAP, "Not many countries accept men. We have had some very successful placements with single men, but unfortunately our options are very limited." She must, after all, comply with the criteria set by the foreign countries.

It's probably not only foreign countries that are not welcoming single dads with open arms. Domestic adoption agencies generally avoid them as well. So much for the importance of fatherhood and all those dads nationwide who *do* get up in the middle of the night with baby, change diapers, kiss "boo-boos," etc.

Survey results of 42 single adoptive fathers published by the Committee for Single Adoptive Parents revealed that nine men felt that agencies were prejudiced against male applicants, and thought that social workers felt "a single man could not be sensitive to the child's needs; 'a boy needs a mother.' "

Twenty-two of the men had been directly or indirectly questioned about their sexual orientation. Many of them were offended by the questioning. Few women receive the same close questioning, and apparently it is assumed that the average woman seeking to adopt is "straight." Since adoption is perceived as a normal "female" thing to do, then a man who wants to adopt may be suspect in his sexuality.

Two of the men in the Committee's survey *were* gay, although only one admitted it to the social worker. He adopted severely disabled children.

For those determined men who *do* want to adopt an infant, despite these additional obstacles, The Committee for Single Adoptive Parents publishes listings of agencies who will allow males to apply.

Advice from Singles

"Perseverance is very important!" emphasized a single mom from South Carolina. "Single people do face a certain amount of prejudice and you need a lot of determination." This advice was echoed by virtually every single (and married) parent.

Advises another, "You never know when the child comes, so line up child care in advance or get on a waiting list." This mom had already planned for a grandmotherly woman to watch her son when he arrived from Honduras. Others get on waiting lists at day-care centers and some lucky few have relatives willing to babysit.

Betsy Burch, Director of Single Parents Adopting Children Everywhere (SPACE), a Massachusetts support group, offers advice to singles new to the adoption scene.

She has over 300 people on her mailing list, and about 80% are female, mostly professionals in their thirties and forties.

"Approximately 40% of our members adopt children from foreign countries," she says.

One option Burch thinks singles should consider is adopting siblings. "If you want more than one child, and you want both children from the same country, you may want to adopt them at the same time," she says.

According to Burch, the international adoption scene is so changeable that a country that accepts singles as adoptive parents this year may close their doors to singles next year.

Another advantage to adopting siblings is that it often speeds up the adoption process.

"If you were interested in adopting, say an infant and a two or three year old, the agency would put you right at the head of their list," she explains.

Independent Adoption

Another route for singles interested in adopting a baby is independent adoption. This may be a door open for you—and may not. If independent adoption is lawful in your state, you must find an attorney or physician willing to work with you.

You may encounter the same resistance singles face through agencies: the lawyer and/or the birthmother may prefer a couple for this child.

One man adopted the baby of a woman he knew who had been raped. She was convinced that he'd make a good father and insisted that the adoption go through.

Sometimes a birthmother decides at the very last minute that she wants to place her child for adoption—at the time of labor or delivery. Attorneys may be hard-pressed to find a good, immediate candidate for parenthood.

This worked out well for one single woman. She had already had a home study completed with the end-view of adopting a special needs child from her state. Then she received a call from a member of her support group that a baby would be immediately available: was she interested?

She was. "It was one week from when I first heard about the birthmother to when I actually received my son!" she said.

"It happened so quickly! I said I was interested and that was on a Monday. On Wednesday, I received a call to go see the attorney and was told the mother was in labor. I brought my son home the following Monday."

This woman was fortunate, and most singles will need to be considerably more aggressive in locating a child.

If you are single and interested in adopting a baby independently, in addition to joining a support group, you'd be well-advised to use your own professional network of friends to get the word out.

Understand that some people will disapprove, and think the babies should only go to childless couples. You'll have to risk that disapproval to make your wishes known and to reach a birthmother or an attorney who will help you achieve your goal of becoming a parent.

"People will say no and you'll be frustrated," says a single mother. "But if you really want to adopt a baby, continue on and there will be a resource for you."

One single mom was so eager to get the word out on her adoption that she had a notice printed out in the handbook given to classmates at her twentieth high school reunion. "It was amazing how many old classmates came up to me and said, 'This is great!' " she laughed.

Agency Adoptions

Says Jeffrey Rosenberg, Director of Public Policy for the National Committee For Adoption in Washington, D.C., "The reason most agencies don't place infants with singles is very simple and straight-forward. As wonderful as a single person might be as a parent, two of you would be all that more wonderful."

He adds, "If you say to a single pregnant woman considering making an adoption plan for her child, 'You can place with couples or you can place with a single woman or a single man,' more often than not, she'll choose a couple."

According to Rosenberg, the reasoning is that if the pregnant woman wanted a single parent for her child, then she'd raise it herself.

Although many international and domestic adoption agencies turn their noses up when it comes to single applicants, there are agencies who will work with singles.

According to Anna Belle Illien, Director of Illien Adoptions International, Ltd., "A good 40% of our parents are single parents, both with domestic and international children."

She continues, "Most are professional women and they don't depend on the marriage structure economically or psychologically to parent. There's been an evolutionary change in the role of women over the past forty years.

"Birthmothers are keeping their babies today, which was not an option before. And single parents are adopting them."

Bryce Hatch, Director of the Southwest Maternity Center of the Methodist Mission Home in San Antonio says his agency places biracial children with single parents.

He says that because his agency allows birthparents to choose adopting parents, it's unlikely a single person would be selected for a White or Hispanic infant.

"The birthmother usually wants her child to go into a two-parent home," he says simply.

Some agencies are willing to place children with severe or multiple handicaps with singles. Yet singles who must work full-time to support themselves and the child may be ill-equipped to handle severe problems. Says one single, "I'm a nurse and can handle disabilities, but I was worried about what if something happened to me? I didn't want to burden my family with a severely disabled child if I died or became ill myself."

Says psychologist Dr. Lorraine Boisselle, Executive Director of The Adoption Centre in Maitland, Florida, an agency which handles both international and domestic adoptions, "One thing that bothers me about some traditional agencies is a sort of a paradox: a single person is not quite good enough to adopt a healthy White infant, but if you take this handicapped or older child, then they'll let you adopt."

She pauses and continues, "What message are you giving to the child? In my opinion, it's much easier for a single person to raise a healthy infant with no problems than to raise a severely handicapped or emotionally disturbed child who really needs two parents."

Concludes Boisselle, "For that reason, I accept single parents. The only problem is, when birthmothers help choose, often they're not going to choose a single parent. But as far as the agency is concerned, it's a completely democratic process and singles are not going to be turned away just because they're single."

Adjustment of Children Adopted by Singles

Many social workers prefer to place female children with women and males with men. When a boy is placed with a female single, will this affect his sexual identity? Because he has no strong male role model, will this damage or delay his development as a man?

According to a June 1986 article in Social Work magazine, longitudinal studies of children who are now eight years old and being raised by single parents have showed that, so far, the children are adjusting well.

The article states, "Among the children of single parents, there seem at this age to be few problems of sexual identity, and single parents have certainly managed the logistics of child care, home, and work with deftness."

The article continues, "the children of single parents are, like the other children in the sample at this age, showing no overt problems with sexual identification. The data gathered from interviews with parents and children suggest that the school-age children identify with children and activities of their own sex." The authors do state that adolescence is a "critical time in the development of sexual identity" and thus the children will be followed up in future years.

The authors of the article speculate that the strong closeness between single parents and their children may cause problems down the road, but as of the study, the kids seemed to be doing well.

After Your Baby Arrives

"The shock was that it was continuous," says one single mom. "If he needs care in the middle of the night—I'm it, the one who does it all."

Says another single mother, "I'll come home at night after work and have intentions of doing laundry or something, but instead, I'll sit and play with the baby for awhile—that's more important than doing the laundry right away."

She continues, "I'd lived alone for so long since my divorce that everything was in its place. I learned that it's okay if the house isn't picked up for a couple of days."

She pauses and reflects, "I think it's a similar adjustment to what couples go through and it's probably the same whether you adopt or not."

Says a Tennessee mom, "The first night with my son was horrible! He didn't like me and I was beginning to wonder what I had done. Then the second day was a lot better and by the third day, everything was fine."

The singles who seemed to make the most rapid adjustment were often those who had close friends and relatives living nearby who thought the adoption was great and who jumped in to pinch-hit with babysitting and moral support.

Conclusion

Singles who are adopting infants and toddlers probably represent a tiny minority of all of today's adoptive parents, but this category has the potential to increase over the future as marriages break up, people age, and the urge to parent a child becomes more powerful every day.

Some single women opt for artificial insemination so they can bear the child they long for, and a handful of single men opt for surrogate mothers to bear their children.

Many singles, however, want to love and care for children who are already here. When they want an infant, their best route appears to be either international or independent adoption. They should also pursue the agencies that handle infant adoptions and will accept singles.

The bottom line is it's definitely possible for single people to adopt healthy infants and toddlers, although much easier for a single woman than for a single man.

They may encounter more obstacles and a closer scrutiny than the average infertile couple, but the singles who have adopted say it's worth all the red tape and hassles.

One single mother sums up her feelings about the adoption of her son this way, "I'm really happy! I feel like my life is finally complete."

CHAPTER 10

A New Openness in Adoption

Twenty years ago, if you were pregnant and unmarried, and didn't *get* married, you were a bad girl. You couldn't go to high school and contaminate the good girls or embarrass the nice boys. So you went off to "visit" your aunt or your married sister for a few months. But often you really went to a home for unwed mothers.

You may or may not have received any counseling or instructions on what childbirth would be like. It was understood that the child would be adopted: there was no other choice.

After the baby was born, if you were very very lucky, you could see him or her. "I never saw my baby, but I figured out she was a girl, because the lawyer never gave me the circumcision papers," said a birthmother who placed her child for adoption twenty years ago.

Then you went back home, the "black sheep" and disgrace of your family. But no one ever talked about it. After all, it was a deep dark secret.

This was the vivid picture painted for me by birthmothers I interviewed who placed their babies in the past. Yet not all felt they had lost control, even then.

"I knew I wanted my baby to be adopted, and I'm glad I did it. I'd do it again if I had to do it over!" asserted a confident birthmother. She added, "I'm amazed at the foresight I showed at the age of twenty!"

Almost everyone was convinced the child had gone to a very good home, even though they received no information about the adoptive parents—other than that it was a "good home."

Back to the Future

Today, pregnant teens and women can receive extensive counseling. They don't have to quit high school or college, and they're not sent off to a phantom relative until it's all over. If they want to keep the baby, they can. If they want the baby adopted, they can do that, too. Often they can specify the type of family they want for their child: religion, age, etc. And sometimes they meet the prospective adoptive parents and can approve or disapprove them.

Today, there's an increasing trend among adoption workers to offer openness in adoption. What exactly is Open Adoption? To some social workers, it means you give a birthmother three or four non-identifying resumes of families, and she picks the one she likes the best.

To others, it means she can peruse many resumes and may even opt to meet the family of her choice, to verify the reality is equal to the printed version of the family.

And still others insist that open adoption means everyone knows who everyone else is. You know the birthmother is Susie Jones and she knows you are Bob and Carol Drake. Or maybe you're on a first-name basis: you know she's Susie and she knows you're Bob and Carol. And there are even more variations than these examples.

For example, one view is that open adoption implies a continuing relationship between the birthparents, adoptive parents, and child.

The National Committee for Adoption in Washington, D.C. views open adoption as an exchange of identities. Says Jeffrey Rosenberg, Director of Public Policy, "We define open adoption as essentially where identifying information is shared and there's the potential for continuing contact."

He continues, "As a result, you cannot have an open adoption and confidentiality, they are mutually exclusive." As a result, the National Committee is opposed to open adoption by this definition.

Says Rosenberg, "We realize it's important to involve the birth-mother in what type of parents are going to adopt that child and, to the extent it is possible, honor her wishes while maintaining confidentiality."

He continues, "But we don't believe in stripping away confidentiality, and we think it's not in anyone's best interest. It's experimental and even its proponents admit they have no idea how its going to affect children and parents."

This chapter will describe the whole continuum of options, ranging from complete confidentiality to the exchange of identities, visits in the home, etc. (There's plenty of ground between those two extremes.)

The good news is that we no longer forbid birthmothers the chance to see their child before relinquishing. Nor is she treated like a social pariah.

The bad news is that there's tremendous disagreement on whether or not openness in adoption is a good idea, and even those who want to open it up disagree on how much information should be exchanged, the degree the agency should be involved, and a wealth of other issues.

Yet there is evidence to suggest that birthmothers support some degree of openness, and providing a gamut of openness could ultimately convince more birthparents to opt for adoption.

According to a release issued by the Office for Adolescent Health and Pregnancy Planning, Department of Health and Human Services, a study performed by Dr. Michael Resnick at the University of Minnesota revealed that about half of the teen parents studied said they would have placed their infants for adoption if some form of open adoption situation had been available to them.

The other half said they might have placed their babies for adoption. Obviously it was a highly favored alternative, with broad implications for the increasing numbers of pregnant teenagers and the social problems associated with them.

Consequently, if we can assume these teenage parents were representative of their peers nationwide, then it's apparent more openness in adoption could lead to more adoptions.

From the Agencies Point of View

Maxine Chalkin is an adult adoptee who owns The Adoption Agency in Ardmore, Pennsylvania. Prospective parents from Pennsylvania and New Jersey can apply to her agency, and birthparents choose who they want to parent their child.

"After a couple applies, we do a home study, and then they write a profile with a picture and just their first names," explains Chalkin. "We take any religion and any race, and age is not a major factor with us."

Many of the birthmothers meet with the adoptive parents before the child is born. "They could meet once or twice and sometimes they go with the birthmother to the hospital when she's in labor," continues Chalkin.

What kind of families are the birthparents looking for? "They're all looking for something different," she says. "Some want big families, some want small families. Sometimes an adoptive parent may look like someone in their family or someone they like. Often it's a gut-level feeling they go by."

Is it scary to meet a birthmother, when you want so desperately to adopt her baby? What if you say something that annoys her, what if you blow the whole thing? "So far that hasn't happened, although I guess it could," says Chalkin.

She sees numerous advantages to meeting the birthmother, from the adopting parents' point of view. "First of all, they realize this birthmother is a regular person like other regular people they know who are pregnant. I really believe it is in the best interest of the child too."

Why the child's best interest? "I think it really benefits a child to know more about his or her background, to know why the parent placed him."

She continues, "And I think it's important, too, for the birthmother who's in so much pain, and nobody really acknowledges that."

Chalkin feels a birthmother engaged in an adoption where she chooses the parents is far less likely to change her mind about the adoption than a birthmother involved in a confidential adoption.

"Not only would she be taking the baby back, she'd be taking the child away from John and Mary who she knows, not faceless people," she explains.

Direct Adoptions is a Midland, Texas adoption agency, which allows birthmothers to choose adopting parents. (Open only to Texas residents.) Owner and administrator Barbara Messinger has a unique perspective on adoption.

"The whole program was based around my personal experiences in adoption, both as being a birthmother who placed a child in a private placement with an open structure, and also as an adoptive parent," she says.

Messinger requires one face-to-face meeting between birthparents and adopting parents. (The birthparents make a first and second choice from non-identifying files on adopting couples.)

"Above that, anything they feel they want to participate in is all right with us," says Messinger.

"If they want direct open daily communication, that's their choice. If they don't want any further communication, that's their choice. And if they want to go through a kind of a middle of the road deal, allowing the agency to be an intermediary for any communications, that's okay too," she explains.

Once a home study is completed, a couple may be chosen the next day, or not for the next year.

"We allow them a two year period of selection, and they can be picked from the day they go into that file to the day they come out," says Messinger.

"We've had a couple selected in thirty days, and we placed one child with a couple this month, which would have been there two years. We do not guarantee placement because you don't come up next on the list. It really depends on a birthmother walking in the door and picking your file," she explains.

Messinger is strongly supportive of this kind of openness in adoption, and can't understand adoptive parents demanding confidentiality.

"For them to say, 'I don't want to know who the birthmother is' is ludicrous! It's like saying, 'I'm ignorant and I want to stay that way.' " She continues, "How can you look at your child sixteen years from now and say, 'that information was not important enough to me to get it for you?' "

Can't information be provided through a third party? "There are certain things you just can't get down in black and white on paper," she argues. "Things like personality, likes and dislikes, so much more."

Messinger also argues for the immediate bonding of the infant to the adopting parents, which her program provides.

"In most traditional placements, parents receive their children three to six weeks after they are born. You're robbing that couple of some really important bonding time," she insists.

She adds, "As for the child, it suffers the separation from its birthmother and goes into foster care. It adapts to the environment, voices, touch, and sound of the foster parents. Then three to six weeks later, it's pulled out and placed with the adopting couple: it's so unfair to do it that way!"

Are there any advantages to adoptive parents when there is openness in an adoption? "About 99% of our adoptive parents are present in the delivery room, and when you're talking about an infertile couple, number one, they'd never otherwise be able to witness or experience childbirth. And number two, you can tell that child, I was there the minute you were born."

She concludes, "Adopting parents walk away with one hell of a respect for the birthmother."

Other agency directors agree that adoptive parents can gain a great deal through an open adoption. "It's like a breath of fresh air!" exclaims Mardell Groth, Director of Florence Crittendon Services, a division of Child Services and Family Counseling in Atlanta.

She continues, "No longer must they worry about this phantom woman. To go to the store and see a young woman and worry that just *maybe* she could be the birthmother of your child can be extremely disturbing and fearful for an adoptive parent. But in an open adoption, you *know* who the mother is and there is no fear!"

Concludes Groth, "New adoptive parents really feel the entitlement to that child, because they've been personally selected. Maybe they've met the birthmother and she has said, 'I want you to take care of my child' to their face. It's so different from some old social worker handing the child over!"

According to Groth, her agency does not handle identified adoptions. Instead, they build openness within a framework of confidentiality. "Last names are not exchanged, and the agency is the intermediary for any new medical updates, letters, pictures, videotapes, whatever."

Groth says an open adoption is a lot harder for caseworkers than a traditional adoption. "The education of the adoptive parents is difficult and requires professionalism, and the other way is a lot easier, I promise you," she says.

"The adopting couple has already learned they are infertile, which means they've had a horrible time and they feel inadequate and incompetent. What they really want is to have their fantasy child, which is the one that would be born to them.

"You have to take that fantasy child away and replace it with a real live child with somebody else's genes. That's no small job," says Groth. In addition, any remaining fantasy is exploded when the parents meet with the birthmother or exchange information with her.

Because it is such a challenge, her agency works in small groups to cover the issues involved in open adoption and adoption in general.

"We bring in adult adoptee searchers and we educate them on what it's like to have grown up adopted and what it's like if you ask your parents something about your birthparents and they get all nervous. The message then is 'Don't ask, it's bad.' "

As a result of this educational process, it's hoped that adoptive parents can feel more confident and open with their children about issues related to adoption.

Social workers say that openness in adoptions can be nerve-racking at first, when it's a new experience.

Says Joellen Williams, Social Worker with Catholic Social Services in Cocoa, Florida, "I was terrified at the first open adoption I did, and said, 'God, please let me be doing the right thing, please let this philosophy hold true.' "

Her agency still supports confidentiality, but adoptive parents and birthparents meet on a first-name basis and correspondence passes through the agency as an intermediary.

How does she feel about openness now? "The more you do them, the more you realize it's a normal process," says Williams. "What we've done in the past is encumber the process."

She explains further, "What ultimately happens is that there is a bond between the adoptive parents and the birthparents, whether they continue to see each other in person or whether it's just a letter once a year—there's a bond. What a gift to give your child!"

Says James Williams, Director of Adoptions for The LIGHT House in Kansas City, Missouri, "We let the girls select the family from written profiles. Usually, they're about two pages long and it's a cross between an autobiography and a resume."

He continues, "When the girl is in her eighth or ninth month of pregnancy, we get information on her background and on the birthfather, if we know him. We take that information along with specific requests.

"For example, she may ask for a Baptist family, or a Methodist family, or a family who lives on a farm, or a family with no kids, or a family with kids. One girl said she wanted a family under thirty, which is hard to do when we start at 25! She also wanted someone with a German background and we had a perfect match."

Williams adds, "We also have the girls write a letter to the baby before or right after the baby is born, explaining why they placed him or her for adoption. We keep a copy and give the original to the adoptive parents so when the child is older, this letter can be shown."

Some of the letters written by birthmothers are real heart wrenchers.

Says Williams, "We do a lot of crying around here!" For example, one birthmother wrote a letter to the adoptive father, telling him how important he was because he was what she couldn't give her child.

"She also talked about how important it is to have a father who cares for the daughter, and that came from her own personal experience, because she had a very poor relationship with her father," says Williams. "She wanted her child to have a father who loved and cared for the child."

According to Williams, one girl felt she couldn't express herself adequately in a letter. "So she did a cassette tape," he said. "On the tape she poured out her heart and told the baby 'I love you enough to give you up.' It was very moving."

Adoptive parents also respond to this kind of "semi-open" adoption. Williams recalls the case when an adoptive mother wanted to give a bracelet to the birthmother.

"The family was relatively poor, and the husband and his wife had both worked part-time for a year to save up enough money for the adoption."

And the significance of the bracelet? "The adoptive mother said when she and her husband had gone to the doctor a few years before, they found out they would never have children. It was crushing to her. Her husband bought her this gold bracelet because of her deep sorrow, and he told her it was a symbol of hope that someday somewhere God would give them a baby."

Continues Williams, "She never took it off and told us it was more important to her than her wedding band. And this was the bracelet she wanted to give to the birthmother. She said the birthmother had given her the best gift she could ever have, and she wanted to give her most precious thing to the birthmother."

After checking out the request with their attorney, the agency complied. "We gave the bracelet to the birthmother with a letter explaining it. The birthmother says she will never take it off," says Williams.

Adoptive Parents Speak

Maybe some agencies are in love with open adoptions, and the advantages to birthparents seem obvious, but what about the parents who have to live with this? Do most of them pretty much go along with it because it may be the only way they can adopt a baby?

"I strongly wanted an open adoption," says a Maryland mother. "I was an adoptee myself who searched for her birthmother. "When I found her, I realized the terrible pain and anxiety and guilt she suffered over my placement. She still apologizes to me, but I had a happy life! There's nothing to apologize for, as far as I'm concerned!"

As a result of this experience, she knew she didn't want another birthmother out there to suffer for twenty years or more wondering what happened to her child.

This Maryland mom advertised in the newspapers for her birthmother and quickly received several responses. To her surprise, most of the birthmothers who replied did NOT want to go for an open adoption. "They were suspicious, they didn't want to get involved, to meet me," she said.

But she did find a birthmother who was willing to meet her, and adopted the child.

A woman in the D.C. area opted for openness and visited her child's birthmother in the hospital shortly after she delivered. The birthmother had told no one she was expecting and it was a secret the adoptive mom helped her keep.

"She was a large girl anyway, and didn't want anyone to know," said the adoptive mom. She laughs and says, "When her relatives came to visit her in the hospital, I had to explain to them the reason she was in the obstetrics ward was because they ran out of room in GYN." (She had told everyone she had a gynecological problem.)

Says the adoptive mom, "We were co-conspirators! Later, her office found out she had a baby and didn't know she placed her for adoption. So they had a baby shower! She brought me as her 'sister-in-law!' Everyone was talking at once and maybe someone suspected, but no one said anything."

The birthmother and adoptive mother left together and the birthmother gave all the gifts to adoptive mom!

An adoptive father is angry at the adoption agencies for not providing the level of openness he thinks is imperative. He and his wife adopted through an attorney, because local agencies couldn't or wouldn't supply the level of openness he and his wife desired. (Although some states require open identified adoptions, others prohibit agencies from handling them.)

"It's arrogant, elitist, and just bad policy to keep adoptions closed!" he insists. He's very glad his adoption is open and he and his wife maintain regular telephone contact with their child's birthmother.

An Illinois mother actually adopted THREE infants over a two-year period, in three separate open adoptions! Her babies all came from California, where she and her husband flew each time to pick up the babies.

"We finalized in six months, which is Illinois law," explains the mother.

What's the story behind this adoption? "Well, we wanted to adopt *A* baby, and never imagined we could actually end up with three!" she laughs. "I sent out hundreds of resumes to doctors in Wisconsin, California, and other states."

It probably didn't hurt that her husband was a doctor. "We received several calls from doctors' secretaries, who wanted to know if we were still interested," she says.

The Illinois mom knows who all the birthmothers are and they each know who she is. "We exchange letters and photographs, and one of them said she'd like to visit, although she never has.

"I think she's testing the waters," speculates the adoptive mom.

Why did she adopt three infants over such a short period? "I wanted my children to be close together," she explains.

"I knew that some social workers think they should be three years apart, but I didn't believe that. I wanted them to have the closeness they would experience by being nearly the same age."

Does she have any feelings of discomfort over the openness in her adoptions. "Well, we do live so far apart from the birthmothers and they can't come over and visit, so that is a factor," she admits.

Among the people I interviewed, the strongest relationship between a birthmother and her child's adoptive parents is between a New Hampshire birthmother, her mother, and the baby's adoptive parents in Arizona. The adoptive parents plan to fly to New Hampshire to attend the birthmother's high school graduation in June 1987, and yes, they will bring the baby.

The birthmother's own mother is very positive about the relationship with "Tom" and "Sue" (not their real names) and says, "They would never have had children if they didn't adopt and they really love the child." She and her daughter freely send the child gifts at Easter, Christmas, and other holidays.

She says, "We've thought about the future. For example, what if when the child is fourteen she says she wants to live with her birthmother? Well, she can't. If she's eighteen and wants to live with her, that might be okay."

Yet, she is glad the adoptive parents are several thousand miles away. "I wouldn't want them to live the next town over or even the next state over!" she says.

"It would be tempting to go visit and see how she's doing. It's better for everyone that they live faraway."

Does she think open adoption is for everyone? "No!" she says emphatically. "It works well for us, but we're all very strong, secure people. My daughter is comfortable with them, they're comfortable with her."

She relates an amusing incident in the courtroom: the day of the adoption hearing, when another birthmother was there relinquishing her child, too, in a closed adoption.

"She was a real scruffy-looking weirdo, and Sue told us that girl was an adoptive parent's nightmare! She was so glad she had the chance to meet my daughter and see how nice she was!"

Was losing her first grandchild painful? "Yes, it was, but we know she's safe! We know that if she ever needs a blood transfusion or if she ever needs us, she can find us and we can find her!"

She proceeded to brag about how intelligent the child sounded on the telephone, in typical grandmotherly fashion, concluding that when you know you can talk to someone or go visit, you don't feel panicky and claustrophobic.

One very positive aspect of openness in adoption is the special feeling the adoptive parents experience at being selected.

"When our son grows up, we can tell him his birthmother chose us, it wasn't like we were number forty-nine on some list," says his mother happily.

As a result of the strongly favorable feelings she has towards the birthmother, it is likely she'll convey good feelings to the son as well.

Says Dorothy Barkley of the Texas Cradle Society, "We do meetings of birthparents and adoptive parents on a first-name basis, and they share information and their feelings. I've seen some real miracles come about when people sit together and share their love for this child and see this is all for the best interests of the child.

She continues, "The adoptive parents are no longer afraid this masked person is going to try to come get their child. You also get the birthmother to see them and relate to them as the parents of her child. I've never had a birthmother want to meet a couple so she could identify them later. Instead, she wants them to see her and understand her, so that this can later be related to the child."

One adoptive mom was deeply moved by a letter she received, through the agency, from her daughter's birthmother. It was to be given to the child when she grows up.

The letter explained why she was placed for adoption, and emphasized how much the baby was loved, yet for a variety of reasons she described, it was impossible for the birthmother to raise the baby.

"Don't ever think they are not your real parents, because they are," she cautioned her daughter in the letter. "They are very good people and they couldn't wait to hold you in their arms."

The adoptive mother said, "I think I cried for a week after I read that letter!" She decided to write to the birthmother and assure her the child was loved. "I told her that the baby gets at least a hundred kisses and a hundred hugs every day," she said.

Negative Aspects of Openness in Adoption

Not everyone is ready to jump on the bandwagon and open up adoptions completely, and many social workers and adoptive parents have serious qualms about whether openness is a good idea. They claim the picture isn't always as rosy as open adoption proponents paint it.

Some fear the birthmother will haunt the family in future years. Even if she's a nice sweet girl now, what if ten years from now she decides she wants her child back and haunts your house, or maybe hangs out by the school, waiting for your little Susie to come out?

Advocates of openness insist that knowing where the child is alleviates fears and anxieties and the obsessive need to see the child. But the evidence still isn't in.

And what if she *isn't* a nice sweet girl now, what if she's a prostitute or a drug addict?

In fact, one of my adoptive parent interviewees knows that her child's birthmother *is* a prostitute. "Her lifestyle causes me great pain, and I hate to think about telling the child someday when she's old enough to understand. But I'm still glad I know her," she says.

And what if adoptive parents are so eager to adopt that they'll agree to anything?

Says Leigh Ann Johnson, Director of Adoptions for Shepherd Care Ministries in Hollywood, Florida, "Adoptive parents will frequently agree to a lot of things out of desperation and naivete. Once they get that baby in their arms and in their home, suddenly they realize what they've agreed to, and they feel trapped.

"If they do honor the request, it's a little bit grudgingly. And they can become over-protective of the child if the mother's demands are too strong."

Here's an example of an extreme request, provided by another social worker: a fourteen year old birthmother said she wanted a letter once a *week* from the adoptive parents. They wanted that baby and they agreed. I don't know about you, but I don't write to anybody once a week, maybe once a month at best.

Yet the adopting parents agreed. How long before that agreement would begin to chafe? How long before the birthmother would quit reading those letters?

Not every adoptive mother would feel comfortable about being a labor coach for a birthmother—but they may be asked. Where do you draw the line?

Some agencies try to create the dividing lines themselves, telling the birthmother she should write a letter to the baby, telling the adoptive parents they should write a thank you letter to the mother, etc. Others say this is preposterous, and the participating parties should decide for themselves how open to make the adoption.

But if you have no experience in such things—and most birthmothers and adoptive parents are new at this—how do you know where to say, "Stop! I don't want to go along with that?"

Think that's an easy one? Well, what if the birthmother is in her eighth or ninth month, you don't want to upset her, do you?

Some experts have hypothesized that open adoptions can interfere with the bonding of an adoptive mother to her child. Constantly aware of the birthmother, she may feel more like a babysitter or an interloper, rather than a "real" mother.

James Timmens, Director of Placements for Adoption Services Associates, an agency in San Antonio, Texas, favors birthmothers selecting the adoptive parents from resumes and even through phone conversations or meetings.

But he has serious qualms about the current vogue of adoptive parents going into the delivery room with the birthmother.

"In some cases, it's probably good," he concedes. But he has observed problems, too. Just after making it through the wrenching pain of labor and delivery, the birthmother may be very emotional and vulnerable.

Seeing the adoptive parents holding her baby and beaming at it may fill her with joy. Or she may experience a surging flood of resentment.

"A birthmother later told me she changed her mind, and said it was because of that," says Timmens. Of course, she might have changed her mind about adoption anyway, even if she were all alone, but Timmens argues the sight of her child in the adoptive mother's arms was clearly a negative psychological factor affecting her decision.

As a result, think carefully before you decide to be a labor coach, go with the birthmother into the delivery room, and the whole nine yards.

Are you comfortable with this yourself, or are you merely agreeing to pacify the birthmother, because you want the baby so bad? This one requires considerable introspection, and you must not allow yourself to be pressured by your social worker, in the event that she or he thinks it's a not-to-be-missed experience.

Some adoption professionals feel openness in adoption does not allow a birthmother to fully accept the adoption and leaves her in a sort of "hanging-on" status. In this instance, open adoption refers to an ongoing personal contact via letters, phone calls, visits, etc.

According to a paper presented to the National Committee For Adoption in 1982, "In all likelihood, the birthmother will still consider the child 'hers' and not be able to relinquish the child from an emotional standpoint. In confidential adoption, the loss experienced can be mourned by the birthmother. This normal process of grieving allows her to begin to be able to relinquish the child from an emotional as well as from a legal standpoint."

Instead, the authors support "confidential" adoption, wherein nonidentifying and medical data is shared through the agency.

Whether you favor openness or not, it takes plenty of hard work and soul searching, on everyone's part: the birthmother, the adoptive parents, and the social worker or attorney.

Both proponents and opponents of openness in adoption generally agree that the jury isn't in yet on whether it will work or not. (Although California's independent adoptions have been open for over 40 years.) After all, the system has been closed a long time, and virtually all our grown-up adoptees were raised under the old system.

"That's the very frustrating part," says Groth of Florence Crittendon Services in Atlanta.

"It sounds logical and sensible to many of us, but we don't know what effect it will have on the children, and we won't know until twenty years from now. Will it all turn out the same way or will it be better? We just don't know."

Open Adoption and Society

How do people in general feel about open adoption? One area where the "outside world" does impact on adoptive parents and birthparents is the hospital where the child is born, and often they can't understand at all when the adoptive parents want to accompany the birthmother into the delivery room. As a result, many hospitals are coming into open adoption kicking and screaming.

"Every person from the cleaning lady on has an opinion which they feel they *must* give to this mother," says Groth wryly.

"They've also gotten used to the confidential adoptions, and then an agency comes along and changes the rules."

Groth says hospitals are horrified at the idea of adoptive parents coming into the hospital to see the birthmother and the baby. "They say, 'Who are these people, what's going on?' " she says.

Even when the agency explains open adoption, there still may be considerable resistance on the part of the hospital staff. Certainly, some confusion is understandable, particularly when some birthmothers are continuing to place in confidential adoptions, while others are opting for open adoptions.

One adoptive mother got around this one in a creative and amusing way. When she and her husband came to see their daughter's birthmother, they were asked, "Are you her mother and father?"

They responded, "Yes," meaning they were the adoptive parents, but knowing full well it was assumed they were the birthmother's parents! Other adoptive parents have had to wait until regular visiting hours, when anyone can come in.

Commitment

If you *do* decide to become involved in an open adoption, follow through on your mutual agreement. Whether you agree to send your child's birthmother pictures once a year, or you communicate over the phone every few months, or—as some people do—you actually visit each other in your homes on Thanksgiving and Christmas—it's important to make a commitment you intend to keep.

The first part of your commitment comes when you decide to adopt a particular birthmother's baby after it is born. Take that commitment very seriously: she does. (Yes, sometimes they *do* change their mind, but assume she probably won't.)

For example, if you agree to adopt a birthmother's baby in four months, and then discover another mother about to deliver in one month, think through your commitment to the first birthmother.

At the very least, you owe her an immediate explanation if you want to go with the other mother, so she can make other plans for her child. The longer you delay, the more shattered she will be, and the harder for her to make a new plan for her child.

Some states will allow you to adopt two unrelated infants, so you might want to consider that option. But you should *tell* her, because the birthmother might want her child to go to a childless couple or a couple with older children, so her baby will get exclusive attention.

Sometimes adopting families will agree to adopt the children of two or more birthmothers, using numbers two and three as emergency backups in case the first birthmother changes her mind. But the adoptive parents only intend to adopt *one* child.

None of the birthmothers knows about each other, and each thinks her child will go to this wonderful loving family who is just dying to adopt a child.

Such a strategy is immoral and unethical, and I strongly discourage readers from stringing along several birthmothers as emergency back-ups, just to make sure you end up with one kid. (Because you're so worried the birthmother may change her mind about adoption.)

Sure, *she* could change her mind, but you know that and she knows that. She doesn't know you have one or more birthmothers waiting in the wings. If she and the other birthmother(s) did know and thought it was all right, that would be another issue altogether.

We're not talking about a sack of potatoes here, we're talking about human life and raising a very precious child. Treat the birthmother and her child with the respect they both deserve.

If you do find the ideal birthmother for you, and then another pregnant woman calls you up to discuss placing her child, don't just say, "Thank you, we're no longer interested." Click.

Politely tell her you've found another birthmother and have made arrangements to adopt her child.

Tell her about adoption agencies in your area, or attorneys who arrange independent adoption. Or give her the name and phone number of your support group, if you think they can refer her to someone who could help.

Give her something to go on. It takes a lot of guts to call strangers and tell them you may want to give them your baby. A little information on your part, and a positive attitude, can make a strong impression.

The second part of your commitment comes after placement. If you agreed to send pictures and letters, then send them. If you agreed to call her at given intervals, call her. A very sad situation occurred in California when a birthmother took her baby back from an adoptive couple after two months.

The reason? She requested the pictures they had initially agreed to send her, but later withheld. She went to court, got the baby back, and placed the child with another adoptive couple who was willing to send her pictures.

This example is *not* to imply that birthmothers can easily take babies back from adopting couples; they can't. California has a longer period than many other states during which the birthmother can sign consent or change her mind.

After finalization of the adoption, adoptive parents can theoretically "cut the cord" and ignore the birthmother forever. But they shouldn't if they made a commitment to her.

Agreements you make with the birthmother are not cast in granite and you can decide to make changes together. For example, in a year or two, she may decide she no longer wants pictures, letters, phone calls, etc. But to make an agreement and then renege just because you're "safe," just isn't fair.

More Openness Is the Coming Thing

Whether you approve or disapprove, it seems apparent that a certain amount of openness is a growing trend. Whether it's choosing adoptive parents from non-identifying resumes, or spending Thanksgiving Day with them, or a whole array of options in between, birthmothers are demanding and getting more openness.

Some states still forbid releasing complete identifying data about adopting parents or birthparents to each other, while other states mandate it.

The good news for adoptive parents is that there are agencies that do closed traditional adoptions, others that regard themselves as "semi-open," and still others that are very open. Just as there are attorneys who support the varied openness options available.

A family opting for closed adoption may find themselves waiting longer than a family who decides they'll apply to an agency where the birthmothers choose the adopting parents. On the other hand, the "open adopters" may get chosen the day their resume hits the files, or they may never get chosen.

Adopting parents should carefully weigh the pros and cons of openness in adoption and, if at all possible, talk to people who've had closed and open adoptions.

Ask penetrating questions: it's amazing how candid adoptive parents are with others interested in learning about adoption.

Then, decide for yourself whether openness is right for your family, and move ahead to achieve the goal for which this book was written: adopting your baby.

CHAPTER 11
Biological Alternatives to Adoption

For couples or singles who feel a strong need for a genetic connection to their child, there are increasing numbers of high-tech biological options available which make it possible to bear an infant. Some are relatively inexpensive, while others cost thousands of dollars and are often not covered by health insurance.

Should You Seek a Fertility Specialist?

Many men and women in their late twenties or thirties want what they want *when* they want it. They've delayed childbearing to establish careers and then decided it's time for children. But even a perfectly normal reproductive system can't always reproduce on demand.

As a result, experts say you should try to become pregnant for at least a year before you start to worry about infertility. Buy a basal thermometer and track your ovulation cycle. (They include directions.) Or purchase a kit to help you pinpoint when ovulation actually occurs.

If you are still not pregnant after a year or so, ask your gynecologist for advice. It may be a simple problem he or she can cure right in the office. Or it may require surgery or some high-tech procedure described in this chapter.

Major biological options include routine or laser surgery, hormone therapy, artificial insemination, surrogate motherhood, and test tube babies; and brilliant physicians are creating new solutions all the time. As a result, people who could never have borne children five or ten years ago are proud mamas and daddies.

Each method has distinct pros and cons to be carefully considered before pursuing. This brief overview of some of the key biological options will discuss the pros and cons of the most popular choices of infertile couples, who finally have a chance to produce a child.

Surgical Alternatives

If a woman's blocked fallopian tubes or a man's varicocele (a varicose vein in the spermatic cord of the testicle) is the problem, surgery may be the answer. Highly sophisticated devices and laser surgery make it possible for surgeons to make microscopic corrections to restore or initiate fertility.

Sometimes a hormonal problem inhibits fertility, and in severe cases, surgery may be warranted. For example, about ten years ago I had a thyroidectomy to eliminate an uncorrectable thyroid problem, which inhibited ovulation.

Two months after surgery, I was pregnant, and 11 1/2 months after our first child was born, our second child arrived. Less severe hormonal problems may be corrected by drug therapy rather than surgery.

Hormonal Solutions

If a woman cannot ovulate at all, her physician may recommend a fertility drug such as Clomid. She may then become pregnant with one or more children. Some women find these drugs have negative side effects, but they insist it's worth the effort—if it works.

Men may have hormonal problems that prevent them from producing sperm when they ejaculate, and drug therapy could be the answer to creating enough sperm to fertilize an egg.

It's important for both the man and woman to be evaluated for fertility. Either (or both) partner(s) could be causing the problem in conceiving.

Physicians may also recommend psychological counseling, so that the partner who is "at-fault" does not feel he or she is letting their partner down.

If medical alternatives do not help, and you are still determined to bear a child with a genetic link to at least one of you, there are several other intriguing choices currently available.

Artificial Insemination

If infertility stems primarily from a problem with the man, and the difficulties cannot be resolved, artificial insemination of the woman may be considered a solution. Sometimes, the husband's sperm can be used. If it is necessary to increase the number and concentration of the sperm, it may be "washed" and then centrifuged and inseminated, as when the man's own semen contains antibodies damaging to the sperm.

If it's not possible to use the husband's sperm, then donor sperm from a sperm bank may be used for the insemination.

Although it has become more popular over the last thirty years, artificial insemination has been used for many years. Still, new refinements, such as freezing sperm, have brought artificial insemination back into the headlines, sharing space with the newer more sophisticated high-tech alternatives.

An estimated 10,000 infants per year are conceived in the United States using this technique.

Women who opt for this method of parenthood contact a sperm bank, and the cost may be as low as $400 per insemination—which is considerably cheaper than an adoption.

Sperm donors are anonymous and the prospective parents can select a donor from non-identifying information, choosing the sperm of a man whose physical characteristics resemble the husband. Donors don't get rich from their donated sperm. They receive about $25 per sample and are often limited on the number of samples they may donate.

According to an April 2, 1987 article in the Wall Street Journal, the Sperm Bank of Northern California in Oakland, run by the Oakland Feminist Women's Health Center, requires new donors to come in a minimum of four times to complete questionnaires, provide semen samples, and undergo interviews and physicals.

Women can either have the sperm cold-shipped to their physician for local insemination, or travel to Oakland for examination and insemination at the Center. The Center accepts couples and singles. Other sperm banks will, often, only inseminate married women, but single women are apparently finding artificial insemination an increasingly popular option.

According to the Wall Street Journal article, a single woman in New York has produced two children through artificial insemination. "She used a sperm bank in Manhattan operated by Daxor Corp's Idant Laboratories division," reported the Journal.

As with singles opting for adoption, most singles who choose artificial insemination are career professionals whose biological clock is ticking away too loudly to ignore.

Many sperm banks use frozen sperm, while others opt for freshly donated specimens. Some physicians argue for frozen sperm, because they say a donor can be retested for disease before the sperm is used. More inseminations may be required to achieve pregnancy when the sperm are frozen because the sperm's ability to move around (motility) is decreased when it is frozen and later thawed out.

The primary disadvantage of using donor sperm from an unknown person is the extreme difficulty of tracking him down later. Should the child grow up and wish to search for his or her biological father, as do some adopted children, it would be impossible to find him unless very accurate records are kept.

And even if a man knows he donated sperm, he will not know if or how many children he fathered, only how many he physically could have fathered through artificial insemination. He will not know the sex of these children or anything about them, unlike a surrogate mother who obviously does possess this information.

In another sense, this very lack of knowledge is seen as an advantage by some donors as well as by some women who have been inseminated.

The obvious advantage of artificial insemination, other than the low cost, is that it will *not* be obvious to the general public that the mother has been inseminated artificially. Everyone will think it's a natural occurrence unless the parents tell people otherwise.

Sometimes the problem of infertility lies with the woman, and she cannot carry a child to term, for any of a variety of reasons. She and her husband may opt to hire a surrogate mother.

Surrogate Motherhood

Surrogate motherhood is an extremely controversial way to get a child. The "surrogate" is usually artificially inseminated with the sperm of the husband and her own egg is fertilized by that sperm. As a result, the child is genetically 50% of the surrogate mother and 50% of the husband.

At the time of this writing, surrogate motherhood is under intense scrutiny, primarily because of the Baby M case in New Jersey. But, in case you were in a coma in 1986, or maybe on an African safari, the gist of this case is that a New Jersey woman was to be paid $10,000 to bear a child for a New Jersey couple. The sperm was provided by the husband of the couple, and the surrogate was artificially inseminated.

Then, after the baby was born, the surrogate mother changed her mind, deciding she wanted to keep it. She ran away to Florida with the baby, the child was forcibly returned, and the whole thing ended up in court.

On March 31, 1987, a judge awarded the baby to her biological father and permitted his wife to adopt the baby. The surrogate mother appealed the case, and the next round will probably take place sometime in late 1987. Whoever loses will probably appeal, and the case may ultimately end up in the United States Supreme Court.

Don't think that surrogate motherhood is a twentieth century phenomenon: surrogate mothers have borne children for other couples for centuries. The Bible tells us that Abraham's infertile wife Sarah asked him to have intercourse with her servant so they'd have a child.

He did and the result was Ishmael. But paying for the surrogate's specific child-bearing services is a modern wrinkle.

Ten thousand dollars is the current "going rate" for surrogate services, although I interviewed a New Hampshire woman who received $15,000.

Expect to pay $25,000 or more, including the fee to the surrogate, the attorney, the agency arranging the surrogacy, the hospital, etc.

If an agency arranges for a surrogate mother, they should make sure she's in good health, and some administer an intelligence test: one agency required an I.Q. of at least 90 for prospective surrogates. Virtually all surrogates have borne children before, and those children are normal and healthy. Many surrogates are married. Sometimes, the couple meets the surrogate, and sometimes they select her from informational resumes.

A considerable amount is required upfront; for example, according to a brochure from the Center for Reproductive Alternatives in Pleasant Hill, California, "An initial deposit of $5,000 is required, plus $1,200 to cover advertising, medical exams, and miscellaneous items." (Paid after a consultation with their staff.)

Attorney Noel Keane claims to be the first attorney who formally arranged a surrogate contract, and he has allegedly arranged for hundreds of babies for happy couples.

An embryo transfer procedure, moving an embryo from the surrogate to the mom, is similar to surrogate parenting. This is a highly unusual procedure which involves a mother with a functioning uterus but no eggs who needs donor eggs. Yet she wants to carry the baby to term and deliver naturally.

In this case, the child is conceived through the artificial insemination of a surrogate's egg which is implanted into her uterus. The resulting embryo is extracted, using special catheters, and then re-implanted into the uterus of the infertile mother-to-be.

The wife will then carry the baby to term and deliver the child. Of course, it will genetically be the child of her husband and the surrogate.

This is an extremely unusual and expensive procedure, although it was successfully accomplished at the Harbor/UCLA Medical Center in 1984.

Test Tube Babies

Only ten years ago, women with blocked or missing fallopian tubes were unable to bear children. Now, scientific techniques can extract the woman's eggs, fertilize them with her husband's sperm outside the body, and then implant the fertilized egg into the womb.

Louise Brown was the world's first test tube baby, born in England in 1978. In the United States, the first test tube baby was born in 1981, "conceived" at the Jones Institute for Reproductive Medicine at Eastern Virginia Medical School in Norfolk.

Fertility specialist Howard Jones and his wife Georgeanna, of the prolific Jones Institute, can proudly point to over 200 babies born so far, with many more to come.

In addition to the highly successful clinic run by the Jones', there are several hundred in vitro clinics in major cities throughout the United States.

In vitro fertilization (IVF) is an option for about a thousand women each year. Success rates run at about 25-50% and IVF costs are in the thousands of dollars for those who wish to try this option. Your insurance may or may not cover this procedure: check first.

Sometimes, in vitro may be attempted jointly with the repair of damaged fallopian tubes, using laser surgery techniques. Another interesting point: the woman need have only one tube to produce a pregnancy.

An Arkansas woman, with only one intact but severely damaged tube, traveled to the Hillcrest Infertility Center in Tulsa, Oklahoma to undergo in vitro fertilization.

It took four tries at about $5,000 each before the woman succeeded in attaining pregnancy. Said her husband simply, "It was worth it." They now have a healthy baby daughter.

Clinics have certain criteria for candidates of in vitro. For example, the Mount Sinai Medical Center In Vitro Fertilization Program considers married couples who have been infertile for two or more years. The wife must be forty years old or younger, and there are other guidelines.

Another unique variation of in vitro was achieved by Australian physicians in 1985. They were able to extract sperm from a man's testes, culture them to maturity, and later fertilize an egg from his wife in vitro. The embryo was inserted into the uterus and a normal birth resulted.

This method was created for cases where the man was unable to ejaculate sperm because of scar tissue or other problems.

Medical science has also recently made it possible to use test-tube baby technology combined with a surrogate mother to create a genetic child of both the contracting father and mother.

If the mother has no uterus but she does have ovaries and can produce eggs, eggs can be withdrawn from the ovaries and combined in a test-tube environment with her husband's sperm.

Since she cannot carry the child herself, the fertilized egg is then implanted into a third party: the surrogate mother. In this case, the child will have the genetic composition of the mother and father, and the surrogate will not contribute any of her eggs or genes.

This is a highly unusual procedure, but it has been done. Such a child was born in April 1986 in Ann Arbor, Michigan.

The Orlando Sentinel blared out a shocker of a headline on surrogate parenting, on April 9, 1987: "Surrogate mother to bear her own triplet grandchildren" was the lead story.

In this rather bizarre case, a South African grandmother made the news in the third month of her pregnancy with triplets: the children of her daughter and son-in-law. It was an in vitro fertilization with the eggs and sperm of the younger people, later implanted into the grandmother.

Other Biological Options

Gamete Intra-Fallopian Transfer is another biological option for a couple seeking a pregnancy. G-I-F-T is a procedure wherein the woman's egg and the man's sperm are injected, separately and directly into the Fallopian tubes during surgery.

As a result, fertilization occurs inside the body, rather than in a test tube, mimicking nature. (Thus, this procedure might be more acceptable to the Vatican than the others described.)

Prior to surgery, the woman receives hormones for a week to stimulate the development of eggs. When the physician determines that ovulation will occur, she is admitted the hospital. Hours before the procedure, her husband's semen is collected and centrifuged so it is highly concentrated. The eggs are retrieved via laparoscopy, which means they are withdrawn during surgery, or by other means.

This procedure is used with unexplained infertility, endometriosis, a failed artificial insemination, and other cases. Of course, the patient must have at least one normal Fallopian tube.

Another high-tech babymaking technique is to combine the egg and sperm and then freeze the resulting embryo for later implantation. A frozen embryo, who grew into a healthy male child, was delivered in Los Angeles on June 4, 1986. The child was a "million dollar baby" born to a couple who had been trying, without success, for fifteen years.

The first frozen zygote baby in the United States was born on March 25th, 1987 in Ocala, Florida. (A zygote is a fertilized egg which hasn't yet begun cell division.) The mother was impregnated at the Reproductive Biology Associates in Atlanta.

Moral Dilemmas

These high-tech alternatives cost many thousands of dollars, and the moral implications have been and will be debated for years to come. For example, what happens to the frozen zygotes or embryos that aren't used?

Is it okay to freeze sperm for insemination years down the road? If your husband dies and you are inseminated with his sperm five years from now, can he legally be cited as the "father" on the birth certificate, would society accept that? These are only a few of the tough questions which lie ahead.

Several years ago, in Australia, an American couple who were patients at an Australian fertility clinic were killed in a plane crash. They had left behind several embryos. Australian officials agonized over what, if anything, to do with the embryos.

Finally, they decided to allow the embryos to be anonymously implanted into a surrogate mother and adopted upon birth.

Surrogate motherhood is controversial because opponents say it creates a breeder class of women. An NBC program on surrogates seemed to partially bear out this opinion: one scene depicted the woman who would adopt the baby showing her friends pictures of the surrogate mother. "Good teeth!" said one, as if the surrogate were a horse she was looking over.

On the other hand, surrogates receive $10,000 or more, and know they are going into this agreement planning to place the child with the couple with whom they sign the contract. Most couples could not have a biological child without the surrogate.

The Vatican has publicly disapproved of surrogate parenting and other "unnatural" forms of conception, thus contributing to the overall controversy surrounding surrogate motherhood.

Significantly, many states are considering legislation to regulate surrogate parenthood. Oregon, for example, is considering a ban on any payment of money or other goods of value to a surrogate mother. Any payment would be a felony.

There are many other issues involved with surrogate motherhood. Each individual must make his or her own informed decision.

A New England surrogate mom I interviewed said she was happy to give her child to a couple who would otherwise never have a child of their own. She was very angry about the Baby M case, and felt the contract should have been honored.

"She already had children and I think she knew what she was doing," the woman said. She speculated that Baby M's birthmother may have been caught up in media hype and felt unable to back down on her decision to fight for the baby.

How did this New England mom make her arrangement? She checked out several surrogate agencies before settling on one she felt was compassionate and fair.

She rejected another she felt was "too businesslike" and claimed that agency insisted on a W-2 income tax form, to be signed upfront, for the surrogate payment. She also said they required surrogates to come to the area three weeks before the due date and induce labor.

"When they make it too much like dollars and cents, I don't like it, it spoils the whole thing," she said.

Her one fear during the pregnancy was what would happen if the baby had a problem, what if it had Down's Syndrome or some other kind of birth defect? "I don't drink or smoke, but you never know!" she said. Her contract required the couple to take the baby even if it did have problems. "Because a problem could have come from his side too," she reasoned.

Everything turned out okay. "She was a beautiful healthy child!" she said.

Did she have any misgivings? "I already had a son and the baby was a little girl," she said sadly. "But she didn't look anything like me at all, and I knew how much they wanted her."

Because she had the child on Christmas Day, the surrogate mom felt that was a sign that she hadn't violated her Christian beliefs and had, instead, done a good thing.

One thing which *did* bother her was the letdown feeling after the baby was gone. "I was so fussed over during my pregnancy and I felt so important!" she said. She claimed that other surrogate moms have immediately opted for another pregnancy so they can again feel important and cherished.

The surrogate mother said she was well-protected and insisted on a lengthy document explaining every element of the agreement. She did have trouble finding an attorney to represent her. "When I finally found one, she'd send me every negative article she could find, even ones from overseas!" she exclaimed.

She faced plenty of flak from disapproving relatives.

"It wasn't talked about much," she admitted, but she did feel a certain chill that wasn't there before.

Will she ever do it again? "Only if I can do it so that I receive the fertilized egg from someone else who can't carry a child," she said. "I won't ever give up one of my own eggs again."

She concludes, "I think having a baby for another family is a really neat thing to do!"

Unspecified Infertility

Sometimes, couples don't know why they are infertile, and this can be extremely frustrating. Everything *looks* good, the sperm count is okay, the Fallopian tubes are undamaged, the uterus seems normal. But pregnancy does not occur. Or worse, it does occur, and the child is lost through miscarriage.

A woman at an adoption seminar described her four pregnancies which ended up in the stillborn deaths of her children. "Everything seemed to be fine, no problems. But I lost every child," she said as her voice broke up.

Realizing they could not bear another loss, the couple decided to adopt, and are now the happy parents of two children.

Other couples never achieve pregnancy and never know why. Some are very disturbed by this and seek counseling. Others either adopt children or remain childless, feeling that someday they may still have a child, since it hasn't been medically ruled out.

If You Want to Try a High Tech Solution

Although your local gynecologist could probably accomplish a simple artificial insemination, he or she may not be adept at the state-of-the-art techniques of achieving pregnancy. As a result, you may have to travel to a large city, in or out of your state.

Ask your doctor for information on where such procedures are done. Call around. Read and do your homework. Some clinics even advertise. For example, The Florida Fertility Institute in St. Petersburg, Florida has advertised in Cosmopolitan magazine, complete with a picture of a beautiful newborn.

Check your local Yellow Pages as well as those of the largest cities in your state and neighboring states. Your local library may have phone directories for cities throughout the country—ask the reference librarian.

Whether your interest is artificial insemination, in vitro fertilization, or any one of the other biological options described here, you can write to The American Fertility Society and ask for a list of recommended fertility experts in your state. (The American Fertility Society, 1608 13th Ave. S., Ste. 101, Birmingham, AL 35256-6199)

Another good source for help in coping with infertility as well as finding medical alternatives, is an organization called RESOLVE, Inc., based in Arlington, Massachusetts. They provide education, referral, and support and operate nearly 50 chapters nationwide. Contact the national office for further information. (RESOLVE, Inc., 5 Water St., Arlington, MA 02174. Phone: [617] 643-2424.)

Can Adopting a Child Make You Pregnant?

It is true that occasionally when a family adopts a baby the adoptive mother suddenly finds herself pregnant. This does not mean that if you adopt you will conceive. Obviously, if the adoptive mother has no uterus or other appropriate internal plumbing, she can't and won't have a child.

Even if the problem is unspecified infertility, it still is no sure thing the couple will ever bear children. If it happens, it happens, and is a blessed event.

If You Are Still Infertile

If all these fancy biological solutions don't work for you, don't give up on raising a child: the adoption option is a wonderful and fulfilling choice! Every adoptive parent interviewed said it was one of the most exciting—if not THE most exciting event of their lives—the day they received their child.

Even those who previously had biological children were thrilled with their adopted baby. Whether it was the first, second, or only child, all agreed, it was an incredible experience. Not second best. Just as good as a biological child.

So work through your infertility problems, physically and psychologically. Then, if you cannot bear a child, rethink adoption. It's a wonderful option.

CHAPTER 12
Conclusion

Hopefully the words between these two covers have by now convinced you that there ARE babies to adopt and that it is possible for you to adopt an infant. I've strongly emphasized the importance of joining an adoptive parents support group, for the information, moral support, and encouragement you can obtain through other adoptive and adopting parents.

This book contains a lot of cheerleading, because people need to hear that it *IS* possible to adopt an infant. Whether you want a healthy White infant, an international child, a special needs child, or whatever kind of infant or toddler you've decided is right for your family—you can do it.

Virtually every adoptive parent I interviewed insisted I stress to my readers NOT TO GIVE UP! They warned me that you will be told it is impossible, and will hear many many discouraging words. But persistence and perseverance will pay off!

So ignore those nay-sayers and "get on with the program" of setting your gameplan for adoption, using the information in this book and information you obtain through your own personal networking process. And charge full speed ahead!

Other Issues

Even though you're planning to adopt an infant, you must realize that the day you hold that child in your arms for the first time isn't the end of adoption: in many ways, it's the beginning of many issues you as an adoptive parent will face.

"At first, I thought everything would be fine after I finally got a baby," reflected one parent. "Then I thought, well, after we finalize, things will be normal forever." She later realized adoption would be a long-term issue in her life and the life of her husband and child. I don't mean to imply that adopted children are less adjusted or happy than children born to a family, or that you must continually agonize over your status as an adoptive parent or your child's status as an adoptee. Studies have revealed that adopted children fare as well as, or even better than, biological kids.

What I do mean is that as your child grows older, he or she will need to learn about the adoption, and face the tough questions. Why did my mother give me up? If it was for love, does that mean if my adoptive parents love me too much, they'll give me to someone else too?

On the surface, that sounds irrational, and yet it could be a logical conclusion for a child to make if adoptive parents rely solely on the explanation, "Your mother gave you up because she loved you."

Of course, she *did* love the child, but the probable reason she placed him for adoption was because she wanted her child to have a better life than she felt she could provide.

When and *how* to tell your child she or he is adopted is beyond the scope of this book, but there are other books and articles that comprehensively address this issue. The important point is that the child SHOULD be told.

"I can't ever remember not knowing I was adopted," an adoptee told a fascinated group, at an adoption seminar in a Florida hospital. "I've just always known." This man had an adopted brother and his adoptive parents later had two biological kids. Did he ever feel jealous because they had a genetic connection to the parents and he didn't?

"Sometimes people would ask my Dad which ones were the 'kids of his own,' " recalls this adoptee.

Melodramatically clapping his hand to his forehead as his father did when asked this question, he recalls his father saying, "I've been *meaning* to write that down!"

Of course, he knew his Dad was joking. But this adoptee was reassured and never felt he was second-best.

Searching for Birthparents

The Search Issue is a major concern to many adoptive parents and birthparents. Does a child have the right to find his or her biological roots? What about the birthmother's rights of confidentiality, assuming she placed her child in a traditional closed adoption? And when should adoptive parents' judgements and control end? Is it fair to require an adoptive parent's signature when an adult adoptee wants to find a birthparent? And how old is old enough to learn about your "past"—eighteen, twenty-one, twenty-five? The whole search issue is extremely controversial, with advocates on the ends of both complete confidentiality and total openness. And some in-between, of course.

Many states have established registries for adoptees or birthparents hoping to find each other. If both are registered, and all requirements are filled, then the state will provide the information.

One adoptee was annoyed by his private adoption agency's extreme openness. He had wanted to send his birthmother a letter through the agency. The social worker told him to drop by the office at his convenience.

When he came by with his carefully-worded letter, the social worker handed him his file. She had obtained a court order without his knowledge and all the information the agency had was in that manila folder. Shaken, angry, and unprepared, he waited awhile.

Then he decided he would find his birthmother. He called every last name that was the same as hers in the directory, with the story that he was planning a family reunion and wondered if this person at the other end was in some way related to him.

He found his birth grandmother very rapidly. She called his birthmother, and within an hour they were speaking to each other. Yet he still feels the closeness to his adoptive parents. "They raised me, and I turned out okay," he said simply.

It takes courage to find this stranger who is your birthmother—who others would call your "real mother." Will your adoptive parents hate you or think you're ungrateful? What if she turns out to be an awful person?

"I want to find my birthmother, but I'm afraid," a female adoptee in her mid-twenties told me. "What if she's a prostitute or a drug addict? What if I hate her, or she hates me?"

Sometimes birthmothers have an intense desire to find their children and make sure that they (a) are alive, (b) are all right, and (c) have "forgiven" them for the adoption.

"I'd like my son to find me, but I won't go looking for him," a birthmother in her late thirties told me. "It would be wonderful to see him and to have the chance to explain. The only thing I'm worried about is, I'm afraid he'll be very mad at me."

Sometimes adoptees *are* mad at their birthparents, at least for awhile. "I told my husband,' If she ever shows up, slam the door in her face!' " remembers an adult adoptee.

Later, she resolved to find her mother and ultimately came to accept that the placement was a good decision. Another adoptee said his birthmother was amazed that he was a college graduate: her other children were all high school dropouts.

One birthmother was very disappointed that she has never been able to establish a closeness with her daughter. Still another birthmother didn't *want* closeness.

She told me that the adoptive parents made a photo album with pictures of the child from the day she came home from the hospital to her graduation from high school, and presented this gift to her.

"I really did appreciate it, but looking at the pictures is like looking at a stranger, she doesn't seem like my daughter but someone else's," she said.

Her daughter found her through an ad in the personals, and is eager to establish a bond. "If I say 'I like chocolate chip ice cream or the color pink', she gets all excited and says, 'So do I!' as if that's where she got it from," says the birthmother.

She added, "She's trying so hard, and I don't want to hurt her, but I just don't feel what she wants me to feel."

One birthmother who found her daughter hopes to establish a very strong relationship. She recalled the first time she called her daughter: "I was sitting on the floor of my bedroom, and it took me two hours to dial the number!" she said. After she dialed, she told herself, "It's okay, I can handle this, I'm cool."

"Then she answered the phone, and I just lost it—I burst into tears!" she recalled. Slowly, the relationship is building and blossoming.

Not all birthmothers want to find their children and not all children want to actually meet their birthmothers. "I hope they told my son I'm dead, that's what I wanted," said one mother.

Another said she doesn't want to meet her daughter but wishes there was some way to convey medical information: she recently had cancer and thinks this information should be shared so her daughter can be on the lookout for any warning signs. A registry could theoretically provide such limited access information to the adopted person.

Others felt guilty and said they don't have any right to meet their children, because they would have had an abortion if that had been an option twenty years ago. So, they figured, they didn't have any rights. (Today's birthparents do have that option, so this issue is more a problem of past generations.)

The whole search issue is intensely personal and emotional, and over the next eighteen to twenty years, as your child grows up, it's likely societal attitudes and state laws will change.

Adoptive parents must realize that a child is not renouncing them by being curious, and a child is not abnormal by *not* wishing to find his/her birthparents.

Attitudes of Others

We've already discussed how family members and strangers may react to your adopting a baby, but there are other influences for which parents should be alert; for example, the school.

Many adoptive children said that the hardest and most embarrassing thing about being adopted was the genetics exercise when the teacher said to "go home and find out what color hair and eyes your mom and dad have so you can figure out where your eye and hair color came from."

If you are fortunate enough to have that information about your child's birthparents, he can use that. Or he can explain to the teacher that he can't do the assignment and he would like to do some related work.

Despite all your best efforts, there will be people who get flustered about adoption, who will make stupid comments about it, and who will anger and irritate you.

They'll ask you personal questions about your child in front of him/her, and act as if the child isn't there. Adoptive parents learn to cope with such behavior.

There's not a constant stream of major aggravations, but adoptive parents can't be super-sensitive to insults, and yet they can't allow people to get away with hurting their children. Use your best judgement about what's right for you and your child, and it'll carry you through most situations.

And Finally

I hope this book has helped you learn about adoption and how you can develop your own adoptive gameplan. I didn't write the book as the "be-all and end-all," ultimate, and final word on adoption. There are other issues I may not have fully explored.

Instead, it should be a springing-off point for you, my readers—future parents. I wrote it because I succeeded at adoption, and I was angry when I heard and read "Them" saying it was impossible.

I resolved to find out if the adoption of my child was a fluke, an accident of fate, or if it is indeed possible to adopt an infant today.

The adoptive parents and the adoption professionals I interviewed, along with the research I did, drew me irrevocably to one conclusion: if you want to succeed bad enough, if you're a "doer" not just a talker, you have a very good chance of adopting your baby. Not a 100% guarantee, but probably far better odds than you ever imagined before you picked up this book.

No, I cannot promise you that reading this book and following the suggestions provided will ensure success. I can only give you some of the informational tools you need, pat you on the back, and wish you luck.

So, that is how I will end this book, fervently hoping that you will go on out there and find your baby, and maybe I will have played some small role in that.

Good luck and God bless.

Bibliography

NOTE: Much of the research was derived through interviews with adoptive parents, social workers, attorneys, birthmothers, and others actively involved with adoption. Below is a list of books and magazine and newspaper articles used to research adopting an infant.

Adamec, Christine. "They Adopted From Afar." Home Life, A Christian Family Magazine. January 1985.

Adamec, Christine. "To Find A Child." The Times Magazine. (Air Force/Army/Navy Times monthly magazine insert.) May 2, 1983.

Administrative Regulations. Department of Children and Youth Services, Connecticut. "Adoption Placement of Children Who Have Been Identified or Located by Prospective Adoptive Parents." Connecticut Law Journal. July 22, 1986.

Bachrach, Christine A. "Adoption Plans, Adopted Children, and Adoptive Mothers: United States, 1982." Published in 1985. Working Paper Series Number 22, National Center for Health Statistics, U.S. Department of Health and Human Services.

Chase, Marilyn. "Sperm Banks Thrive Amid Debate Over Medical and Ethical Issues." Wall Street Journal, April 2, 1987, p. 31.

Children's Home Society of California, State Headquarters. "The Changing Picture of Adoption." Los Angeles. 1984.

Committee for Single Adoptive Parents." Who Wants to Be a Single Adoptive Parent?" Update Number 1. February 1986.

Committee for Single Adoptive Parents. "Survey of Single Adoptive Fathers." Update Number 2. July 1986.

Department of Health & Human Services release on research performed by Dr. Michael Resnick, Assistant Professor and Research Coordinator of Adolescent Health Program at University of Minnesota. Release by Lucy Eddinger, Public Information Officer, U.S. Department of Health and Human Services, Office of Population Affairs. "Adolescent Family Life Program Adoption Research." 1987, Washington, D.C.

Florida TODAY newspaper. "First Frozen Zygote Baby Born in U.S." March 28, 1987.

Fullerton, Paul. "Independent Adoption: The Inadequacies of State Law." Washington University Law Quarterly, Winter 1985, Vol. 63, pp. 753-775.

Gaiter, Dorothy. "Red Tape vs. Black-White Adoption." Miami Herald. September 19, 1986.

General information on infertily, in vitro fertilization, G.I.F.T., and other advanced procedures provided by The Florida Fertility Institute, a Division of Stein Womens Center in St. Petersburg and by Mt. Sinai Medical Center, Department of Obstetrics, Gynecology, and Reproductive Science in New York.

Herr, Kathleen Mary. "What Am I Going To Do About My Baby?" An Analysis of the Cost-Effectiveness of Decision-Making Groups for Pregnant Adolescents" (Teenage Pregnancy, Program Evaluation). Ph.D. dissertation at Brandeis University. 1986.

Holtan, Barbara and Laurel Strassberger, eds. *They Became Part of Us: The Experiences of Families Adopting Children Everywhere.* F.A.C.E. Inc., Baltimore, Maryland. 1985.

Infertility-United States, 1982. "Morbidity and Mortality Weekly Report." Published by the U.S. Centers for Disease Control.

Johnson, Penny R. "A Longitudinal Study of Black Adoptions: Single Parent, Transracial, and Traditional." Social Work, May/June 1986, p. 172-176.

Johnston, Patricia Irwin. *Understanding: A Guide to Impaired Fertility for Family and Friends.* Perspectives Press, Fort Wayne, Indiana. 1983.

Kraft, Adrienne D., Joseph Palombo, Patricia K. Woods, Dorens Mitchell, and Anne W. Schmidt. Some Theoretical Considerations on Confidential Adoptions, "Part I: The Birth Mother." A paper presented to the National Committee For Adoption in October 1982.

Lee, Elliott D., "White Couples Battle Obstacles to Adoption of Nonwhite Children." Cover story. The Wall Street Journal, February 27, 1987.

Lindner, Elizabeth. "Maternal-Fetal Attachment in the Pregnant Adolescent, Self-Esteem, Relationship with Mother, and the Decision to Keep or Release the Infant for Adoption." Ph.D. dissertation at the University of Wisconsin, Madision, in 1984.

Lindsay, Jeanne Warren. *Open Adoption: A Caring Option.* Morning Glory Press, Buena Park, California. 1987.

Mann, Peggy. "New Help for the Childless." Reader's Digest. January 1986.

Marindin, Hope. *The Handbook for Single Adoptive Parents.* Committee for Single Adoptive Parents, Chevy Chase, Maryland. 1985.

Melina, Lois Ruskai. *Raising Adopted Children: A Manual for Adoptive Parents.* 1987: Harper & Row, Publishers, NY.

"Motherhood Minus Mom." (Article on in vitro fertilization.) Time Magazine, April 28, 1986, p. 39.

Mosher, William D. "Reproductive Impairments in the United States, 1965-1982." Demography, Volume 22, Number 3, pp. 415-430.

National Committee For Adoption. *Adoption Factbook: United States Data, Issues, Regulations and Resources.* 1985. Washington, D.C.

National Committee For Adoption. *1985-1986 Directory of Resources.* Washington, D.C. 1986.

The Office of Population Affairs. "The Adolescent Family Life Demonstration Projects: Program and Evaluation Summaries." Washington, D.C. 1986.

Pendarvis, Leah Vorhes. "Anxiety Levels of Involuntarily Infertile Couples Choosing Adoption" (Adoptive Parents, Children, IPAT 8-Parallel-Form Anxiety Battery, State Trait Anxiety Inventory) Ph.D. dissertation, Ohio State University, 1985.

Port, Bob. "Baby Broker or Savior? Father of Surrogate Parenting." St. Petersburg Times, March 7, 1987. Section D, pp. 1-2D.

Project SHARE, A National Clearinghouse for Improving the Management of Human Services. *The Adoption Option: A Guidebook for Pregnancy Counselors.* Developed by Office of Population Affairs, U.S. Department of Health and Human Services. Published 1986, available from Project SHARE in Rockville, MD.

Reid, Barbara Moulden. "Characteristics of Families Who Adopt Children with Special Needs." (Parenting, Traits.) Ph.D. dissertation, The University of Texas at Austin. 1983.

International Concerns Committee for Children (ICCC). *Report on Foreign Adoption* 1986. Boulder, Colorado.

International Concerns Committee for Children (ICCC). *Report on Foreign Adoption* 1987. Boulder, Colorado.

Schmich, Mary T. "When Adopted Children Know Their Roots." Chicago Tribune, December 18, 1985.

Silber, Kathleen and Speedlin, Phyllis. *Dear Birthmother: Thank You for Our Baby.* Corona Publishing Company, San Antonio, Texas. 1983.

Simon, Rita James and Altstein, Howard. *Transracial Adoption.* 1977: John Wiley & Sons, New York.

South Carolina Department of Health and Environmental Control, Vital Records Division. "Report on Adoptions for the Year 1986." January 8, 1987.

State of California Department of Social Services. "Characteristics of Relinquishment Adoptions in California, July 1983-June 1984." Program Information Series Report 1986.

State of Connecticut, Department of Children and Youth Services Licensing Division. "A Guide for Writing Your Life Story."

Strassberger, Laurel. (Compiler of readings.) *Family Building Through Adoption: Families Adopting Children Everywhere.* 1987, published by Families Adopting Children Everywhere support group. (F.A.C.E.)

Stone, Allyn. "When A Mother Changes Her Mind." The San Francisco Chronicle, July 21, 1986.

U.S. Department of Justice, Immigration and Naturalization Service. "The Immigration of Adopted and Prospective Adoptive Children." Form M-249. November 1984.

Wallace, Bill and Allyn Stone. "Special Report/States's System for Adoptions Breaking Down." The San Francisco Chronicle. July 21, 1986.

"Whose Baby is That?" interview with Dr. Edward Wallach in People Weekly, Nov. 3, 1986.

Wisconsin Office for Children, Youth and Families. Issue Paper on Openness in Adoption. October 1986.

Further Recommended Readings

READERS: If you order a book through the mail, be sure to include at least $1 for postage and handling and any applicable tax.

Adoption Factbook: United States Data, Issues, Regulations and Resources.
Comprehensive look at adoption, including statistics and key issues. Check with NCFA on price

> National Committee For Adoption
> Suite 512, 2025 M St. NW
> Washington, DC 20036

The Changing Picture of Adoption
A compendium of opinions and information on adoption from a variety of social workers, attorneys, birthparents, adoptees, etc. Covers agency adoption, private adoption, special needs, infertility and many other subjects. Heavily slanted to Californians, it is still of interest to others because of sweeping scope. 1984 $14.95

> Children's Home Society of California
> State Headquarters
> 2727 West 6t St.
> Los Angeles, CA 90057

Dear Birthmother: Thank You For Our Baby
by Kathleen Silber and Phyllis Speedlin
Book on open adoption and how two adoption professionals came to accept this practice. Letters from and to adoptive parents and birthmothers. 1983 $7.95

> Corona Publishing Company
> 1037 South Alamo
> San Antonio, TX 78210

The Handbook for Single Adoptive Parents
Compiled and edited by Hope Marindin
The Mechanics of Adoption, Managing Single Parenthood, Adoption Experiences, and Professional Social Workers Look at Single Person Adoption.

Committee for Single Adoptive Parents
P.O. Box 15084
Chevy Chase, MD 20815

Open Adoption: A Caring Option
by Jeanne Warren Lindsay.
Interviews with agencies using open adoption practices, as well as with adoptive parents and birthmothers. 1987 $9.95

Morning Glory Press
6595 San Haroldo Way
Buena Park, CA 90620

Raising Adopted Children: A Manual for Adoptive Parents
by Lois Ruskai Melina
Comprehensive and well-researched book covering breast-feeding adopted infants, transracial adoptions, telling child he or she is adopted, and many other topics. 1986

Harper & Row, Publishers
10 E. 53rd Street
New York, NY 10022

Report on Foreign Adoption, 1987 (or whatever year my reader is in!)
A must for parents interested in foreign adoption. Includes monthly updates. 1987 $15.00

International Concerns Committee for Children (ICCC)
911 Cypress Drive
Boulder, CO 80303

They Became Part of Us: The Experiences of Families Adopting Children Everywhere
Edited by Barbara Holtan and Laurel Strassberger
Experiences of F.A.C.E. members in Baltimore area. Foreign adoption, special needs adoption, private adoption, sibling adoption, etc. A Mini-World Publication. $7.95

F.A.C.E.
P.O. Box 28058 Northwood Station
Baltimore, MD 21239

Adoption Agencies

NOTE: This listing does NOT include all adoption agencies in the United States, but will get you started. Contact your state social services agency for a complete listing.

ALABAMA

Agape of North Alabama
2733 Mastin Lake Rd.
Huntsville, AL 35810

Catholic Social Services
137 Clayton St., P.O. Box 454
Montgomery, AL 36101

ALASKA

Fairbanks Counseling & Adoption
222 Front St.
Fairbanks, AK 99701

LDS Anchorage
201 E. 56th Ave., Ste. 125
Anchorage, AK 99502

ARIZONA

Globe International Adoption, Inc.
6334 West Villa Theresa Rd.
Glendale, AZ 85308

House of Samuel
11777 S. Old Nogales Hwy.
Tucson, AZ 85706

ARKANSAS

Bethany Christian Services
1501 N. University
Little Rock, AR 72204

Friends of Children
2024 Arkansas Valley Drive
Little Rock, AR 72211

CALIFORNIA

Adoption Horizons
P.O. Box 247
Arcata, CA 95521

Adoptions Unlimited
P.O. Box 462
4724 Brooks St.
Montclair, CA 91763

Children's Home Society of California
State Headquarters
2727 West 6th St.
Los Angeles, CA 90057

COLORADO

Christian Family Services
1399 S. Havana #204
Aurora, CO 80012

Colorado Adoption Services International
3333 Quebec ST., #4030
Denver, CO 80207

Family Builders by Adoption
3033 South Parker Rd., #222
Aurora, CO 80014

Hand-In-Hand
4965 Barnes Rd.
Colorado Springs, CO 80917

Parent Resource Center
7025 Tall Oak Drive
Colorado Springs, CO 80919

Special Child Placement Agency
(New agency—foreign adoptions)
1300 Vrain St.
Denver, CO 80204

Walk on Water Adoption Agency
2821 Remington
Fort Collins, CO 80525

CONNECTICUT

Child and Family Agency of
Southeastern Connecticut, Inc.
255 Hempstead St.
New London, CT 06320

Family and Children's Services,
Inc.
60 Palmer's Hill Rd.
Stamford, CT 06902

International Adoptions, Inc.
96 Chapel St.
Stratford, CT 06497

International Alliance for Children
23 South Main St.
New Milford, CT 06776

LDS Social Services
57 Quornhunt Rd.
West Simsbury, CT 06092

DELAWARE

Catholic Social Services
1200 North Broom St.
Wilmington, DE 19899

Child and Home Study Associates
101 Stonecrop Rd.
Wilmington, DE 19899

Children's Bureau of Delaware, Inc.
2005 Baynard Blvd.
Wilmington, DE 19899

Welcome House
146 Brackenville Rd.
Hockessin, DE 19707

DISTRICT OF COLUMBIA

Adoption Service Information
Agency/ASIA
7720 Alaska Ave., NW
Washington, DC 20012

Associated Catholic Charities
2800 Otis St. NE
Washington, DC 20009

The American Adoption Agency
1228 M St. NW
Second Floor
Washington, DC 20005

Lutheran Social Services
5121 Colorado Ave. NW
Washington, DC 20011

FLORIDA

The Adoption Centre
500 N. Maitland Ave. Ste. 305
Maitland, FL 32751
(New agency)

Shepherd Care Ministries, Inc.
Christian Adoption Services
5935 Taft St.
Hollywood, FL 33021

Suncoast International Adoptions
P.O. Box 332
Indian Rocks Beach, FL 33535

Universal Aid for Children, Inc.
P.O. Box 610246
North Miami, FL 33161

GEORGIA

Child Service & Family
Counseling Center, Inc.
1105 West Peachtree St.
Atlanta, GA 30309

Christian Homes for Children, Inc.
288 Lawrence St.
Marietta, GA 30060 Georgia

AGAPE, Inc.
790 Church St.
Smyrna, GA 30080

Illien Adoptions International, Ltd.
1254 Piedmont Ave. NE
Atlanta, GA 30309

Jewish Family Services, Inc.
1605 Peachtree St. NE
Atlanta, GA 30309

The New Beginning Adoption
and Counseling Agency
3564 Forrest Rd.
Columbus, GA 31907

HAWAII

Child and Family Service
200 North Vineyard Blvd.
Honolulu, HI 96817

Hawaii International
P.O. Box 13
Hawi, HI 96719 LDS

Social Services of Honolulu
1500 S. Britania St.
Honolulu, HI 96826

IDAHO

Catholic Counseling Services of
Idaho
2316 N. Cole Rd., Ste. F
Boise, ID 83704

Christian Counseling Services
545 Shoup Ave., Ste. 226
Idaho Falls, ID 83402

Idaho Youth Ranch Adoption
Services
P.O. Box 8538
Boise, ID 83707

L.D.S. Social Services
10740 Fairview, Ste. 100
Boise, ID 83704

WACAP
2320 N. 9th
Boise, ID 83702

ILLINOIS

The Baby Fold
108 East Willow St.
Normal, IL 61761

Bensenville Home Society
331 S. York Rd.
Bensenville, IL 60106
(Foreign Adoption)

Catholic Social Services
P.O. Box 817
2900 W. Heading
Peoria, IL 61625

The Cradle Society
2049 Ridge Ave.
Evanston, IL 60204

Family Counseling Clinic, Inc.
19300 West Highway 120
Grayslake, IL 60030

INDIANA

NOTE: The agencies listed below provide statewide adoption services

Adoption Resource Services, Inc.
810 West Bristol
Elkhart, IN 46514

Bethany Christian Services
9595 Whitley Dr., Ste. 210
Indianapolis, IN 46240

Chosen Children Adoption Services
305 Bank St.
New Albany, IN 47150

Jewish Family and Children's Services
1717 West 86th St.
Indianapolis, IN 46260

IOWA

Bethany Christian Services
322 Central Ave., Box 143
Orange City, IA 51041

Catholic Charities of Sioux City
1825 Jackson St.
P.O. Box 2025
Sioux City, IA 51104

Lutheran Family Service
230 9th Ave. N
Fort Dodge, IA 50501

Tri-County Counseling Service
Adoption Program
1514 Mulberry
Muscatine, IA 52761

KANSAS

Lutheran Social Service-
Spaulding Midwest, Inc.
1855 N. Hillside
Wichita, KS 67214

Adoption and Counseling Services, Inc.
5400 Lackmon Rd.
Shawnee, KS 66217

Gentle Shepherd Placement Services
304 S. Clairborne
Olathe, KS 66062

International Adoption &
Counseling Services of Kansas
7012 Hallet
Shawnee, KS 66216

Jewish Family & Children's Services, Inc.
4550 W. 90th Terr.
Shawnee Mission, KS 66207

Inserco, Inc.
445 N. Dellrose
Wichita, KS 67207
(Foreign Adoptions)

KENTUCKY

Bluegrass Christian Adoption Services
42 Waller Ave.
Lexington, KY 40504
(New Agency—1987)

Catholic Social Services Bureau
3629 Church St.
Covington, KY 41011

Chosen Children Adoption Services, Inc.
5227 Bardstown Rd., #111
Louisville, KN 40291

Community Services of the
Kentucky Baptist Homes for
Children
10801 Shelbyville Rd.
Middletown, KY 40243

Holt International Childrens
Services
P.O. Box 18266
Louisville, KY 40208

LOUISIANA

Children's Bureau of New Orleans
226 Carondelet St.
New Orleans, LA 70130

LDS Social Services of New
Orleans
2000 Old Spanish Tr.
Pratt Center, S.203
Slidell, LA 70458

Sellers Baptist Home
2010 Peniston St.
New Orleans, LA 70115

Volunteers of America
354 Jordan
Shreveport, LA 71101

MAINE

Coastal Adoption Placement
Service
P.O. Box 85
Addison, ME 04606

Community Counseling Center
622 Congress St.
P.O. Box 4016
Portland, ME 04101

Growing-Thru-Adoption
P.O. Box 7082
Lewiston, ME 04240

International Christian Adoption
Agency
60 West River Rd.
Waterville, ME 04901

St. Andre's Home, Inc.
283 Elm St.
Biddeford, ME 04005

MARYLAND

Bethany Christian Services
114 Annapolis St.
Annapolis, MD 21401

Episcopal Social Services
105 West Monument St.
Baltimore, MD 21201

Jewish Family and Children's
Services
5750 Park Heights Ave.
Baltimore, MD 21215

Maryland Children's and Family
Service
303 W. Chesapeake Ave.
Towson, MD 21204

MASSACHUSETTS

Boston Children's Services Assn.
867 Boylston St.
Boston, MA 02116

Hermandad of Guadeloupe
Adoption Services, Inc.
185 Meadow Lane
West Barnstable, MA 02668

International Adoptions, Inc.
282 Moody St.
Waltham, MA 02154

Jewish Family Service of
Worcester, Inc.
646 Salisbury St.
Worcester, MA 01609

Lighthouse Child Placement
Agency
345 Main St.
Oxford, MA 01540

World Adoption Services, Inc.
161 Auburn St.
Newton, MA 02166

MICHIGAN

Bethany Christian Services
901 Eastern Ave.
Grand Rapids, MI 49503

Catholic Family Service
1008 South Wenona
Bay City, MI 48706

Community, Family and
Children Services
1000 Hastings
Traverse City, MI 49684

Foreign Adoption Consultants
1850 N. Livernois
Rochester Hills, MI 48063

MINNESOTA

Building Families Through
Adoption
P.O. Box 550
Dawson, MN 56232

Children's Home Society of
Minnesota
2230 Como Ave.
St. Paul, MN 55108

Crossroads, Inc.
7703 Normandale Rd., 100B
Edina, MN 55435

Hope International Children's
Services
421 S. Main
Stillwater, MN 55082

New Life Homes & Family Service
3361 Republic Ave.
St. Louis Park, MN 55426

MISSOURI

Family Adoption & Counseling
9378 Olive St., Rd., Rm. 305
St. Louis, MO 63132

Family & Children's Services of
Kansas City
3217 Broadway
Kansas City, MO 64111

Jewish Family and Children's
Services
9358 Olive Blvd.
Saint Louis, MO 63132

The LIGHT House
1409 East Meyer Blvd.
Kansas City, MO 64131

Love Basket, Inc.
8965 Old Lemay Ferry Rd.
Hillsboro, MO 63050

MONTANA

Catholic Social Services
530 North Ewing
Box 907
Helena, MT 59601

Lutheran Social Services of
Montana
P.O. Box 1345
Great Falls, MT 59403

AID in Montana
554 West Broadway
Missoula, MT 59802

LDS Social Services
2001 11th Ave.
Helena, MT 59601

Montana Intercountry Adoption,
Inc.
109 South 8th.
Bozeman, MT 59715

NEBRASKA

Catholic Social Service Bureau
P.O. Box 2723
Lincoln, NE 68502

Child Saving Institute
115 South 46th St.
Omaha, NE 68132

Holt International Children's
Services
P.O. Box 12153
2582 Redick
Omaha, NE 68112

Jewish Family Service
333 South 132 St.
Omaha, NE 68154

Nebraska Children's Home Society
3549 Fontenelle Blvd.
Omaha, NE 68104

NEVADA

Catholic Community Services of
Nevada
P.O. Box 1926
Las Vegas, NV 89125

Catholic Community Services of
Nevada
P.O. Box 5415
Reno, NV 89503

LDS Social Services
1906 Santa Paula Dr.
Las Vegas, NV 89105

LDS Social Services
507 Casazza Dr., Ste. C
Reno, NV 89502

NEW HAMPSHIRE

Adoptive Families for Children
26 Fairview St.
Keene, NH 03431

LDS Social Services
131 Route 101 A, #204
Amherst, NH 03031

New Hampshire Catholic
Charities
215 Myrtle St.
Manchester, NH 03014

NEW JERSEY

Adoption Placement Services
R.D. 2, 375 Fergeson Ave.
Franklinville, NJ 08322

The Children's Home Society of
New Jersey
929 Parkside Ave.
Trenton, NJ 08618

Children's Services International
P.O. Box 2176
Westfield, NJ 07091

Christian Homes for Children
275 State St.
Hackensack, NJ 07601

Family and Children's Counseling
and Testing Center
40 North Ave., P.O. Box 314
Elizabeth, NJ 07207

NEW MEXICO

Chapparal Home and Adoption
Services
4401 Lomas, Northeast
Albuquerque, NM 87110

Christian Placement Service
West Star Route, Box 48
Portales, NM 88130

LDS Social Services
7800 Marble, Northesast #1
Albuquerque, NM 87110

Rainbow House
1709 Moon St. NE
Albuquerque, NM 87112

NEW YORK

Adoption & Counseling
Services, Inc.
One Fayette Park
Syracuse, NY 13202

Catholic Family Center
50 Chestnut St.
Rochester, NY 14604

Family Resources Inc.
226 North Highland Ave.
Ossining, NY 10562

International Social Service
95 Madison Ave.
New York, NY 10016

Jewish Board of Family &
Children Services
130 West 57th St.
New York, NY 10019

Sheltering Arms Children's
Services
122 East 29 St.
New York, NY 10016

Spence Chapin Adoption Services
6 East 94 St.
New York, NY 10028

NORTH CAROLINA

Bethany Christian Services
25 Reed St., P.O. Box 15436
Asheville, NC 28813

Catholic Social Services
75 Blue Ridge Ave.
Asheville, NC 28806

Children's Home Society of
North Carolina
Med. Ctr. Bldg., 86 Victoria Rd.
Asheville, NC 28801

NORTH DAKOTA

Building Families Through
Adoption
P.O. Box 550
Dawson, MN 56232
(Licensed in ND)

Catholic Family Service
3003 South 11th St.
Fargo, ND 58107

Christian Family Life Services
Case Plaza, Ste. 222
One North Second St.
Fargo, ND 58102

Covenant Children
120 West Thayer Ave.
P.O. Box 2344
Bismarck, ND 58502

New Horizons Foreign Adoption
Service
2876 Woodland Place
Bismarck, ND 58501

The Village Family Service
Center
P.O. Box 7398
Fargo, ND 58103

OHIO

Child and Family Service, Inc.
616 South Collett St.
Lima, OH 45805

Catholic Social Services, Inc.
197 East Gay St.
Columbus, OH 43215

Family Counseling and Crittenton
Services
185 South Fifth St.
Columbus, OH 43215

Families for International
Adoptions, Inc.
1303 Starbrook SW
Massillon, OH 44646

Family Service Association
184 Salem Ave.
Dayton, OH 45406

LIMIAR: USA
2373 Brunswick Lane
Hudson, OH 44236

OKLAHOMA

The Adoption Center of
Northeastern Oklahoma
Box 3941
Bartlesville, OK 74006

Catholic Social Services
739 North Denver
Tulsa, OK 74106

Dillon Childrens Services
2525 E. 21st St.
Tulsa, OK 74114

LDS Social Services of Oklahoma
4717 S. Yale, Ste. 17
Tulsa, OK 74135

Small Miracles International
7430 SE 15th., Ste. 220
Midwest City, OK 73110

OREGON

Holt International Children's
Services
P.O. Box 2880
Eugene, OR 97402

Open Adoption and Family
Services, Inc.
239 East 14th
Eugene, OR 97401

Plan Loving Adoptions Now
(PLAN)
P.O. Box 667
McMinnville, OR 97128

PENNSYLVANIA

The Adoption Agency
63 West Lancaster Ave.
Ardmore, PA 19003

Adoption Center of Delaware
Valley
1218 Chestunut St., Ste. 204
Philadelphia, PA 19107

Catholic Social Services of
Luzerne Co.
15 S. Franklin St.
Wilkes Barre, PA 18701

Golden Cradle Home
555 East City Ave.
Bala Cynwyd, PA 19004

Tressler Lutheran Service
Association
25 W. Springettsburry Ave.
York, PA 17403

Welcome House
Route 202 & Beulah Rd.,
P.O. Box 836
Doylestown, PA 18901
(Foreign and Domestic Special
Needs)

RHODE ISLAND

Catholic Social Services
433 Elmwood Ave.
Providence, RI 02907

Childrens Friend and Service
2 Richmond St.
Providence, RI 02903

Jewish Family Service
229 Waterman St.
Providence, RI 02906

SOUTH CAROLINA

Bethany Christian Services
300 University Ridge
Ste. 114
Greeneville, SC 29601

LDS Social Services
5624 Executive Center Drive,
Ste. 109
Charlotte, NC 29205
(Licensed in SC)

The Children's Bureau of South
Carolina
1001 Harden ST., Ste. 225
Columbia, SC 29205

Family Counseling Service
P.O. Box 10306
Greeneville, SC 29603

SOUTH DAKOTA

Casey Family Program
3435 West Main
Rapid City, SD 57262-2321

Catholic Family Services
3200 West 41st St.
Sioux Falls, SD 57105-4223

Children's Home Society
3209 S. Prairie Ave.
Sioux Falls, SD 57105-5633

LDS Social Services
2525 W. Main St. #310
Rapid City, SD 57702-2423

Threshold
514 W. Minnesota
Sioux Falls, SD 57101

TENNESSEE

AGAPE
2702 Nolensville Rd.
Nashville, TN 37211

Covenant Children
P.O. Box 341490
Memphis, TN 38184-1490
(Foreign Adoption ONLY)

Holt Adoption
5347 Flowering Peach
Memphis, TN 38115
(Foreign Adoptions ONLY)

Holston United Methodist Home
for Children, Inc.
P.O. Box 188
Holston Drive
Greeneville, TN 37743

Jewish Family Service, Inc.
P.O. Box 38268
6560 Poplar Drive
Memphis, TN 38138

TEXAS

Adoption Services Associates
8703 Wurzbach Rd.
San Antonio, TX 78240

Agape Social Services, Inc.
3200 Maple, Ste. 400
Dallas, TX 75201

Direct Adoption Center
1108 N. Big Spring
Midland, TX 79701

Edna Gladney Home
2300 Hemphill Rd.
Fort Worth, TX 76110

James Kirby Read Child Placing
Agency
604 Myrtle Ave.
El Paso, TX 79901

Los Ninos International
Adoption Center
1110 W. William Cannon, Ste. 504
Austin, TX 78745-5460

Texas Cradle Society
8222 Wurzbach Rd.
San Antonio, TX 78229

UTAH

Children's Aid Society of Utah
652 26th St.
Ogden, UT 84401

Children's House International
P.O. Box 2321
Salt Lake City, UT 84110

LDS Social Services
718 South Main St., P.O. Box 835
Cedar City, UT 84720

VERMONT

Casey Family Services
Box 413
Lebanon, NH 03766
(Licensed in VT)

Elizabeth Lund Home
Box 4009
Burlington, VT 05401

International Adoptions
P.O. Box 3115
Burlington, VT 05402

Rootwings Ministries, Inc.
Box 197
Cabot, VT 05647

Vermont Catholic Charities
311 North Ave.
Burlington, VT 05401

Vermont Children's Aid Society
P.O. Box 127
Winooski, VT 05404

VIRGINIA

Bethany Christian Services
246 Maple Ave. E
Vienna, VA 22180-4631

Children's Home Society of
Virginia
4200 Fitzhugh Ave.
Richmond, VA 23230

L.D.S. Social Services of
Virginia, Inc.
8110 Virginia Pine Ct.
P.O. Box 34361
Richmond, VA 23234

Pan American Adoption Agency
12604 Kahns Rd.
Manassas, VA 22111

WASHINGTON

Adoption Advocates International
658 Black Diamond Rd.
Port Angeles, WA 98362

Adoption Services of Western
Association of Concerned
Adoptive Parents (WACAP)
P.O. Box 88948
Seattle, WA 98188

Open Arms
16429 NeE 133rd Court
Redmond, WA 98052

WEST VIRGINIA

Children's Home Society of West
Virginia
1118 Kanawha Blvd. E
Charleston, WV 25301

United Methodist Child Placement
Services
4013 Teays Valley Rd.
Scott Depot, WV 25560

WISCONSIN

Adoption Choice
2542 North Terrace Ave.
Milwaukee, WI 53211

Adoption Option
1804 Chapman Drive
Waukesha, WI 53186

Building Families Through
Adoption
Route 4, Box 21B
Wautoma, WI 54982

Community Adoption Center
101 E. Milwaukee , Ste. 322
Janesville, WI 53545

Pauquette Children's Services
1835 Stevens St., P.O. Box 237
Rhinelander, WI 53901

WYOMING

Catholic Social Services of
Wyoming
P.O. Box 2247
Casper, WY 82601

Holt International Children's
Services
1080 Horizon Drive
Casper, WY 82601

Wyoming Parenting
P.O. Box 3033
Jackson, WY 83001

Wyoming Children's Society
716 Randall
Cheyenne, WY 82001

Addition as we were going to
press.

MASSACHUSETTS

Adoption Center
55 Wheeler Street
Cambridge, MA 02138

Table I
Independent Adoption

State	Legal?	Home Study Required?*	Advertise OK?**	No. in FY 1986
AL	yes	yes	no	unknown
AK	yes	???	???	???
AZ	yes	yes	yes	1,094 in 1985 including small percentage step-parent adoptions
AR	yes	yes	yes	unknown
CA	yes	yes	no	2220
CO	yes	if court orders	yes	unknown
CT	no***	yes	no	unknown
DC	???	???	???	???
DE	no	n/a	n/a	n/a
FL	yes	yes	yes	1113
GA	yes	yes	yes	about 500
HI	???	???	???	???
ID	yes	yes	yes	98
IL	yes	yes	yes	unknown
IA	yes	yes	yes	97
IN	yes	yes	yes	170
KS	yes	yes	no	about 1500
KY	yes	yes	no	about 350

State	Legal?	Home Study Required?*	Advertise OK?**	No. in FY 1986
LA	yes	yes	yes	unknown
ME	yes	yes	yes****	about 100
MD	yes	yes	yes	unknown
MA	no***	yes	no	unknown
MI	no	n/a	n/a	n/a
MN	no	n/a	n/a	n/a
MS	yes	if judge orders	yes	unknown
MO	yes	yes	yes	unknown
MT	yes	???	no	unknown
NE	yes	yes	yes	unknown, maybe 600
NH	yes	yes	yes	unknown
NJ	yes	yes	yes	unknown
NM	yes	yes	yes	62
NY	yes	yes	yes	unknown
NC	yes	if court orders	no	130
ND	no	n/a	n/a	n/a
NV	yes	yes	no	79
OH	yes*****	yes	no	unknown
OK	yes	yes	yes	unknown
OR	yes	yes	yes	286
PA	yes	yes	yes	unknown
RI	yes	yes	no	29
SC	yes	yes	yes	152
SD	yes	yes	yes	about 150

State	Legal?	Home Study Required?*	Advertise OK?**	No. in FY 1986
TN	yes	yes	no	282
TX	yes	yes	yes	unknown
UT	yes	if court orders	yes	unknown
VT	yes	no	yes	unknown
VA	yes	yes	no	336
WA	yes	yes	no	unknown
WV	???	???	???	???
WI	yes	yes	yes	182 in 1985
WY	yes	if judge orders	yes	69

*Check with your state to find out if the home study is required BEFORE or AFTER placement. States vary greatly on this requirement.

***Ads such as "Happily married couple wishes to adopt baby," etc.

***Massachusetts and Connecticut don't view "identified adoption" as independent adoption for various reasons, e.g., an agency does home study, etc. See chapter on agency adoption.

****Requires special wording.

*****Many Ohio probate courts do not allow independent adoptions.

NOTE: Check CURRENT state laws! They may have changed.

Table II
Additional State Adoption Data

State	Birthfather Consent Required*	Time to Finalize	Est. # of Agency Adoptions+
AL	yes	6 months	55
AK	???	???	???
AR	???	6-12 months	unknown
AZ	yes	1 year	61 under 1 yr.
CO	varies	6-12 months	unknown
CA	yes	6-24 months	1150 under 3 yr.
CT	yes	1 year	72 under 5 yr.
DE	yes**	1 year	20
DC	???	???	???
FL	yes	3 months plus	unknown
GA	yes	varies	unknown
HI	???	???	???
IA	yes	6 month plus	205
ID	yes	6 months	53
IN	varies	varies	unknown
IL	yes	6 months	unknown
KS	yes	immediate	unknown
KY	yes	6 months plus	unknown
LA	???	???	???
ME	varies	6 months plus	unknown
MD	yes	6 months	unknown
MA	yes**	6 months plus	unknown

State	Birthfather Consent Required*	Time to Finalize	Est. # of Agency Adoptions+
MI	???	???	???
MN	yes	6-9 months	230
MO	varies	9-12 months	about 145
MS	yes	6 months	22 public, unknown private
MT	yes	varies	unknown
NE	no	6 months	unknown
NJ	yes	6 months plus	159 under 1 yr. via NJ agencies 48 under 1 yr. via other agents
NM	yes	under 1 yr.—4 mos. over 1 yr.—6 months	62
NV	yes	6 months	118 public, unknown private
NH	yes	6-12 months	unknown
NY	If he lived with or supported child	6 months	unknown
NC	yes	1 year	unknown
ND	yes	6 months plus	439
OH	varies	6 months plus	unknown
OK	no	varies	unknown
OR	yes	unknown	58 under 3 yr.— public, 272 private
PA	no	6-9 months	unknown
RI	yes	6 months	unknown
SC	yes	infants—6 months special needs— 12 months	160 under 1 yr.

State	Birthfather Consent Required*	Time to Finalize	Est. # of Agency Adoptions+
SD	yes, if known	6 months	unknown
TN	yes	12 months	unknown
TX	no	6 months plus	unknown
UT	yes	6 months	11 public, unknown private
VT	yes	6 months	unknown
VA	yes, unless waived	varies	134 under 11 months, 297 1-4 years
WA	yes	6 months	unknown
WV	???	???	???
WI	no	???	???
WY	yes	6 months plus	48

*Rules vary greatly on whether birthfathers must sign consent. Check current state laws.

**These states (and possibly others) require birthfathers to surrender child for adoption or court will terminate parental rights for cause.

+Unless otherwise noted, figures represent estimated or actual number of infants, under two years-old, adopted through licensed agencies. All figures are for 1985 or 1986.

State Social Service Offices

NOTE: Although state social service offices are not generally good sources for adoptable infants and toddlers, they CAN provide listings of adoption agencies throughout your state. Some states produce booklets with detailed information, while others offer photocopied listings: both are useful to the prospective parent. I recommend you address your letter to the State Adoption Supervisor, to ensure it is quickly routed to the right person.

Alabama Department of Pensions and Security
64 N. Union St.
Montgomery, AL 36130

Division of Family and Youth Services
Department of Health and Social Services
State of Alaska
Pouch H-05
Juneau, AK 99811

Arizona Department of Economic Security
1400 West Washington, 940A
Phoenix, AZ 85005

Arkansas Department of Human Services
P.O. Box 1437
Little Rock, AR 72203

Adoptions Branch
California Department of Social Services
744 P St.
Sacramento, CA 95814

Colorado Department of Social Services
717-17th. St.
P.O. Box 181000
Denver, CO 80218-0899

Department of Children & Youth Services
170 Sigourney St.
Hartford, CT 06105

Division of Child Protective Services
330 East 30th St.
Third Floor
Wilmington, DE 19802

District of Columbia Department of Human Services
500 1st St./8th Floor
Washington, DC 20001

Florida Department of Health and Rehabilitative Services
1317 Winewood, Building 8
Tallahassee, FL 32301

Georgia Department of Human Resources
878 Peachtree St., NE
Atlanta, GA 30309

Hawaii Department of Social Services and Housing
P.O. Box 339
Honolulu, HI 96809

Idaho Department of Health and Welfare
Statehouse
Boise, ID 83720

Department of Children and Family Services
Program Operations—Adoptions
Chicago Regional Office
100 West Randolph St., Ste. 6-100
Chicago, IL 60601

State of Indiana
Department of Public Welfare
Child Welfare/Social Services Division
141 South Meridian St.-6th Floor
Indianapolis, IN 46225

State of Iowa Department of Human Services
Hoover State Office Building
Des Moines, IA 50319-0114

The Department of Social and Rehabilitation Services
Youth Services
Smith-Wilson Building
2700 West Sixth St.
Topeka, KS 66606-1898

Kentucky Cabinet for Human Resources
Department of Social Services
275 East Main St., 6th Floor West
Frankfort, KY 40621

Louisiana Department of Health and Human Services
Division of Youth and Families
P.O. Box 3318
Baton Rouge, LA 70821

Maine Department of Human Services
State House, Station 1
221 State St.
Augusta, ME 04333

Maryland Department of Human Resources
Social Services Administration
300 West Preston St.
Baltimore, MD 21201

Massachusetts Department of Social Services
150 Causeway St.
Boston, MA 02114

Michigan Department of Social Services
P.O. Box 30037
Lansing, MI 48909

Adoption Unit
Department of Human Services
Centennial Bldg., 4th Floor
St. Paul, MN 55155

Mississippi Department of Public Welfare
P.O. Box 352
Jackson, MS 39205

Missouri Department of Social Services
Division of Family Services
P.O. Box 88
Jefferson City, MO 65103

Montana Department of Social and Rehabilitative Services
P.O. Box 4210
Helena, MT 59604

Nebraska Department of Social Services
P.O. Box 95026
501 Centennial Mall South
Lincoln, NE 68509

Nevada Department of Human Services/Welfare Division
251 Jeanell Drive
Carson City, NV 89701

New Hampshire Department of Health and Welfare
Hazen Drive
Concord, NH 03301

New Jersey Department of Human Services
Division of Youth and Family Service
1 South Montgomery St., C.N. 717
Trenton, NJ 08625

New Mexico Human Services Department
Social Services Division
P.O. Box 2348, Rm. 515
Santa Fe, NM 87504-2348

State Adoption Service
New York State Department of Social Services
40 North Pearl St.
Albany, NY 12243

North Carolina Department of Human Resources
Division of Social Services
325 North Salisbury St.
Raleigh, NC 27611

North Dakota Department of Human Services
State Capitol Building
Bismarck, ND 58505

Ohio Department of Human Services
30 East Broad St.
Columbus, OH 43266-0423

Oklahoma Department of Human Services
P.O. Box 25352
Oklahoma City, OK 73125

Oregon Children's Services Division
198 Commercial St. SE
Salem, OR 97310

Commonwealth of Pennsylvania
Department of Public Welfare
Office of Children, Youth and Families
P.O. Box 2675
Harrisburg, PA 17105-2675

Rhode Island Department of Children and Their Families
610 Mt. Pleasant Ave.
Providence, RI 02908

Office for Children's Services
South Carolina Department of Social Services
P.O. Box 1520
Columbia, SC 29202

South Dakota Department of Social Services
Child Protection Services
Richard F. Kneip Bldg.
700 Governors Drive
Pierre, SD 57501-2291

State of Tennessee
Department of Human Services
400 Deaderick St.
Citizens Plaza Building
Nashville, TN 37219

Policy and Program Development Division
Texas Department of Human Services
P.O. Box 2960
Austin, TX 78769

Utah Department of Social Services
Division of Family Services
150 West North Temple
Salt Lake City, UT 84110

Department of Social & Rehabilitation Services
Division of Social Services
Adoption Unit
103 South Main St.
Waterbury, VT 05676

Adoption Reports Unit
Commonwealth of Virginia
Department of Social Services
Blair Building
8007 Discovery Drive
Richmond, VA 23229-8699

Washington Department of Health and Social Services
Office Building -2
Olympia, WA 98504

West Virginia Department of Human Services
1900 Washington Street E
Charleston, WV 25305

Wisconsin Department of Health and Social Services
P.O. Box 7851
Madison, WI 53707

Wyoming Department of Social Services
Hathaway Building
Cheyenne, WY 82002

Adoptive Parent Support Groups

NOTE: These listings were obtained from a variety of support group newsletters and state social service departments. Hopefully they are current but all have not been verified so there may have been changes. If you cannot make contact with one of these groups, write or call your state social services department for current information. Another good tactic is to contact another group in your state: most support groups within a state know about each other.

ALABAMA

AFOA
4968 Springbrook Rd.
Birmingham, AL 35223

ARIZONA

Advocates for Single Adoptive Parenting (ASAP)
Phoenix Branch c/o Jan Rose
P.O. Box 5288 #162
Phoenix, AZ 85010

Tucson Branch c/o Sarah Kenner
1701 E. Linden
Tucson, AZ 85719

CALIFORNIA

Adoption Avenues
c/o Joel & Pam Hart
3027 Sylvia Lane
Redding, CA 96002

Inter Country Adoption Network
c/o Barbara Weaver
8506 Matilija Ave.
Panorama City, CA 91402

COLORADO

Families for Adoption
c/o Peg Mussard
2124 Ford Lane
Ft. Collins, CO 80524

Single Adoptive Parents:
c/o Judy Stewart
6451 South Lakeview
Littleton, CO 80120

CONNECTICUT

The Open Door Society of Connecticut
P.O. Box 478
Hartford, CT 06141

Latin America Parent Association (CT chapter)
P.O. Box 523
Unionville, CT 06085

Single Parents Adopting Children Everywhere (SPACE)
c/o Betty LiLiberte
64 Elida Court
East Hartford, CT 06108

Miracles
c/o Nancy Coughlin
3 Hampden Circle
Simsbury, CT 06070

DELAWARE

Adoptive Families with Information and Support (AFIS)
c/o Susan Ford, Membership
Box 146, RD #2
Hockessin, DE 19707

DISTRICT OF COLUMBIA

Families for Private Adoption
P.O. Box 6375
Washington, DC 20015-0375

FLORIDA

Building Families Through Adoption
c/o Bob & Beth Van Rhee
7202 9th Ave. W
Bradenton, FL 33529

Families Adopting Children Today (FACT)
c/o Mary Ellen Ramsay
7285 Abby Lane
Winter Park, FL 32792

The Lifeline for Children, Inc.
P.O. Box 17184
Plantation, FL 33318

IDAHO

Lewis-Clark Adoptive Families
3628-16th St.
Lewiston, ID 83501

Adoptive Families of Idaho
1000 Sweetwood Circle
Nampa, ID 83651

Forever Families
899 Saratoga
Boise, ID 83706

Families Through Adoption
150 Center Bldg.—ABC Services
Pocatello, ID 83201

ILLINOIS

Chicago Area Families for Adoption
c/o Kathy Levitan
9 S. Wright St.
Naperville, IL 60540

Heart of Illinois
c/o Marsha Thompson
1017 W. Scottwood
Peoria, IL 61615

South Central Illinois Adoptive Parents Assoication
c/o Nancy Weitekamp
406 S. Oak St.
Raymond, IL 62560

INDIANA

Families Adopting Children Today
819 North Rensselaer
Griffith, IN 46319
Attn.: Mrs. Karen Scheeringa

Adoptive Parents Together (APT)
3312 Ivory Way
Indianapolis, IN 46227
Attn.: Mrs. Roberta Decker

Rainbow Families of OURS
1745 Rainbow Bend Blvd.
Elkhart, IN 46514-2028
Attn.: Mrs. Jan Parrish

Adoptive and Foster Parent Support Group of Delaware County
R.R. #1, Box 60A
Daleville, IN 46334
Attn.: Ms. Cindy Michael

IOWA

F.A.I.T.H.
c/o Linda Davis
RR 2, Box 279
Wapello, IA 52653

International Adoptive Parents
c/o Rita Grafft
345 Crandall Dr. NE
Cedar Rapids, IA 52402

Iowa Foster and Adoptive Parents Association
c/o Phyllis Nielsen
RR 1
Everly, IA 51338

KENTUCKY

Parents & Adoptive Children of Kentucky (PACK)
c/o Carolyn Brown
47 Comer Drive
Madisonville, KY 42431

MAINE

Adoptive Families of Maine chapters
Sue Curran, AFM
11 Chandler St.
Calais, ME 04619

Sharon Pierce, AFM
21 Glenwood Ave.
Augusta, ME 04330

Edie Keller, AFM
19 Roosevelt Ave.
Waterville, ME 04901

Fran Brotka, AFM
4 Brook St.
Houlton, ME 04730

MARYLAND

Committee for Single Adoptive Parents
P.O. Box 15084
Chevy Chase, MD 20815

Families Adopting Children Everywhere (F.A.C.E.)
P.O. Box 28058
Baltimore, MD 21239

Single Adoptive Parents Society
c/o Clotilde Vidoni
7595 Earnshaw Drive.
Brandywine, MD 20613

MASSACHUSETTS

The Open Door Society of Mass. Inc.
867 Boylston ST., 6th Floor
Boston, MA 02116

Single Parents Adopting Children Everywhere
6 Sunshine Ave.
Natick, MA 01760

Single Parents for Adoption of Children Everywhere
95 Poplar
Roslindale, MA 02131

Stars of David (Jewish families)
c/o Rabbi Susan Abramson
Temple Shalom Emeth
14-16 Lexington St.
Burlington, MA 01803

MICHIGAN

A.D.O.P.T.
c/o James & Maxine Berden
6939 Shields Ct.
Saginaw, MI 48603

Families Through Adoption
c/o Lynne Moffitt
34250 Ramble Hills Dr.
Farmington Hills, MI 48018-3055

International Families Through Adoption
c/o Cher & Marshall Cronican-Walker
3001 Larkin
Muskegon, MI 49441

Michigan Association of Single Adoptive Parents (MASAP)
2830 Old Plank Rd.
Milford, MI 48042

Singles for Adoption
c/o Carol Powell
619 Norton Dr.
Kalamazoo, MI 49001

MINNESOTA

Minnesota Single Adoptive Parents Association
c/o Margie Scott
4137 Abbott Ave. S
Minneapolis, MN 55410

OURS
3307 Highway 100 N., STe. 203
Minneapolis, MN 55422
(A must for families adopting internationally.)

MONTANA

Yellowstone International Adoptive Families
c/o Arlon Peda
3126 Turnberry Circle
Billings, MT 59101

NEBRASKA

Kearney Area Adoption Association
c/o Jan Shanahan
3459 Lakeview Drive
Kearney, NE 68847

NEW HAMPSHIRE

Open Door Society of New Hampshire
c/o Coppolas
11 Wilders Grove Rd.
Kingston, NH 03848

NEW JERSEY

Adoptive Single Parents of New Jersey
c/o Diane Veith
117 Spencer Rd.
Basking Ridge, NJ 07920

Concerned Persons For Adoption
P.O. Box 179
Whippany, NJ 07981

NEW MEXICO

Alliance for Children Today
c/o Cindi Eldred
208 West Ash
Bloomfield, NM 87413

NEW YORK

Adoptive Parents Committee, Inc./State Association
210 Fifth Ave.
New York, NY 10010

Black Adoptive Parents Association
A. Peter Bailey
P.O. box 104
Lincolnton Station
New York, NY 10037

Latin American Parents Association
National Headquarters
P.O. Box 72
Seaford, NY 11783

New York Singles Adopting Children
2448 Stuart St.
Brooklyn, NY 11229

Single Adoptive Parents for Adoption
c/o Maggie Schultz
1013-91st ST.
Niagara Falls, NY 14304

NOTE: The State of New York provided names and addresses for nearly 80 support groups, far too many to list here. Write to the state for further information.

NORTH CAROLINA

Triangle Area Ours Thru Adoption
c/o Judity Geyer
6609 Chantilly Place.
Bahama, NC 27503

OHIO

Rainbow Families of Toledo
c/o Debra Graf
3714 Douglas Rd.
Toledo, OH 43613

Western Reserve Adoptive Parents
c/o Mr. and Mrs. Richard Novak
8517 Kinblewick NE
Warren, OH 44484

OKLAHOMA

Council on Adoptable Children
c/o Dwe Williams
2609 NW 38th
Oklahoma City, OK 93112

FACT Families Adopting Children in the Tulsa Area
c/o SuDawn Peters
47 N. Victor
Tulsa, OK 74110

OKC
c/o Linda Babb
P.O. Box 7242
Moore, OK 73153

OREGON

Northwest Adoptive Families Association, Inc.
P.O. Box 25355
Portland, OR 97225-0355

PENNSYLVANIA

Keystone Adoptive Families
c/o William & Terry Bow
21 Sylvan Drive
Hollidaysburg, PA 16648

Single Adoptive Parents of Delaware Valley
c/o Judy Volk
45 W. Stratford Ave.
Lansdowne, PA 19050

The Adoptive Parents Group of Delaware County
c/o Rosemary Hughes
904 Westdale Ave.
Swarthmore, PA 19081

SOUTH DAKOTA

c/o Donna Bieber
RR2, Box 86
Sioux Falls, SD 57103

TENNESSEE

Papoos
757 Darden Place
Nashville, TN 37205

TEXAS

North Texas for Adoption
c/o Candice Rea
5317 Buckner Drive
·Flower Mound, TX 75028

UTAH

Families Involved in Adoption (F.I.A.)
P.O. Box 746
Centerville, UT 84014-0746

H.O.P.E. of Utah
P.O. Box 1146
Provo, UT 84601

VERMONT

Friends in Adoption
Box 87
Pawlet, VT 05761

Parents for Private Adoption
P.O. Box 7
Pawlet, VT 05761

Vermont Families Through Adoption
c/o Lorraine Dindo
Box 241-A, RD 1
Graniteville, VT 05654

VIRGINIA

COAC
c/o Mary Shanley
1025 S. Ironwood Rd.
Sterling, VA 22170

F.A.I.T.H.
c/o Sandra Daniels
P.O. Box 7302
Roanoke, VA 24019

Fairfax County Adoptive Parents
c/o Janet Hale
3212 Burgundy Rd.
Alexandria, VA 22303

Rappahannock Adoptive Parents
c/o Kay Roscoe
Rt. 3, Box 703
Fredericksburg, VA 22401

Shenandoah Valley Adoptive Parents
c/o Linda Lemay
548 Massanutten Heights
Woodstock, VA 22664

WASHINGTON

Advocates for Single Adoptive Parents, Northwest
c/o Laurelle Nickles
2201 East Roanoke
Seattle, WA 98112-2241

W.A.R.M.
220 Kirkland Ave. #10
Kirkland, WA 98033

WEST VIRGINIA

Appalachian Families for Adoption
c/o Martha Nunley
1502 Brentwood Rd.
Charleston, WV 25314

Northern West Virginia Council on Adoptable Children,
Single Parent Comm.
c/o John Zirkle
1103 Fourth St.
Fairmont, WV 26554

WISCONSIN

Adoption Parent Group of Southern Wisconsin
c/o Marilyn Holshuh
1408 Vilas Ave.
Madison, WI 53711

Adoptive Families of Western Wisconsin
c/o Deborah Timmerman
433 N. Wasson La.
River Falls, WI 54022

Adoptive Parent Association of Greater Milwaukee
c/o Dee Loomis
11327 W. Clarke
Wauwatosa, WI 53226

Open Door Society
c/o Jackie Omdahl
5215 W. Townsend St.
Milwaukee, WI 53216

Wisconsin Association of Single Adoptive Parents (WASAP)
c/o Mary Cissoko
2111 Barton Ave., #3
West Bend, WI 53095

WYOMING

Wyoming OURS Inc.
c/o Mary Patrick
1654 Bellaire Drive
Casper, WY 82601

Important Related Organizations

American Fertility Society
1608 13th Ave. South, Ste. 101
Birmingham, AL 35256-6199

A professional group which provides referrals to physicians expert in the latest high-tech techniques to help infertile couples bear children.

National Coalition to End Racism in America's Child Care System
22075 Koths
Taylor, MI 48180

A national organization which concentrates on transracial placements in foster care and adoption. In favor of placing Blacks and biracial children in White homes when Black homes unavailable.

National Committee For Adoption
Suite 512, 2025 M Street NW
Washington, DC 20036

North American Council on Adoptable Children (NACAC)
National Parents Group
Box 14808
Minneapolis, MN 55414

OURS
3307 Highway 100 North, Ste. 203
Minneapolis, MN 55422

National support group for adoptive parents

RESOLVE, Inc.
5 Water St.
Arlington, MA 02174
Phone: (617) 643-2424

A national organization for infertile couples and professionals who assist them. Has chapters nationwide and offers referral services to physicians, adoption services, support groups, and others.

Photo of author by J.M. Adamec.
Cover design by Lyrl Ahern.
Composition by CopyRight, Inc., Bedford, Massachusetts.
Printing/Manufacturing by Little River Press, Miami Florida.

Other Books from Mills & Sanderson

Fifty and Fired! How to Prepare for It; What to Do When It Happens by Ed Brandt with Leonard Corwen. The authors lead the middle-aged, middle-manager through the trauma of age motivated job dismissal using actual hard-hitting case histories to show what can be done before and after the fact to defend your career and dignity, and rebuild your livelihood. **$9.95**

Your Astrological Guide to Fitness by Eva Shaw. Find out what your astrological sign has to say about your ideal exercises, sports, and menus. There are also astrologically keyed gift ideas and comparison charts to help you choose your ideal mate or traveling companion. **$9.95**

Bachelor in The Kitchen: Beyond Bologna and Cheese by Gordon Haskett with Wendy Haskett. From Beer Jello to Duck with Cherries, San Diego chef Gordon Haskett shows you quick and easy recipes for yourself and/or that special someone in your life; also, how to be the hit of any party or Pot Luck. **$7.95**

60-Second Shiatzu: How to Energize, Erase Pain, and Conquer Tension in One Minute by Eva Shaw. The author explains how acupressure relief can be self-administered amidst the frustrations of commuter rush hours, college exams, family fights, or office hassles. It's fun, it's easy, and it works! **$7.95**

Smart Travel: Trade Secrets for Getting There in Style at Little Cost or Effort by Martin Blinder. The author's thirty years of globe-spanning travel have taught him many secrets for getting the best of everything for as little expense as feasible, and he wants to share those secrets with you. **$9.95**

The Cruise Answer Book: A Comprehensive Guide to the Ships and Ports of North America by Charlanne F. Herring. This book offers a tremendous amount of information about ships, itineraries, shore excursions, and ports that is not included in other cruise guides, and that will help you decide which cruise is best for you at any particular time. This book concentrates on cruises around North America, the Caribbean, Bermuda, Hawaii...the areas where most Americans choose to cruise. **$9.95**

Adventure Traveling: Where the Packaged Tours Won't Take You by T.J. "Tex" Hill. Whether you're looking for the keen edge of real danger or trips that invoke the tingle without the threat, here's an international menu of itineraries and guidelines for the vacationer who is looking for a "different" kind of vacation. **$9.95**

Order Form

If you are unable to find our books in your local bookstore, you may order them directly from us. Please enclose check or money order for amount of purchase plus handling charge of $1.00 per book.

( ) Fifty and Fired! @$9.95   _____

( ) Your Astrological Guide to Fitness @$9.95 _____

( ) Bachelor in The Kitchen @$7.95   _____

( ) 60-Second Shiatzu @$7.95   _____

( ) Smart Travel @$9.95   _____

( ) The Cruise Answer Book @$9.95   _____

( ) Adventure Traveling @$9.95   _____

     Add $1.00 per book handling charge   _____

     Add 5% Sales Tax if MA resident   _____

     Total Amount enclosed   _____

Name _____

Address _____

City/State/Zip_____

Mail to: Mills & Sanderson, Publishers
         442 Marrett Road, Suite 5
         Lexington, MA 02173